MANCHESTER MEDIEVAL LITERATURE

LANGUAGE AND IMAGINATION
IN THE *GAWAIN*-POEMS

Manchester University Press

MANCHESTER MEDIEVAL LITERATURE

J. J. ANDERSON, GAIL ASHTON *series editors*

This series is broad in scope and receptive to innovation, bringing together a variety of approaches. It is intended to include monographs, collections of commissioned essays, and editions and/or translations of texts, with a focus on English and English-related literature and culture. It embraces medieval writings of many different kinds (imaginative, historical, political, scientific, religious) as well as post-medieval treatments of medieval material. An important aim of the series is that contributions to it should be written in a style which is accessible to a wide range of readers.

Language and imagination
in the *Gawain*-poems

J. J. ANDERSON

Manchester University Press
MANCHESTER AND NEW YORK

distributed exclusively in the USA by Palgrave

Published by Manchester University Press
Oxford Road, Manchester M13 9NR, UK
and Room 400, 175 Fifth Avenue, New York, NY 10010, USA
www.manchesteruniversitypress.co.uk

Distributed exclusively in the USA by
Palgrave, 175 Fifth Avenue, New York, NY 10010, USA

Distributed exclusively in Canada by
UBC Press, University of British Columbia, 2029 West Mall, Vancouver, BC, Canada V6T 1Z2

British Library Cataloguing-in-Publication Data
A catalogue record for this book is available from the British Library

Library of Congress Cataloging-in-Publication Data applied for

ISBN   0 7190 5353 6 *hardback*
EAN   978 0 7190 5353 5

ISBN   0 7190 7102 X *paperback*
EAN   978 0 7190 7102 7

First published 2005

14 13 12 11 10 09 08 07 06 05   10 9 8 7 6 5 4 3 2 1

Typeset by Northern Phototypesetting Co Ltd, Bolton
Printed in Great Britain
by Bell & Bain Limited, Glasgow

Contents

Preface

This is the first study to be published in the series *Manchester Medieval Literature*, a new series of studies and texts brought out by Manchester University Press. In accordance with the brief for the series I have made reader-friendliness a high priority, and so where possible have avoided critical jargon and technical language.

Writing a more or less open-ended critical account of the *Gawain*-poems after all the critical and scholarly attention they have received in the course of many decades has meant that I have had no chance of reading everything that may possibly be relevant, though I have read a lot. But much of what I have read, including some of the editions, monographs, and journal articles which have helped shape my thinking, and to whose authors I am grateful, does not get a mention here. I have cut down on the amount of scholarly reference and the number of footnotes in order to make the study more readable and to keep its length within bounds. I ask for forgiveness if some of the points I make have already been made by others whom I have failed to acknowledge.

My thanks are due to many colleagues and students who have shared their enthusiasm for the *Gawain*-poems with me over several decades. In particular I wish to thank Grevel Lindop for reading a draft of the chapter on *Pearl*, and Susan Powell for her thoroughgoing criticism of the whole study in an earlier incarnation. Derek Pearsall, the reader for Manchester University Press, has given me great encouragement, and I owe thanks too to the Department of English and American Studies and the Faculty of Arts and Humanities in the University of Manchester for awarding me a sabbatical semester, and for research grants which enabled me to buy out some of my teaching.

My wife Joy is entitled to special thanks not only for her many invaluable suggestions, but for supporting me so well in every way while I was writing the book. I am very glad to have the opportunity at last to put my great gratitude to her on record.

Introduction

The four poems of MS Cotton Nero A.x, Art. 3, are untitled in the manuscript, but titled by modern editors, in manuscript order *Pearl, Cleanness* (or *Purity*), *Patience*, and *Sir Gawain and the Green Knight*. This is the only manuscript containing any of them, and it gives no clear information as to by whom and for whom it, or they, were produced, and whether or not they are all by the same author. There is no external evidence either which settles any of these matters. They must to a degree be regarded as poems without contexts. All that can be gleaned about authorship comes from the poems themselves. My conviction that a single individual wrote all four poems informs my approach to them. Without going over again the arguments and counter-arguments that have been put forward, I believe that my conviction is well, though not conclusively, supported by the balance of the evidence.

The poems testify that he was cultivated, with an appreciation of the finer points of chivalric life, and also deeply religious – a cleric, no doubt, given his biblical knowledge, his interest in Christian doctrine, and his understanding of sermon style. They demonstrate some learning and reading, though, with a few exceptions, apart from the Bible, which is the source of most of the three religious poems, they give no clue to the particular works which he read.[1] The alliterative long line metres of *Cleanness, Patience*, and *Gawain* are refined, and the metre of *Pearl*, syllabic with alliteration added, is inventively elaborate. They share a rich literary language (with an alliterative poetic diction which goes back to Old English poetry) based on a north-west midlands dialect of Middle English. The poet's use of this language suggests that he was more concerned to find/create a suitably elevated language for his subject matter than to give his work the widest possible circulation. The paucity and uncertainty of early references to the poems and of signs that other authors made use of them, together with the fact that only one manuscript has survived, indicates that they never achieved wide currency.

Just as the wider world did not pay much attention to the poems, so the poems did not concern themselves directly with the doings of the wider world. Of course the poet did not write in a vacuum, but there is no explicit or obvious reference to contemporary people, events, or political or social issues (though there is to features of architecture, dress, and other aspects of material culture). The three religious poems largely keep intact the teaching of Augustine which still shaped orthodox church doctrine in the fourteenth century. I cannot find any evidence of Wycliffite or Lollard attitudes. In *Gawain* the poet's view of chivalry is conservative and literary, less influenced by 'newer' more prosaic attitudes to knights and knighthood than his contemporary Chaucer, with his rather dull pilgrim-knight and his mockery of romance chivalry in the Tale of Sir Thopas,[2] or, a century or so later, Malory, whose Arthurian compendium, *Le Morte Darthur*, is infiltrated by the politics of the Wars of the Roses and the values of contemporary gentry culture.[3] As Putter has shown, *Gawain* 'is a conventional romance, deeply rooted in the tradition of the Old French *roman courtois*'.[4] The poet is more interested in what he sees as the essence of chivalry than in chivalry's contemporary manifestations.

The poems are thematically linked by a religious view of all human enterprise as ultimately unsatisfactory, for the reason that all human beings are fallen. They convey the message that all, whatever their status, whether they are Christians trying to come to terms with loss, prophets on a dangerous errand for God, or knights struggling against temptation to uphold their honour, find the going hard. They bring out the difficulty of understanding and keeping to the rules, whether of the Christian faith or of chivalry. The idea that a penitential attitude offers hope is important in all four poems, but it is not demonstrated to be a sufficient answer to human weakness.

There is no evidence that the poet was ever attached to a court or great house (though he may have been),[5] that he had a patron, or that his poems were commissioned. He was not important enough to be mentioned in any records, as far as is known, and the physical ordinariness of the manuscript and the religious emphasis of its contents suggest an educated middle class audience rather than a predominantly aristocratic one. But this audience, though a step down from Chaucer's, still deserves to be called 'courtly' in the sense of being interested in courtly matters. The discourse of chivalry and courtesy is central in *Gawain*, important in *Pearl*, and significant in *Cleanness* and *Patience*, and no doubt this interest reflects audience interests and aspirations. But the poems lead their audiences to consider courtly values critically.[6]

Langland's *Piers Plowman*, the great religious poem written at about the same time as the *Gawain*-poems over the last four decades of the fourteenth century, and a point of comparison in many ways, is obviously more involved than they are in the contemporary political, social, and intellectual environment, including the everyday world. In comparison the *Gawain*-poems are not topical. As their otherwordly, biblical and Arthurian settings indicate, they take little interest in contemporary events and in everyday life. Their centre is elsewhere.

However it may be that, at bottom, the *Gawain*-poet is driven by the same kind of personal crisis of faith as Langland, a crisis which to some extent reflects the strains on the highly developed doctrines and practices of late medieval Catholicism in the pre-Reformation years. Both poets see a gap between what is theoretically and actually possible for human beings to achieve in the moral and religious sphere – the difficulty or impossibility of comprehending in other than an intellectual way the mysteries of Christian doctrine, that is, of ever succeeding in applying that doctrine meaningfully to their own lives. Like Langland the *Gawain*-poet is perhaps trying to write out his own anxieties as much as to give his readers food for thought.

If the poems are fundamentally conservative in outlook, this is not to say that they are unoriginal. On the contrary they are in many ways markedly individual, even idiosyncratic. Doctrinally orthodox, the three religious poems yet have some unusual doctrinal emphases, and in form they strongly challenge horizons of expectation. No other work besides *Pearl* sets religious debate in such a complex allegorical and metrical matrix, and, though there are many other vernacular paraphrases of biblical narrative, including verse paraphrases, there are no parallels to the intricate merging of narrative and concept in *Cleanness* and *Patience*. *Gawain* too has formal aspects which are unusual in medieval romance, notably its tightly structured one-plot-inside-another narrative.

Given that (as I believe) the poems are by the one author, they read very differently. This is not so remarkable when they belong to different genres, like *Cleanness* and *Gawain*, but it is when they share not only the same genre but the same approach and kind of material, as in *Cleanness* and *Patience*. With these two it is as though the poet wants to show how different the 'feel' of two works which follow the same formal and conceptual pattern can be. The distinctiveness is constructed by the matching of differing underlying ideas to appropriate narrative, expository, and linguistic, detail. Though more interested in essences than particularities, the poems are full of specific detail which, in line with medieval rhetorical practice, is used not so much for graphic effect *per se* as to give support to the various ideas. This is a poet who, on the evidence of his small surviving output, is capable of pouring himself into very different imaginative moulds. There may be an element of self-challenge about this; there are hints, in the metrical and numerological constraints he works with,[7] that he is interested in setting himself a difficult task and then seeing how well he carries it out.

What implications, if any, does the fact that the poems occur together in the same manuscript have for their meaning? Until recently, the usual view was that they were best considered as separate works, and that there was no particular significance in their manuscript order. However Prior's monograph, *The Fayre Formez of the Pearl Poet,* sees the poems, in their manuscript order, as moving 'progressively further and further away from visualized and apocalyptic images of the divine'.[8] Blanch and Wasserman's monograph, *From Pearl to Gawain*, takes the view that the four poems are essentially a unity, between them delineating the whole course of providential history from Creation to Apocalypse.[9] They compare the makeup of the manuscript with that of Malory's 'book' of *Le Morte Darthur*, with its famous attendant question: one tale or many? Condren's monograph, *The Numerical Universe of the Gawain-Pearl Poet*, which considers the poems as they are set out in the manuscript, sees their meaning, as individual poems and as a group, as a product of the complex mathematical patterns according to which they are written.[10] I do not go as far as these latter two studies towards seeing the four poems as a unity, but I argue that there are significant connections between them and that the manuscript arrangement matters. I have no doubt, either, that numerology plays an important part in the design of the poems, as Condren shows, though I approach them from another point of view.

The most fundamental connection is between *Cleanness* and *Patience*, which, as second and third in order respectively, take up the central positions in the manuscript. All four poems are structured by patterns of parallel and contrast, but in the case of *Cleanness* and *Patience* these patterns work not only intra- but intertextually, in that the two poems contrast with each other and may be seen as reciprocal.[11] Between them they see God, implicitly, in terms of the traditional opposition between his justice and his mercy, an opposition often expressed in literature by the motif of the debate of the four daughters of God, which has the personified Justice and Truth arguing for divine justice, Mercy and Peace for divine mercy. In the terms of this debate, *Cleanness* presents God as justice and truth, *Patience* as peace and mercy. But it is the idea of the opposition, not the details of the debate, which interests the poet, and there is no overt reference to either.[12] The connection between these two poems is reinforced by parallels of detail, notably the fact that both in their discussions quote from the same two passages, one from the Psalms and the other from *The Romance of the Rose*.

One may also see a structural complementarity between the two outer poems, *Pearl* and *Gawain*. The protagonists of both, after a testing event, go on a quest or journey (*aventure*, *Pearl* line 64 and *Gawain* line 489) which challenges them in unexpected ways. They are left, after a decisive lapse on their part, in an ambiguous situation which is never resolved. The complementarity consists in the fact that *Gawain* operates this traditional romance pattern on the secular level, while *Pearl* translates it to the spiritual level. There is an evident numerological link between these two poems. Both have one hundred and one stanzas, and it seems that *Pearl* was fine-tuned to achieve just this number.[13] Structurally, they are similar in that they both begin and end with symmetrical framing passages, and the narratives in between are carefully patterned, with threefold patterns prominent.

I do not wish to put forward a hypothetical biography of the poet as Gollancz and others did around the turn of the twentieth century[14], but it seems likely that, rather than inventing the whole scenario of *Pearl*, the poet wrote in response to the trauma of the death of his infant daughter. One may speculate that all four poems proceeded from this single life-event.[15] Writing *Pearl* gave him the chance to articulate the struggle he had, less than successful according to the poem, as a Christian believer trying to find Christian consolation for his loss. In the poem the struggle is transmuted into a symbolic mode and generalised. The dreamer is an everyman figure, a representative of all Christians trying to make their faith work for them in the face of personal tragedy, and beyond that of all human beings looking for a transcendental solution.

Cleanness and *Patience* may be seen as growing out of *Pearl*, and *Gawain* as a response to all three. *Pearl* embraces the whole sweep of Christian history and doctrine, and it establishes the connecting theme of the three religious poems, the dichotomy between earth and heaven. The narratives in *Cleanness* and *Patience* are more specifically historical, together tracing Old Testament history through from Noah to Jonah. In them the poet looks at the issues of *Pearl* from another point of view, asking in *Cleanness* and *Patience* whether Christians can ever understand God's justice and mercy, and implying that they cannot. *Cleanness* focuses on the next world and God's justice, *Patience* on this world and God's mercy. Between them the two poems present the two opposing sides of God in dialogic fashion, leaving the reader to grapple with the paradox of his nature, though God offers his resolution of the matter (imaged in debate of the four daughters literature when the daughters kiss and make up) in the last two lines of his concluding speech in *Patience*.[16]

In *Gawain* the poet turns to chivalry, the dominant secular ethos of the day, espoused by the ruling classes, to see what sense it can make of life. The late medieval issue of the rivalry between religious and secular forces for control of men's minds relates to the whole group of poems. *Gawain* does for chivalry what *Pearl* does for Christianity, putting chivalry's basic tenets on show and relating them to its (mythic) origins and history. The poet does not however conclude that chivalry is 'better' than Christianity, or vice versa. Instead he is profoundly drawn to the idealism of both systems, even as he is forced to concede that both are fundamentally at odds with human nature (see further pp. 247–9.

By the time of the *Gawain*-poet some of the greatest imaginative writers in Europe had taken up the matter of Britain and King Arthur, attracted not only by the story-telling possibilities but also by the nobility of the code of honour which governed the lives of the Arthurian knights. It is obvious from the three religious poems that the poet is no ascetic, and in *Gawain* he not only, through the story, considers the moral and spiritual status of chivalry, but expresses his delight in its colourful world. In this last, longest, and most substantial of the poems, he gives chivalry the chance to have its full say.

The design of the manuscript, in which the first poem is the key to the others, mirrors the design of the individual poems, each of which has a preliminary section constituting a key to the meaning of what follows. *Cleanness* and *Patience* both begin with quotation and explanation of a New Testament text, which leads into the main Old Testament narratives and confirms their New Testament relevance. *Pearl*'s first section is a waking episode which sets up the dream, and *Gawain*'s is its version of the historical myth of the founding of Britain, which introduces both the story and the underlying theme of *blysse and blunder*. These first sections define their poems' parameters as *Pearl* defines the manuscript's. All four poems end by returning to the language and ideas of their first lines, and in *Pearl*, *Patience*, and *Gawain* the last line (the last long line in the case of *Gawain*) closely echoes the first. Possibly the concluding prayer to Christ in *Gawain* is meant not only to play a part in the reader's evaluation of Gawain's quest, but to throw the reader back to the beginning of the manuscript and the spiritual quest of *Pearl*.

In terms of their construction of meaning the poems are the product of the poet's dialogical imagination (to borrow Holquist's title for the standard collection of Bakhtin's essays on dialogics translated into English).[17] As Chaucer characteristically does, the poet prefers to set up a dialogue between two (or more) discourses, without explicit favouring of one over the other(s). Although his dialogues between earth and heaven are, as one would expect, weighted in favour of the heavenly side, the weighting is left implicit and the human side is far from eclipsed.

The poet is not in the business of providing clear-cut answers or telling the reader what to think.[18]

Of the individual poems, *Pearl* is the most obviously dialogic, with the case for humanity and the case for God put by the dreamer and the maiden respectively in the course of their long dream-vision debate. *Cleanness* in itself is assertively non-dialogic. *Patience*, in a less systematic way than *Pearl*, presents another dialogue in which the earthly and the heavenly points of view are set against each other without any final resolution of their differences, with the narrator and Jonah speaking for earth and God for himself. *Gawain*, the most complex of the poems, sets up various discourses which may be thought to be in dialogic relationship with each other, for instance masculine and feminine (symbolised by the shield and the girdle), and religious and magical (symbolised by the image of the Virgin on the inside of Gawain's shield and the pentangle on the outside). Again, Gawain, Arthur's court, and the shape-shifting Green Knight/Bercilak exhibit three different views of chivalry, which issue in three different judgements of Gawain's conduct, with the reader left to choose between them if he so wishes.[19] But the most important dialogue in *Gawain*, between chivalry and Christianity, is less explicitly articulated. In this poem chivalry is the foregrounded discourse, and Christianity (as opposed to chivalry, not as part of it) is in counterpoint with it. This situation is the reverse of that in the first poem, *Pearl*, in which the foregrounded discourse of Christianity is counterpointed by that of courtesy.[20]

This dialogic method is the product of a mind which sees the world in a binary or multiple way, aware of alternative ways of looking at things and alternative possibilities of meaning. Meaning itself is not so much crystallised out as implied and suggested. In different ways in the different poems, implication operates at all levels – ideas, actions, descriptions, situations, dialogue, details, words. The poet's dialogic method is underpinned by his remarkable skill with language, involving a highly developed sensitivity to words and their multiple meanings and implications. So more or less distinctive styles or sub-styles are constructed for the various dialogic positions. Thus in *Pearl* the essence of the dreamer's 'earthly' position is expressed by his emotional language, and the maiden's 'heavenly' position by language that is coolly rational. In *Cleanness* the different voices, principally those of the narrator and God, come together in a designedly over-wrought rhetoric. In *Patience* the narrator's voice is worldy-wise, Jonah's extravagant, God's authoritative. In *Gawain* there are several dialogic positions, all relating to chivalry, and several chivalric languages: so Gawain's language in the first fitt is to be differentiated from that of Arthur and again from that of the Green Knight, and from his own language in the fourth fitt, after the Green Knight's revelations.

In terms of their interrelations, each poem has a distinctive linguistic colouring which expresses its main idea. Thus the reader of *Pearl* is made aware of the large number of words, par-ticularly metrical link-words (including *perle* itself), which have both 'earthly' and 'heavenly' meanings, so that these words them-selves lead the reader to think about the division between earth and heaven which the poem focuses on[21] *Gawain* also exploits the fact that many words have more than one meaning or shade of meaning, but in this poem verbal ambiguity goes along with other ambiguities of many kinds to express the central idea of the deceptiveness of the appearances of chivalry and the instability of its doctrines. The overall linguistic colouring of light irony in *Patience* is apt for both the forgiving nature of the story and the idea of impatience as folly rather than crime or sin. *Cleanness* is different from the other poems in that it is an example of the dia-logic method in reverse. It is not only monologic, but deliberately and relentlessly so. In this it images the totally uncompromising nature of God's justice, and at the same time helps set up its rela-tionship with *Patience*.

The poems invite consideration of other possible relationships between them. If *Cleanness* is about justice and *Patience* about mercy, *Pearl* and *Gawain* may both be thought of as holding the balance. In *Pearl* the relationship between God's justice and mercy is expounded by the maiden and figured by the Lamb. In *Gawain* the Green Knight balances justice and mercy in his judgement of Gawain. *Pearl* and *Cleanness* may be paired off against *Patience* and *Gawain* in that essentially the first two work metaphorically, the last two literally. *Patience* is on its own against the other three poems in that, miracles apart, its world is ordinary. Thus dirt or filth is excluded from *Pearl* and *Gawain* and is a metaphor in *Cleanness*, but it is 'real' in *Patience*, as in the descriptions of the whale's insides and the penitential actions of the Ninevites.

I do not mean to imply by anything I have said that the poet drew up a plan of dialogic relationships as his first step in composing his four poems, or that he expects the reader to be aware of all possible relationships. It seems to me more in line with his whole approach, particularly his readiness to exploit the multiple meanings and ambiguities of words, that he should want to give the reader room to read the individual poems and the manuscript interactively, room to make his own connections and come to his own conclusions. The reader finds himself at the intersection of the dialogic voices.

I consider the poems as openly as possible, as though the texts were spread out in front of me, with a view to saying something useful about their meanings as poems. Though I take account of relevant literary and intellectual contexts where the poems signpost them, especially the Bible for the three religious poems, I see meaning as primarily constructed by patterns of words rather than by ideas and scripts which lie beyond the texts. There may be much in the three religious poems which possibly connects with the figural and allegorical interpretations of biblical commentators and other medieval expositors, and with the poet's religious *milieu*, but mine is not one of the many studies which take a theological approach to them, or any other extra-textual approach. As indicated above, little is known of their circumstances, and they seem less firmly grounded in actuality and more in literary worlds of their own than, say, *The Canterbury Tales* or *Piers Plowman*. Though all the *Gawain*-poems have been subjected to cultural/historical interrogation, they do not respond as readily to it as many medieval writings do.[22]

A major stumbling-block for approaches from outside the texts is that they have to work with broad brush-strokes, and this means that they are difficult to combine with the close reading which I see as necessary for these particular poems if any sort of justice is to be done to them. Not all agree. Thus Francis Ingledew, in suggesting that *Cleanness* is concerned with the degenerate state of the medieval English priesthood, asserts the direct opposite of my own position, that the poem requires a reading which gives priority to 'specifiable liturgical, historiographical, and prophetic discourses' instead of one based on its words.[23] But he has to leave much of the poem out of consideration. It is of course open to a reader to read a text (from a cultural theoretical or any other point of view) by focusing on some parts or aspects of it and subordinating or ignoring others. To a degree every reader must do this. But not to attend to the highly-wrought nature of these particular poems, with their studied use of words, is to run the risk of serious oversimplification or misinterpretation.

An influential line of interpretation of *Cleanness* builds on the standard eschatological reading of the parable of the wedding feast as a figure for the Last Judgement and sees the whole poem as being about the Last Judgement. But *clannesse* is the poem's first word, and it recurs, in one form or another, throughout the poem, in discussion as well as story. As the poem gives such striking prominence to the word, it is hard not to see the word itself, and the ideas contained in it, as the central focus. True, the word *clannesse* and the concept of 'cleanness' are archaic and difficult; the fact that *Purity* is an accepted alternative editorial title for the poem is a good indication of that. Interpreting the poem as not about *clannesse* but the Last Judgement moves it to more familiar and manageable ground, but at the cost of evading much of its challenge.[24] *Cleanness* has also been much examined by critics interested in gender studies, who usually see it as homophobic and idealising heterosexuality. They are naturally struck by the remarkable speech in which God celebrates the joys of heterosexual lovemaking. But if they take the speech at face value as demonstrating the poem's preoccupation with the issue of heterosexual *versus* homosexual lovemaking, they are in danger of moving the poem off-centre through paying insufficient regard to its rhetorical and metaphorical basis.[25]

Another, rather different, example of the need for careful examination of the poet's use of words comes from critical work on *Pearl*. Every generation of critics seems to have had difficulty with the maiden's long expository speeches and the dreamer's description of the New Jerusalem. A recent study claims that 'one of the problems with the Maiden's (theological) discourse' is 'her impersonal, legalistic, or doctrinal language', and that some readers have found the description of the New Jerusalem 'flat and insipid, an example of a lack of attention on the poet's part'.[26] Many other critics have indeed come to the same or similar conclusions.[27] But the maiden's language, when examined closely, is *not* 'impersonal, legalistic, or doctrinal'. On the contrary, it is demonstrably vivid and metaphorical. She uses simple language to express the commonplaces of Christian history and doctrine in lines which are memorable even out of context, as *Ryche blod ran on rode so roghe* 'rich blood ran on the rough cross' (line 646), or *Adam with inne deth uus drounde* 'Adam drowned us in death' (line 656). But to quote the lines out of context does not do justice to them, for the stylistic effects of *Pearl* are cumulative. Passages like the maiden's long speeches and the dreamer's description of the city develop their own momentum, and when read with the movement of the whole earlier part of the poem behind them are very powerful. The dreamer's listing of the twelve precious stones which make up the twelve layers of the foundation of the heavenly city, a listing which takes up two stanzas and which out of context may seem merely repetitive, may also be seen, in extended context, as purposefully expansive, conveying the brightness of the city, its solidity, and its otherness.

As highly self-conscious works of art, the poems invest a great deal in literary effects, both large-scale, as in careful structural patterning of the narratives and lengthy descriptions, and small-scale, as in the precise use of a rich vocabulary in descriptive details. They are indeed almost Shakespearian in their sense of the dramatic, in their fusing together of the intellectual and emotional, in the inventiveness of their treatment of ideas, and in the energy and assurance of the writing. Shakespeare writes as a Renaissance humanist, and the *Gawain*-poet too, from his late medieval religious perspective, writes with understanding of the human condition. They express their vision in the literary forms most available and congenial to them: Shakespeare writes poetic plays in the Renaissance genres of tragedy and comedy, and the *Gawain*-poet writes religious poems and a high-level romance. For both, language is all-important. On the one hand they have their linguistic showpieces (Shakespeare's soliloquies, the *Gawain*-poet's 'set-piece' descriptions), and on the other they are able to generate great power from the simplest word sequences. For readers and audiences of works of such verbal sophistication, alertness to the possibilities of language is a primary requirement for anything approaching full appreciation.

The fact that the *Gawain*-poet's language is thoroughly archaic is a considerable barrier to reading and understanding, and helps to explain why his work is so little known to the world at large. One wonders how 'alive' Shakespeare's work would be today if it were not for the fact that he wrote mostly plays. As it is Shakespeare is largely kept alive by performance, in spectacular productions which draw attention away from his archaic language. If today Shakespeare's language is a problem, the *Gawain*-poet's is much more so, based as it is on a remote dialect of Middle English which was not the ancestor of modern standard English, and with a complex vocabulary. It is a language which is difficult to translate successfully into modern English. Unlike Shakespeare or any other playwright, the *Gawain*-poet must rely entirely on his language in order to communicate. I believe, therefore, that the reader who does *not* read him closely, down to the individual word, must miss important meaning. Naturally my own study is shaped by this belief.

Notes

1   References in *Gawain* show that the poet had a good knowledge of Arthurian traditions, especially French. In addition *Cleanness* makes considerable use of 'wonders of the East' passages in *Mandeville's Travels* as a source, and both *Cleanness* and *Patience* make use of a passage from *The Romance of the Rose*. *Cleanness* refers explicitly to 'Clopinel and his clene Rose', i.e. Jean de Meun (also known as Jean Clopinel) and *The Romance of the Rose*. This uncharacteristically specific reference has literary point; see below, pp. 102–3.

2   Chaucer may see the Gawain of tradition as representing old-style chivalry when he has the Squire refer to 'Gawain with his olde curteisye' (*Canterbury Tales*, V. 95).

3   See Raluca L. Radulescu, *The Gentry Context for Malory's Morte Darthur* (Cambridge: Boydell & Brewer, 2003).

4   Ad Putter, *Sir Gawain and the Green Knight and French Arthurian Romance* (Oxford: Oxford University Press, 1995), p. 244.

5   Despite the lack of hard evidence, others have speculated that he was. With reference to the north-west midlands dialect, which is the basis of the language of the manuscript, J. R. Hulbert in a seminal study posited that the poet was attached to the provincial court of a north-west midlands noble which sought to establish its independence of the royal court in London, and that this court constituted the original audience of the poems (J. R. Hulbert, 'A hypothesis concerning the alliterative revival', *Modern Philology* 28, 1931, 405–22). More recently Michael J. Bennett, in a number of papers, has argued that there is no evidence of the existence of a north-west midlands court of sufficient size and wealth, and that the *milieu* of the poems is the royal court of Richard II itself, with its considerable and favoured retinue of Cheshiremen; see, e.g., Michael J. Bennett, 'The historical background', in Derek Brewer and Jonathan Gibson, eds, *A Companion to the Gawain-Poet*

(Cambridge: D. S. Brewer, 1997), pp. 71–90.

6 Nicholas Watson, 'The *Gawain*-poet as a vernacular theologian', and David Aers, 'Christianity for courtly subjects: reflections on the *Gawain*-poet', in Brewer and Gibson, *Companion*, pp. 293–313 and 91–101 respectively, take up a different position. They argue that religion in the poems is assimilated to courtly values in such a way as to make it comfortable for their courtly audiences. Both see, in Watson's words, 'the life of the aristocracy . . . carefully presented as coterminous with Christian life in general' (p. 313). Here I only have space to note that the poet appears to see a division between courtesy and religion (*Gawain*), and earthly and heavenly courtesy (*Pearl, Cleanness, Patience*), and that courtesy in its 'earthly' contexts is somewhat suspect: the language of courtesy is used by the dreamer in *Pearl* to curry favour with the maiden, by Lot in *Cleanness* to appease the Sodomites, by Jonah in *Patience* to criticise God, and by Gawain and others in *Gawain* as, amongst other things, a means of hiding thoughts and feelings.

7 The metre of *Pearl* must have been difficult to manage (there are signs of this in unusual word-forms, etc.), likewise the numerological patterning, most obvious in *Pearl* (e.g. in its many 'twelves'), though all four poems exhibit it. See below, pp. 4–5.

8 Sandra Pierson Prior, *The Fayre Formez of the Pearl Poet* (East Lansing: Michigan State University Press, 1996), p. 67.

9 Robert J. Blanch and Julian N. Wasserman, *From Pearl to Gawain: Forme to Fynisment* (Gainesville: Florida University Press, 1995).

10 Edward I. Condren, *The Numerical Universe of the Gawain-Pearl Poet* (Gainesville: Florida University Press, 2002).

11 I take this point further in the chapters on *Cleanness* and *Patience*, especially p. 149 below. There is a similar kind of reciprocating relationship, made up of contrasts and parallels, between the descriptions of the Knight and the Squire in the *General Prologue* (each representing one 'half' of the idea of knighthood, the two together making up the whole), and between the *Knight's Tale* and the *Miller's Tale*, which represent complementary world views. In my article 'The narrators in the *Book of the Duchess* and the *Parlement of Foules*', *Chaucer Review* 26 (1992), 219–36, I argue that these two narrators complement each other in that they express a 'practical' and 'academic' approach respectively, rather like the narrators of *Patience* and *Cleanness*.

12 The idea that God is both justice and mercy is particularly prominent in *Piers Plowman*, which has a full version of the debate between the four daughters in the context of the Crucifixion, Harrowing of Hell, and Resurrection (B-text, ed. A. V. C. Schmidt, 2nd edn (London: Dent, Everyman, 1995), 18.110–427). The *Gawain*-poet nowhere alludes to the four daughters, but his complementary pairing of *Cleanness* and *Patience* may owe something to this debate motif.

13 *Pearl* is metrically divided into twenty sections of five stanzas each, with the exception of section fifteen, which has six stanzas.

14 See Malcolm Andrew, 'Theories of authorship' in Brewer and Gibson, *Companion*, p. 25.

15 Another poet who transmuted a female close to him in life into a heavenly personage whom he meets in his dream-vision is Dante, who does this with his beloved Beatrice in *The Divine Comedy*. As has long been noticed, there are several affinities between *Pearl* and *The Divine Comedy*.

16 See below, pp. 149–50.

17 Michael Holquist is responsible for the title of the standard English edition of Mikhail Bakhtin's writing on dialogics and heteroglossia. See Michael Holquist, ed., *The Dialogical Imagination: Four Essays* [by M. M. Bakhtin], trans. Caryl Emerson and Michael Holquist (Austin: Texas University Press, 1981). My study is concerned with the poems, not Bakhtin, and I came to see the relevance of Bakhtin's ideas only after the study was already well advanced. I use the term 'dialogic' to refer to the pattern of voices that I find is set up in the individual poems and in the manuscript as a whole, each voice distinctive and expressing a distinctive point of view. There is no controlling voice so the effect is of different voices juxtaposed with each other and competing with each other, on more or less equal terms, for the reader's attention and approval. For a helpful introduction to Bakhtin and ideas of monologic and dialogic texts in a medieval literature context see S. H. Rigby, *Chaucer in Context* (Manchester: Manchester University Press, 1996), especially pp. 18-77. There is also a collection of essays: Thomas J. Farrell, ed., *Bakhtin and Medieval Voices* (Florida: Florida University Press, 1996).

18 In *Pearl* and *Patience* especially the human side is presented sufficiently attractively to make it possible for a reader to be drawn towards it and, consequently, away from God's. Jim Rhodes, *Poetry Does Theology: Chaucer, Grosseteste, and the 'Pearl'-Poet* (Notre Dame: Notre Dame University Press, 2001), goes some way along this road, seeing all three of the religious poems as participating in an 'incarnational theology'. Ad Putter, *An Introduction to the 'Gawain'-Poet* (London and New York: Longman, 1996), discusses the complexity of such issues in *Pearl* (pp. 177–98), and argues that 'God's manners in *Patience* are indeed thoroughly off-putting' (p. 136), until he redeems himself in his 'mercy' speech. It seems to me that in all three poems the reader is placed in a kind of catch-22 situation. If he moves towards sympathy for the human side and criticism of God, then he may be accused of falling into the same trap as the dreamer and Jonah and not taking the point that the ways of God run counter to 'fallen' human nature and are therefore difficult or impossible for human beings to comprehend.

19 On this point see my article, 'The three judgments and the ethos of chivalry in *Sir Gawain and the Green Knight*', *Chaucer Review* 24 (1990), 337–55.

20 J. A. Burrow, *The Gawain-Poet* (Tavistock: Northcote House, 2001), notes that *Pearl* and *Gawain* both insist on the *endeles* aspect of their main symbols, the pearl and the pentangle (p. 52). This link, like other binary links in and between the *Gawain*-poems, indicates both sameness and difference. The insistence on the endlessness of the symbols confirms that both relate to ideals of perfection. But the endlessness has a heavenly reference in *Pearl*, suggesting the nature of heaven, and an earthly one in *Gawain*, suggesting the integrity of the ideal of chivalry and of Gawain as its representative.

21 See James Milroy, '*Pearl*: the verbal texture and the linguistic theme',
   Neophilologus 55 (1971), 195–208.

22 This may help explain why David Wallace, ed., *The Cambridge History of
   Medieval English Literature* (Cambridge: Cambridge University Press,
   1995), with its broadly New Historicist approach, has much less to say on the
   Gawain-poems than on Chaucer and *Piers Plowman*, as a glance at its index
   will reveal.

23 Francis Ingledew, 'Liturgy, prophecy, and Belshazzar's Babylon: discourse
   and meaning in *Cleanness*', *Viator* 23 (1992), 247–79.

24 Thus Cindy L. Vitto, 'Feudal relations and reason in *Cleanness*', in Liam O.
   Purdon and Cindy L. Vitto, eds, *The Rusted Hauberk: Feudal Ideals of Order
   and their Decline* (Florida: Florida University Press, 1994), pp. 5–28, appears
   to see the difficulty of pinning down the meaning of the word *clannesse* as a
   reason for looking elsewhere for meaning. She notes that if 'the poem is
   designed to define *clannesse*', then 'we are still arguing over that definition',
   and she refers to the different 'definitions' of Menner, Spearing, Brewer, and
   Morse (p. 8). She accepts that the poem is in fact 'primarily eschatological in
   nature' (p. 22), and refers in the course of her argument to studies that put
   this point of view by, *inter alia*, Morse, and Clark and Wasserman (for which
   see below, p. 122, note 8).

25 The most substantial study is Elizabeth B. Keiser, *Courtly Desire and
   Medieval Homophobia: The Legitimation of Sexual Pleasure in Cleanness and
   Its Contexts* (New Haven and London: Yale University Press, 1997). Keiser
   refers to the poem's 'undertow of homophobic hatred that comes in the wake
   of such idealization of heterosexual passion' (p. 70). For my own discussion
   of the 'heterosexual passion' passage see below, pp. 106–7.

26 Rhodes, *Poetry Does Theology*, p. 143.

27 So Putter, *Introduction*, who seems to see the description of the heavenly city
   as 'largely a string of quotations from [the] biblical text' (p. 194). Burrow,
   Gawain-Poet, writes of sharing 'the disappointment most readers feel . . .
   with [the] lengthy description of the New Jerusalem, taken avowedly and in
   detail from chapters of Revelation' (p. 11). Much the same point is made, at
   greater length if with less consistency, by an earlier critic, P. M. Kean (*The
   Pearl: An Interpretation*, London: Routledge, 1967, pp. 210–17), and Kean's
   lukewarm response is endorsed by A. C. Spearing (*The Gawain-Poet: A Critical Study*, Cambridge: Cambridge University Press, 1970, pp. 165–6).

1

Pearl: the last shall be first

Introduction

Pearl is a religious dream-vision in which the dream is largely
taken up by dialogue between the narrator or dreamer, as a figure
in his dream, and a woman who is a fount of divine wisdom. The
closest analogy in fourteenth-century English writing is the
dream-dialogue between the dreamer and Lady Holy Church in
Passus I of the B-text of *Piers Plowman*.[1] In both the dreamer figure struggles with the great question of how to make the church's
teaching on salvation meaningful to him. *Piers Plowman* is vast
and multi-faceted but *Pearl* is relatively small-scale, focussed, and
personal in tone. It is an indication of the difference between the
two that in *Piers Plowman* the lady personifies a great institution,
and in *Pearl* the maiden is the resurrected form of his dead infant
daughter. Everything in the poem stems from the anguish which
his daughter's death has caused him.

Lady Holy Church holds forth on the great virtues of truth
and love, which *Piers Plowman* goes on to relate to faith, hope, and
charity, the seven deadly sins and the four cardinal virtues. But
these (and other) schemes and concepts, though they are central
to much medieval religious literature, are absent from *Pearl*. The
poem is little interested in morality. It is not interested either in
the finer points of Christian doctrine, or in controversial religious
issues. Unlike *Piers Plowman*, it does not engage significantly with
the fourteenth century.[2] Its interest lies rather in relating Christian doctrine to universal life-experience, and particularly in the
problem that some of the basic tenets of that doctrine fly in the
face of basic human instincts and attitudes. Langland's dreamer
in front of Lady Holy Church does not understand her, has little
to say, and is full of humility. He functions largely as a foil to his

instructor. The dreamer in *Pearl*, who also does not understand, has much more to say and is often assertive and challenging. His point of view as well as the maiden's is given weight. A dialogic relationship between two opposed positions emerges in the cut and thrust of their debate.

The narrative of *Pearl* is multi-layered, with the poet creating a dreamer-figure separate from himself whose attitudes differ significantly before, in, and after his dream. Before the dream (so the dreamer relates) he is the victim of conflicting emotions, and especially of a conflict between his will and his reason. He is to be seen, before, during, and after the dream, not only as a bereaved father but as a medieval Christian and, more generally still, as anyone brought by personal loss to a crisis of faith. In the dream he is also the embodiment of human will, and his transformed daughter the embodiment of human reason. This central opposition of abstractions may be extended to include others, for example earth and heaven, emotion and reason, body and mind. *Pearl* creates a strong sense of the anguish which drives the dreamer to make his demands and ask his questions, and it may well have been written out of the poet's own experience. But, if so, the poet is careful to keep all personal reference out of the poem. Like every aspect of the dreamer, his anguish is to be seen as representative of the human condition, bound up with human will and desire, not as an expression of the poet's own personal suffering. The poem is fundamentally metaphorical, moving always from concrete to abstract, specific to general. The poet may make the pearl-jewel his central image because of the multiplicity of metaphorical meanings which are available to it. He avoids particularising details which might take the reader in the wrong direction.

The poem is very highly wrought, with a complex metre, numerological patterning, and a carefully worked out and balanced structure. The metre is both syllabic and alliterative, with a four-stress pattern and an ornate rhyme scheme.[3] Its most striking feature is the linking of one stanza to another in five-stanza sections, and the linking of one section to another, by the use of the same word (the 'link-word') in the last line of each of the five stanzas, and in the first line of the stanza following. As in *Patience* and *Gawain* the last line of *Pearl* closely echoes the first, though the last group of five stanzas has a different link-word from the first. Numerologically it is not difficult to see the highlighting of the number twelve (twelve lines per stanza, 1212 lines in the poem, corresponding to the twelve tables and gates of the heavenly city, the twelve fruits that the trees of life bear twelve times per year, the 144,000–strong company of heavenly virgins), and there are other numerological significances, some obvious, some less so.

As with *Gawain*, and the manuscript as a whole, the key to *Pearl*'s complicated thematic structure is to consider it as tripartite, with an inner part contained within two framing parts. In *Pearl* there is intricate symmetry between the opening and closing frames, each of which consists of four sections of grouped stanzas; thus the four sections at the beginning are mirrored by the four at the end (17–20). In sections 1 and 20 the dreamer is awake and in the garden where he lost his pearl. In sections 2 and 19 he expresses his pleasure at the wonderful things he sees in his vision, and in sections 3–4 and 17–18 he describes two heavenly sights, the maiden and the heavenly city itself. Significantly, in expressing his sense of these two sights as overpowering, he twice uses the image of a stunned bird. The central sections (5–16) consist of dialogue between the dreamer and the maiden, and this inner part can be seen to have its own carefully constructed tripartite structure. The metrical and structural patterns make the poem a perfect correlative of its central image, the beautiful pearl in its elaborate and beautiful setting.[4]

Earth (1)

> Perle, plesaunte to prynces paye
> To clanly clos in golde so clere;
> Oute of oryent, I hardyly saye,
> Ne proved I never her precios pere.
> So rounde, so reken in uche araye,
> So smal, so smothe her sydes were,
> Quere-so-ever I jugged gemmes gaye,
> I sette hyr sengeley in synglere.
> Allas! I leste hyr in on erbere;
> Thurgh gresse to grounde hit fro me yot.
> I dewyne, fordolked of luf-daungere
> Of that pryvy perle wythouten spot. (lines 1–12)[5]

[Pearl, pleasing to a prince's taste, fit to be finely set in brightest gold; from out of the east, I say with certainty, I never found her precious equal. So round, so beautiful in every setting, so small, so smooth were her sides, wherever I judged bright gems I set her apart as unique. Alas! I lost her in a garden; through grass to the ground it went from me. I pine away, grievously wounded by the power of (frustrated) love for that special pearl without spot.]

The poem's first word is its focal point. When the dreamer refers to his pearl he means, as gradually becomes clear, a person, specifically his daughter who died in infancy and who appears to him in his dream in adult form. In referring to her in this way he draws on a common metaphorical usage in which the word 'pearl' denotes a person of excellent or pre-eminent qualities.[6] When he says he has lost a pearl, therefore, he expresses his sense of his lost one's jewel-like beauty and preciousness. Also, as an inanimate object, a pearl may be possessed entirely, as no human being can be. His metaphor may thus point to the way he thinks of his daughter, objectifying her as something precious which belonged to him in the way that a jeweller owns a jewel. It emphasises her materiality to him, the fact that he responds more to her apprehensible being than her inner or spiritual self; pearls do not have inner selves. In the repeated refrain line he refers to his pearl as *privy* 'special to me' (as in *my privy perle* 'my own special pearl', line 24), as *precios*, and also as *wythouten spot*, 'flawless, of spotless beauty and purity'.

The fact that the dreamer introduces the association between pearl and daughter obliquely, and never at any stage makes it fully explicit, makes the point about her preciousness to him in a different way. It seems from the first four lines that the poem is to be about a jewel, the most beautiful of pearls, worthy of a prince and the finest gold setting. But the pearl is not particularised as a jewel. Instead the dreamer reiterates its singular excellence, twice stating that he has never found its equal (lines 4, 7–8). When he does describe it, he confines himself to conventional adjectives of general import (*rounde, reken* 'beautiful', *smal, smothe*). Moreover, the adjectives belong to a vocabulary used for the description of courtly ladies in Middle English literature, and one phrase in particular (*so smothe her sydes were*, line 6) suggests a woman rather than a jewel.

This meaning seems to be corroborated by the fourfold use of the feminine pronoun in the first nine lines. In line 10 the neuter pronoun appears instead of the feminine pronoun, but then in lines 11–12 the dreamer seems to be confirming the hint in lines 5–6 that his pearl is a woman. Line 11 contains the commonplace metaphor of the lover, wounded by love, languishing for his mistress, and the noun *luf-daungere* evokes the great medieval love-allegory *The Romance of the Rose*. Variation between feminine and neuter forms of the pronoun continues through the first section of the poem. The pearl is *hit* in line 13, *hir* in line 22, *hit* again in line 41. Later there are oblique indications that the pearl is not a mistress but a daughter (*Ho was me nerre then aunte or nece* 'she was closer to me than aunt or niece', line 233), who died in infancy (*Thou lyfed not two yer in oure thede* 'you did not live two years in our land', i.e. on earth, line 483). But the idea of a daughter is only confirmed, and still only indirectly, in the poem's last stanza.

The dreamer's lack of explicitness and his wavering between thinking of his daughter as a jewel and a person may be explained in terms of the psychology of grief. He tries to cope with the pain of her death by blurring the identity of jewel and daughter in his mind, hiding the person in the jewel. He tries to keep the harsh fact of the death of his loved one at a distance from himself.[7] In this he is like the Man in Black in the dream in Chaucer's *The Book of the Duchess*, who to begin with is equally unable to confront the loss of a loved one and whose first response to the dreamer's questioning him about his sorrow is to present the death of White in terms of a game of chess, which he loses when his queen is captured. Eventually, prompted by a series of further questions from the dreamer to say more about her, the Man in Black is able to cut through his various self-defensive circumlocutions and to remember White as a woman and not a chess piece. He ends by finding words which state the fact of her death in the bluntest way possible: 'She ys ded!'.[8] The Man in Black seems to 'talk it out', with the help of the dreamer, and this seems to help him to face his loss.

Like Chaucer's dreamer, the dreamer in *Pearl* asks a series of questions, but he addresses them to his own lost loved one. His permanent inability to acknowledge the father-daughter relationship directly and to admit that his daughter is dead suggests that the raw pain of his bereavement never moderates to the same extent as the Man in Black's. Thus in terms of the dreamer's perceptions, the pearl-metaphor seems to have four functions. It

suggests his high valuation of the dead girl's beauty and preciousness, his objectifying and possessive attitude towards her,
the intensity of his love for her, and his inability to come to terms
with her death.

The dreamer's attitude to the garden in which he finds himself is similarly mixed. He sees it as a place of love and frustrated
love, like the garden in *The Romance of the Rose,* and also as a
place of consoling beauty. As the dreamer is caught between
thinking of his daughter as a pearl and as a person, so in the garden he is caught between conflicting emotions. He recalls how in
the past his pearl was always able to lift (*heven*) his mood (line 16),
whereas now his watching for her weighs his heart down (line 17).
There is contrast between his anguish and the soothing effect of
the beauty of the garden, beauty of sound, sight, and scent (lines
18–20). He sees the soil, where his pearl is buried, as ruining its
beauty (line 23), but at the same time he sees the soil as creating
new beauty from it (lines 25–6). His words express the biblical
paradox (John 12. 24)[9] that out of death comes life, that it is only
when a seed dies that it brings forth fruit. The miracle of transformation is obscurely conveyed by more contrasts: between
ryches and *rot* (line 25), between the brightness of the flowers
(lines 28, 42) and the darkness of the earth in which the pearl lies
(line 30), between the downward motion of the pearl as it falls to
the ground (lines 30, 41) and the springing up of the spice plants
(line 35). But the dreamer does not spell out the consolatory
implications.

The dreamer says that he entered the garden in a *hygh seysoun*
(major religious festival) in August. The festival is not specified,
but all three August festivals which qualify as *hygh* (Lammas on 1
August, the Transfiguration on 6 August, and the Assumption of
the Virgin on 15 August) imply the transformation of the earthly
into the heavenly. However, the dreamer also associates August and
the festival with harvest: *Quen corne is corven wyth crokes kene*
'when corn is cut with sharp sickles' (line 40), and this may guide
the reader to think principally in terms of Lammas, the harvest festival. In a religious poem the harvesting of the corn suggests the
harvest of souls which brings the dead to their heavenly home and
eternal life.[10] The dreamer has already found a shadowy consolation in the biblical idea that, without the death of a seed, no wheat

would be brought into the barn (line 32). But the detail that the sickles are sharp helps bring to mind also the contrasting image of death as the grim reaper with his scythe. The cutting of the corn, therefore, continues the idea of the conflicting messages, of despair in this world and hope in the next, which come to the dreamer from the garden. Only his references to the wheat in the barns and the cutting of the corn acknowledge life outside the garden. In his grief, he appears to have cut himself off from the world.

The garden is where the dreamer's daughter is buried: line 10 refers to the pearl slipping from him through the grass into the ground, line 22 to *hir color so clad in clot* 'her colour so clad in clay', line 23 to the (grave-) earth which spoils his *myry juele*, and line 41 to the (grave-) mound where the pearl had rolled down. It was usual in the middle ages for a person to be buried in a church or churchyard, or a burial-ground associated with a church. But it is not clear that *erbere* 'garden' means also 'churchyard' here; the word does not have this meaning elsewhere. It may be that just as the dreamer prefers to envisage his dead daughter as a pearl, so he prefers to see the churchyard in which she is buried as a garden. This may be another attempt to escape harsh reality, and also, in the light of the pragmatic attitudes which his dream-self reveals, it may be taken to indicate that he is ill at ease with spiritual things (and places) and mentally reframes their spirituality when he can.

In the last stanza of the first section, the dreamer explains himself as pulled in two directions by inner conflict:

> A devely dele in my hert denned,
> Thagh resoun sette myselven saght.
> I playned my perle that ther was spenned
> Wyth fyrce skylles that faste faght;
> Thagh kynde of Kryst me comfort kenned,
> My wreched wylle in wo ay wraghte. (lines 51–6)

[A heavy grief lay deep in my heart, though reason reconciled me (to my loss). I mourned my pearl that was imprisoned there with fierce arguments that fought hard (against each other). Though the nature of Christ offered me comfort, my wretched will laboured on in sorrow.]

The reader seems to have arrived at a clear statement of the dreamer's dilemma. He blames his will as responsible for his negative feelings. He describes it as *wreched*, which has the immediate meaning 'sorrowful', but which from his post-dream perspective might also have the derogatory sense 'of little value, useless'. His will is to be identified with his sense of his daughter as a pearl, an object to be desired, and with his sense of the garden as a place of loss, where the pearl he longs for lies beyond his reach in the soil. Reason here evidently means religious right-thinking, or understanding of Christian doctrine.[11] It appears to be equated with the *kynde of Kryst*, a phrase of imprecise import but which may be taken in context to refer principally to that central tenet of Christian doctrine which asserts that Christ overcame, and enabled others to overcome, death. If so it follows that *resoun* and *kynde of Kryst* are to be associated with the mysterious consolatory beauties of the garden, and with the dreamer's dim perception that what seems to have been lost has not in fact been lost at all. The syntax, in which *resoun* and *kynde of Kryst* belong to the two *Thagh* clauses and *devely dele* and *wreched wylle* to the two main clauses which resolve them, indicates that the internal battle is not an even one and that the dreamer's will has the ascendancy over his reason.[12]

The dreamer's inner conflict is representative of that which any Christian believer is likely to go through when faced with the death of one dearly loved. The subsequent dream, in which the two figures of the dreamer and the maiden confront each other, may be regarded as an externalisation of this inner conflict. The maiden expresses the wisdom of the *kynde of Kryst*, that is, the truths of Christian doctrine, and the dreamer in the dream expresses the force of the human will, the perceptions of the body rather than the mind. *Pearl* thus chronicles the struggle of the Christian individual to come to terms with a distressing life-event which challenges his deepest beliefs. The dreamer finds before his dream that, though he knows the teachings of the faith, they are at odds with his feelings and his whole sense of loss. He cannot make them work for him. His dream articulates his attempt to do so.

Paradise

The dreamer explains that in the midst of his anguish he falls asleep, on the spot where he lost his pearl. He dreams, or, as he puts it, his spirit, through God's grace, is taken out of his body on a journey to a place of marvels (lines 61–4). He responds to his dream-environment in two distinct stages. In the first his will is in abeyance, as he reacts with amazement and pleasure to what he sees. In the second his will returns, as his joy mutates to desire. Out of the body he may be, but he retains his human attributes, and behaves in the dream-world as though his dream is a continuation of his waking life.

Thus in lines 85–6 and 121–4 he recollects (from his post-dream standpoint) that the beauty of the dream-landscape made him forget his grief. In contrast to the garden in which he fell asleep, it brings him no mixed messages. Its beauty is supernatural, timeless and perfect, like that of a work of art. Whereas the garden was small-scale and conventionally pretty, with its individually named spice-plants, the landscape is on a large scale and has everything in abundance. It has the same physical features as natural landscapes, but they are made unnatural.[13] Rocks are of glass and precious stones, vegetation is of precious metals. In the garden the dark earth (line 30) is set against the beauty of the plants, but in the landscape all is dazzlingly beautiful. The ground itself consists of pearls (lines 81–2), which contribute to the general bejewelled effect. In the description of the garden the reader is made aware of the passing year and the cycle of growth and decay. The landscape by contrast has an inorganic quality of fixity and permanence. The description of the garden has an uncertain movement, reflecting the garden's mixed nature and the mixed effect it has on the dreamer, while that of the landscape is controlled and purposeful.

As the dreamer moves through the landscape and nears a stream, the description builds towards a climax (lines 103–5). The stream he finally comes to fits in with its setting (the pebbles in the stream-bed are of precious stones), and the country on the far side of the stream is in keeping. Crystal cliffs had taken his eye when he first entered the dream-landscape (line 74), and he eventually sees the maiden sitting under one on the opposite side (line 159). He sees the far side of the stream as still more beautiful than the near side (line 148), to the point where he thinks that the *mote* (walled city) of paradise must be located there (lines 137–8, 141–2). Indeed he later sees the Heavenly City across the stream.

The dreamer makes several statements to the effect that the beauty of the landscape is beyond human experience and beyond human powers of description. He states that no man might believe the glory of the light coming from the rocks (lines 69–70), and that no man might ever have such pleasure as to hear and see the birds there (lines 95–6). He makes two statements of inexpressibility, of the kind 'no man might describe its glory' (lines 99–100, 133–6).[14] He interprets the strange by the familiar: rich woven fabrics do not have half the splendour of the shining rocks, tree-trunks are as blue as indigo,[15] leaves are like burnished silver, and the gravel on the ground consists of pearls from the orient, compared with the light of which sunbeams are dark. No musical instrument, neither citole nor cithern, might compete with the beauty of the paradisal birdsong, and the steep slopes of the land near the river are as though woven from pure gold thread. The brightness of the precious stones shining in the stream-bed is conveyed by a climactic double comparison:

> In the founce ther stonden stones stepe
> As glente thurgh glas that glowed and glyght,
> As stremande sternes, quen strothe-men slepe,
> Staren in welkyn in wynter nyght. (lines 113–16)

[Bright stones were set in the bottom there, that glowed and gleamed like a beam of light through glass, as streaming stars, when men of this world are asleep, shine in the sky on a winter's night.]

In the context of the many other 'earthly' metaphors and comparisons these two similes, evocatively put but unoriginal, suggest an ordinary consciousness struggling to express a supernatural beauty which is beyond it. The reader is not allowed to forget that his perception remains earthbound.

The second stage of the dreamer's experience of paradise begins when he describes how his joy grows as he walks along the stream. For the first time he uses the word *more* (line 128), and in line 132 the phrase *more and more* becomes the metrical link-word of section 3. In line 144 the link-word conveys his ever-increasing longing: *And ever me longed ay more and more.* His experience of pleasure has led him to want still more pleasure. Specifically, he wants to cross the stream to the even more beautiful country on the other side. He looks for a ford, but finds only dangers. He pictures himself as in a dilemma, put off by the dangers and at the same time telling himself that, because the land across the stream is so full of delights, he should not be put off. So the reawakening of will and desire generates frustration, which in turn generates indecision.

The dreamer is led further into confusion by his sighting of the maiden. She too, like the rocks and trees, is more than earthly. She is a woman and at the same time a thing of supernatural beauty, an otherworldly creature not of flesh and blood. The shining white of her robe matches the shining of the *crystal clyffe ful relusaunt* (line 159) underneath which she sits, and the golden colour of her hair matches the gold of the river banks, which the dreamer describes as like fine gold thread (*fyldor fyn*, line 106), such as would be woven into a tapestry. She is a vision of pearls and gold in the setting of a bejewelled otherworldly landscape, a transformation into supernaturally beautiful human form of the pearl in its setting of gold which the dreamer envisions in the first lines of the poem.

The dreamer's response to the maiden is complicated. He recognises her at once: *I knew hyr wel, I hade sen hyr ere* (line 164). His language indicates that he sees in front of him both a child (*faunt*, line 161) and an adult (*mayden of menske* 'noble maiden', line 162). His mind seems to register her heavenly and her earthly appearance simultaneously, that is, to superimpose the image of his daughter, the child he knew in life, on the image of the adult figure who confronts him. His perception of the earthly child in the heavenly woman stays with him throughout his dream.

In his description of the maiden, as of the landscape, the dreamer several times uses conventional 'earthly' comparisons. He compares her hair to cut gold (line 165), and her face to polished ivory (line 178). When later she comes to meet him he is able to see her more clearly and to describe her in more detail. He presents her dress as a dazzlingly decorated version of one which might be worn by an aristocratic lady, with the *lappes large* 'broad hanging sleeves' (line 201) of the gown giving it a contemporary touch. Her gown and other garments are of shining white material, decorated with pearls, and she wears a crown of pearls. Conventional comparisons reminiscent of, for example, the Harley Lyrics, once more emphasise the whiteness of her face and the gold of her hair:

> Her ble more blaght then whalles bon.
> As schorne golde schyr her fax thenne schon. (lines 212–13)[16]

[Her complexion (was) whiter than whale's bone. Her hair shone then like bright cut gold.]

White complexion and hair like gold are usual attributes of beautiful women in medieval lyrics and romances, but here the exclusion of other colours (a woman's beautiful complexion conventionally has white and red mixed together) contributes to an effect of unearthly radiance. The description culminates with the great pearl on her breast which is the most distinctive feature of her dress. It calls from the dreamer a double statement of inexpressibility:

> A mannes dom moght dryyly demme
> Er mynde moght malte in hit mesure.
> I hope no tong moght endure
> No saverly saghe say of that syght,
> So was hit clene and cler and pure,
> That precios perle ther hit was pyght. (lines 223–8)

[A man's reason might be utterly eclipsed before his mind could take its measure. I believe no tongue might suffice to utter any meaningful words about that sight, it was so bright and clear and pure, that precious pearl in its setting.]

Pearl and pearl-maiden seem to merge in one overwhelming vision which defeats both his mind and tongue, leaving him lost for any descriptive words other than the simplest (line 227). He makes no attempt to make meaning out of what he sees, apart from his cryptically-conveyed recognition of the maiden as his daughter (line 233). The symbolisms which are latent in the details of the maiden's dress are for the reader, not for him. Her white *beau biys* 'gown of fine linen' is primarily the 'fine linen, clean and white' which is the bridal garment of the wife of the Lamb in Revelation 19.8, and it also has associations with innocence and with baptism.[17] Her crown of pearls marks her out as an inhabitant of heaven, and she herself later (lines 733–44) explains the great pearl at her breast as a symbol of the kingdom of heaven.

Predictably, the dreamer's sighting of the maiden produces a powerful response in him. The struggle between his desire to cross the stream to speak to her, and his fear that if he tries to do so he will lose her (lines 169–88), is heightened. His emotions, together with the shock of seeing her (line 174), leave him in a state of paralysis (lines 182–4). But when instead of withdrawing the maiden comes towards him, he is reassured. His confused feelings give way to unalloyed pleasure, and his awareness of their former relationship now simply adds to his joy (lines 231–4). Her greeting to him, formal but friendly as he describes it, in which she takes off her crown and bows to him (lines 235–8), confirms him in his delight (lines 239–40).

Emotion and reason

The stage is now set for the long dialogue which follows. In it the dreamer tells the maiden of his pain at losing her and looks forward to joining her across the stream. She tells him that he has not lost her but that he cannot join her (lines 241–360). The dreamer then changes direction, asking her a series of questions about her position in heaven, which she answers (lines 361–976). He, the embodiment of will, takes the initiative in their conversation, while she, the embodiment of reason, does not assert her own agenda but is content to respond to his.

The maiden's style of speech befits her appearance. Her words have a commanding authority which distances them from earthly confusions. Whereas the dreamer constantly uses terms of endearment to her, she never calls him 'father' or otherwise speaks affectionately. She usually does not call him anything, but occasionally she addresses him as *sir* or *burne* (*jueler* several times in Section 5, where it is the metrical link-word). She maintains an attitude of formality which fluctuates only within narrow limits. As the stream keeps them physically apart, so her attitude puts off his various advances.[18] She does confirm his identification of her as his lost pearl, thereby acknowledging the bond between them:

> Thow wost wel when thy perle con schede
> I was ful yong and tender of age. (lines 411–12)

> [You know well that when your pearl slipped away I was very young and of tender age.]

Her purpose in doing so is not however to remind the dreamer of her earthly existence but to make the point that, despite her youth

when she died, she is now married to Christ the Lamb (lines
413–14). Her indirect reference to her death as the slipping away
of his pearl is no doubt for reasons very different to the dreamer's
when he uses similar language (as in line 10). She does not want
to remind him of his pain any more than is necessary, not out of
sensitivity to his feelings but because she wants him to see her as
she is. Throughout the dream, without denying their former relationship, she tries to prise the dreamer loose from the past which
he clings to. The new situation has brought about a reversal of
their status *vis-à-vis* each other. Her position, formerly one of
dependence, is now one of authority. The reversal gives difficulty
to both of them. He cannot accept it, and she has to try to find a
way of managing and changing his non-acceptance. Her attitude
manifests itself as responsible concern for a loved one on whom
one has, however unintentionally, inflicted pain. Although the
maiden makes only this one brief reference to their relationship
on earth, the reader is left to infer that it informs all her efforts to
help the dreamer to understand. But whereas to him their bond is
emotional and means everything, she takes a cooler, more rational
view of it. It is true that in the first part of their dialogue she
clearly expresses both pleasure (lines 397–400) and severe frustration (lines 289–94). But it may be that she carefully manages
her language the better to manage the dreamer, and in any event
her emotions are always under control. There is an urgency about
her words, but it is the urgency of one who has an important truth
to communicate, not a sign of emotional agitation.

In the first part of the dialogue the dreamer is at his most
direct, as he tells the maiden how *joyles* he is and how *joyfol* he
could be. As throughout their dialogue, the dreamer's words
reflect primary physical perceptions and emotions and an immediate, common-sense logic; the maiden's, the more intellectual
voice of reason in the service of spiritual truth. The immediate
problem for the maiden is that the dreamer always fails to take her
meaning, and for the dreamer that the emotional engagement
which he longs for never eventuates. He tries to reach her through
various emotionally based stratagems, such as challenges and
appeals, and she tries to make him see reason by adopting one
style of argument after another as she seeks to convince him of the
wrongness of his way of looking at things. The underlying difficulty is that they can only try to connect with each other on their

own terms. Thus the dreamer speaks to the maiden not as an embodiment of heavenly wisdom but as his dear daughter, and the maiden does not respond to him as her loving father so much as a Christian in need of spiritual enlightenment.

Error and correction

The maiden's first three speeches to the dreamer have a kind of descending order, in both matter and manner. She seems to lower her intellectual sights progressively as she becomes increasingly aware of the dreamer's inability to comprehend what she is saying. The three styles she uses may be described as allegorical, scholastic, and homiletic respectively, all styles which are part of the equipment of the medieval preacher.

When he begins to speak the dreamer does not admit to his delight at seeing the maiden. In the manner of a parent whose child has gone missing and is then found again he disguises his relief and grumbles at her.[19] He talks of his longing for her and of the pain he has endured at being parted from her. Self-pity manifests itself when he contrasts her life in heaven with his own wretched existence on earth. He gives no sign of being glad for her, but seems to accuse her of thoughtlessness towards him:

> Pensyf, payred, I am forpayned,
> And thou in a lyf of lykyng lyghte,
> In Paradys erde, of stryf unstrayned. (lines 246–8)

[Sad, worn out, I am in great pain, and you are in a life of easy pleasure, in the land of Paradise, untouched by trouble.]

He ascribes what has happened not to God but to a malign fate (*wyrde*, line 249). In its mixture of love and self-regard the dreamer's first speech to the maiden sets the underlying tone for his part of the ensuing dialogue. He calls himself *a joyles juelere* (line 252).

In her reply (lines 257–76) the maiden employs allegorical imagery to try to convince the dreamer that his way of seeing things is back to front. Her first action and words point to the gap of understanding between them. Whereas a moment before, as he records, she had taken off her heavenly crown and greeted him with friendly words, she now replaces her crown and speaks to him severely, using at first the formal plural of address: *Sir, ye haf*

your tale mysetente 'Sir, your words are misconceived' (line 257).
She makes powerful use of a classic symbol of earthly transience
to suggest the heavenly reversal of natural processes. She explains
that the pearl he thought he had lost was not a true pearl at all but
a rose *that flowred and fayled as kynde hyt gef* 'that flowered and
failed as its nature required' (line 270), and that the rose only
became a true pearl in heaven, achieving jewel-like permanence
by becoming part of the heavenly eternity. If he were a true jeweller, she says, he would appreciate this.

The words 'pearl', 'jewel', and 'jeweller' are used frequently
in this opening exchange, and they focus the differing viewpoints
of dreamer and maiden. The dreamer in the dream associates a
jeweller particularly with his delight in the jewel(s) in his keeping.
A jewel is amongst the most beautiful and precious of all objects,
and if an object is beautiful and precious it is natural to want not
to lose it. He thinks of his daughter as a pearl, or a jewel, and himself as a jeweller (he uses the word of himself first in line 252) who
has suffered the misfortune of such a loss. His response to his loss
is the 'natural' one of sorrow, followed by joy when he thinks he
has found his jewel again and will be able to take it back into his
possession.

But the maiden has a different view of pearls, jewels, and jewellers, which strikes radically at the dreamer's 'natural' assump-
tions. She challenges his thinking of her (or anyone else) as a pearl
or jewel because the aspect of pearls or jewels which for her
defines their 'pearlness' or 'jewelness' is, as becomes progressively
clearer, their permanence, their imperviousness to decay.[20] Later
she associates pearls with the 'spiritual' meanings of righteousness, innocence, virginity (lines 767–8), and purity.[21] For her the
pearl or jewel is a symbol of her transformed self, and the risen
Christ, and heaven, and the state of innocence. In short, it is a
symbol of transcendental perfection. She expounds this view
(lines 729–39) on the authority of the biblical text of the parable
of the merchant who gives all that he has to purchase the pearl of
great price, in Matthew 13. 45–6: 'Again, the kingdom of heaven
is like unto a merchant man, seeking goodly pearls: Who, when he
had found one pearl of great price, went and sold all that he had,
and bought it.' The parable not only identifies the pearl with
heaven (an identification which the maiden elaborates) but also
cuts across the idea of the 'natural' possessiveness of the jeweller,

for the emphasis of the parable is on the jeweller's letting go of the jewels that he possesses, giving up all that he has accumulated for the sake of the one great prize, the kingdom of heaven. For her a *gentyl* or *kynde* jeweller (lines 264, 276) is one who behaves like the jeweller in the parable, not like the dreamer, who wants to keep his jewel and get it back when he has lost it.[22] For the dreamer the pearl is a symbol of the best of the material world, for the maiden the perfection of the spiritual.

The maiden's meaning passes him by. As the context makes clear, to him she is a *juel* (line 277) and her words are *jueles* (line 278) because they are precious, not because they are eternal. His reply begins with a term of endearment:

> 'Iwyse,' quoth I, 'my blysfol beste,
> My grete dystresse thou al todrawes.' (lines 279–80)

['Indeed,' I said, 'my blessed darling, you entirely dispel my great distress.']

He is happy not for the reason she wants him to be (that is, because he understands she is safe in heaven), but because he thinks she has told him that she has not gone from him after all. Like Lear with Cordelia he appears to think that by a stroke of good fortune she has been given back to him and that the two of them will henceforth be together, each finding sufficiency in the other's company. He accepts her rebuke to him for blaming fate by announcing that he is now happy to praise the Lord, for the reason that the Lord has made it possible for him to be with her again (lines 285–6). He constructs his own meaning out of what the maiden says, looking forward to the joy of joining her (lines 287–8).

The dreamer's determination to get close to the maiden only makes her withdraw herself further. In the second of her three speeches (lines 289–336) she begins with an exasperated comment on the folly of the human race in general: *Wy borde ye men? So madde ye be!* 'Why do you men jest? You are so mad!' (line 290). Faced with his incomprehension, she abandons her attempt to make him see what has happened to her in a positive light and concentrates on exposing the errors she finds implicit in his statements. To do this she turns away from allegorical imagery and adopts techniques of scholastic analysis. She points to three separate errors and does not mince her words:

> Thre wordes has thou spoken at ene;
> Unavysed, for sothe, wern alle thre.
> Thou ne woste in worlde quat on dos mene;
> Thy worde byfore thy wytte con fle. (lines 291–4)

[You have said three things (lit. words) all at once; ill-considered, in truth, were all three. You do not know at all what one (of them) means; your words have flown ahead of your understanding.]

Systematically, she goes on to particularise the three errors. The first, she says, is that he believes she is in the valley with him because he sees her (lines 295–6); the second (*Another thou says*) that he believes he will be able to live with her there (lines 297–8); the third (*The thrydde*) that he believes he will be able to cross the stream (line 299).

Not content with this brief listing, she then deals in detail with each of the errors in turn, accusing him of disrespect for God in each case. She first takes him to task for his lack of faith in that he does not trust God's promise of resurrection and believes only what he can see and understand (lines 301–12). Secondly she accuses him of presumption in assuming that he will be able to live where she lives without first asking permission of God (lines 313–17). Finally she accuses him of rash misapprehension in thinking that he will be able to cross the stream, explaining that, because of the Fall, God has decreed that the stream may only be crossed through death (lines 318–24).

She expounds her first point in general terms:

> I halde that jueler lyttel to prayse
> That leves wel that he ses wyth yye. (lines 301–2)

[I consider that jeweller little to be praised who trusts fully what he sees with his eye.]

In continuing her exposition she uses the second person plural, which makes her seem, as in line 290, to be addressing the human race in general rather than the dreamer in particular:

> Ye setten hys wordes ful westernays,
> That leves nothynk bot ye hit syye. (lines 307–8)

[You (people) set his words very much askew, you who believe nothing unless you see it.]

For her second and third points she homes in on the dreamer, using the second person singular:

> Deme now thyself if thou con dayly
> As man to God wordes schulde heve. (lines 313–14)

[Now judge (for) yourself whether you have spoken in the way that a man should offer up words to God.]

She ends her third point with another generalisation:

> Thurgh drwry deth bos uch man dreve
> Er over thys dam hym Dryghtyn deme. (lines 323–4)

[Every man must go through cruel death before the Lord will allow him over this water.]

There is no comfort here for the dreamer. Her movement between the general and the particular is the mark of a preacher's rhetoric. He has become the target of a sermon, whose meaning for him is as uncompromising as its tone: he will not be able to join her.

The maiden's severity turns the dreamer's joy to dismay. He continues to see their relationship exclusively in personal terms. Endearments are again prominent in his speech: *my swete* (line 325), *my precios perle* (line 330), *perle myne* (line 335). Driven on by emotional need he counters her points with points of his own, expressed not by reasoned statements but by rhetorical questions which all amount to the same question: having found her, how can he be expected to let her go again? As before her reasonings have passed him by, and he understands only that she has told him that he cannot after all be with her. He blames her for making him miserable again (*My precios perle dos me gret pyne* 'my precious pearl causes me great pain', line 330), as though he thinks it is her decision, not God's as she has tried to explain, that he cannot join her. When *he* uses the third person, in an attempt to match her reasoning with reasoning of his own, the effect is not to depersonalise, but to make his anguish all the more apparent:

> What serves tresor bot gares men grete,
> When he hit schal efte wyth tenes tyne? (lines 331–2)

[What use is treasure but to make a man weep, when he must lose it again through (strokes of) misfortune?]

This is argument from the heart, not the head. His questions, and his statement that he no longer cares what happens to him (lines 333–4), constitute a powerful emotional appeal to the maiden.

In her third response (lines 337–60), the maiden narrows her focus and at the same time distances herself still further from the dreamer. She attempts no longer to explain her situation, nor indeed does she even refer to herself. Having failed to make an impression on his attitude first by the use of allegory and then by the use of logic, she resorts to exhortation. Poetic metaphor and reasoning give way to emphasis. She exhorts him to focus not on his sorrow, nor on her, but on loving God, for the reason that no other course will gain him anything.

This is a central idea in *Patience*, which draws on homiletic traditions, and the maiden's language, now down-to-earth and idiomatic (e.g. *For anger gaynes the not a cresse* 'For anger profits you not a jot', line 343, and *Of the way a fote ne wyl he wrythe* 'He will not turn aside from the way one foot', line 350) shares something of the linguistic register of *Patience* also.[23] The difference is that the maiden's language is more dramatic and emphatic, an effect created particularly by her use of pairs of alliterating words, of parallel or contrasting meaning, linked by a conjunction: *wele and wo* (line 342), *braundysch and bray* (line 346), *swefte and swythe* (line 354), *to ne fro* (line 347). This verbal pattern is used three times in the last two lines of the speech:

> For, marre other madde, morne and mythe,
> Al lys in hym to dyght and deme. (lines 359–60)

[For (though you may) lament or rage, mourn and fret, all lies with him to dispose and decree.]

One imagines the maiden speaking the alliterating syllables with particular force to drive her point home. Whereas earlier she had used the complex imagery of the pearl and the rose to try to give the dreamer a sense of the miracle of her transformation, she now confines herself to the simplest imagery, comparing his behaviour to that of a mortally wounded doe thrashing and braying in agony, to no avail (lines 345–8). All her efforts are directed towards convincing the dreamer of one general point, which she urges on him relentlessly. The point is a commonplace of Christian homiletics: people have no choice but to accept God's will and ask for his mercy. Their dialogue has reached a crisis point. Unless the dreamer changes his attitude, it has nowhere further to go.

Redirection (1)

The dreamer gives every sign of being shaken by the maiden's exhortation. His reply to it is three stanzas long, agitated and contradictory. Without saying so in so many words, he appears at last to accept that he is not going to be able to join the maiden in heaven. He retreats, whether strategically or otherwise. He confesses to his failings, and asks her to be tolerant of them. He says that the sight of her has lessened his pain (line 377), and he ends his reply with an extravagant assertion to the effect that the maiden's new happy situation is the foundation of his own happiness (lines 393–6). There is however still a strong current of self-justification in what he says. His request to her not to be angry with him (line 367) and his admission that he has gone astray (line 368) are tempered by his continuing sense that she is responsible for causing him the pain which led him to speak as he did (lines 371–2). It matters to him greatly that she is displeased with him, and he strikes a note of pathos as he appeals to the way they once were:

> And, quen we departed, we wern at on;
> God forbede we be now wrothe,
> We meten so selden by stok other ston. (378–80)

[And, when we parted, we were at one; God forbid we should be angry now, we meet so seldon by stump or stone.]

The simplicity of this appeal, particularly in the understatement of the last line, is touching. But it may not be an artless simplicity; the dreamer deploys his emotional weapons with skill. An accusing self-pity creeps back into his contemplation of the difference between her state and his:

> In blysse I se the blythely blent,
> And I a man al mornyf mate.
> Ye take theron ful lyttel tente,
> Thagh I hente ofte harmes hate. (385–8)

[I see you joyfully placed in bliss, and I a man all sad and dejected. You take very little notice of that, though I often endure burning sorrows.]

He loves her, and wants her, but he is human, and, as is evident
throughout their dialogue, his love for her does not eliminate feelings of resentment and jealousy at her 'success'. In the face of
such agitation his statements that he now looks not to her but to
divine mercy, as she had urged him to do, ring hollow:

> Bot Crystes mersy, and Mary and Jon,
> Thise arn the grounde of alle my blisse. (lines 383–4)

[But Christ's mercy and Mary and John, these are the foundation of
all my happiness.]

Mary and John (who in John 19.26 stand together at the foot of
the cross) seem to be added as an afterthought, to make his statement of acceptance sound more impressive.

To end his speech the dreamer puts a request to the maiden:

> Bot now I am here in your presente,
> I wolde bysech, wythouten debate,
> Ye wolde me say in sobre asente
> What lyf ye lede erly and late. (lines 389–92)

[But now that I am here in your presence I would ask, without any
argument (between us), that you would tell me in quiet concord
(with me) what life you lead day and night.]

His words express his new dilemma. He wants her to be pleasant
to him, but his phrases *wythouten debate* and *in sobre asent* indicate
his anxiety that she might speak to him severely again. His request
is so general that it effectively hands the initiative to her, and in
the next phase of the dialogue his three questions arise out of his
growing disenchantment with her explanations. The principal
underlying reason for his questioning, however, is that after the
shock of his realisation that he is not going to be able to join her
immediately he wants to keep in communication with her. A mixture of subsidiary motives is also evident, all connected with her
and all more or less self-regarding, amongst them curiosity, desire
to please, sense of unfairness, puzzlement, and a determination to
speak his mind. The dreamer in *Piers Plowman* asks Lady Holy
Church how he may save his soul, and is interested in what she has
to teach him more than he is in her as his teacher. But the dreamer
in *Pearl* is interested only in the maiden. Though she tries to use
their dream-encounter to impart to him an understanding of
heaven and how he may get himself to heaven, he gives no sign of

wanting this knowledge, or of acting upon what she says. The only knowledge he wants, it seems, is knowledge of her, and this only as second-best to being with her. His questions betray not only an inability to comprehend the divine, but a lack of interest in it, except insofar as it impinges on her.

Rank

The maiden's replies to the narrator's questions make up most of the second part of the dialogue. Her discourse describes a circle, beginning and ending with what she regards as the most important aspect of her situation in heaven: her marriage to Christ the Lamb. In between, as in the first three-speech cycle of their dialogue, she progresses through three stages of argument which reflect different techniques of the practised preacher, in descending order of difficulty: allegory (with reference to Saint Paul's allegory of the Christian community as the body of Christ, lines 433–68), parable (with reference to the parable of the labourers in the vineyard, lines 493–588), and exposition (with reference to her explanation of the saving power of innocence, lines 601–744). As in the first cycle the dreamer and the maiden draw progressively apart. The dreamer's third question lacks the courteous introduction of the first two, and the maiden's tone hardens in the course of their exchanges, until towards the end of her third reply she mixes exposition with warning directed specifically to the dreamer, in a less emphatic version of her style at the end of the first cycle.

The maiden speaks less urgently than before because the narrator's questions, now that he has accepted that he cannot join her, put her under less pressure. Her priority no longer has to be to bring him to his senses, and her speeches become more expansive. Her tone is serene, her language simple and dignified, appropriate to the expression of divine truths. By comparison with the dreamer her language in this part of the dialogue holds more or less consistently to a middle range, without the variations which characterise the dreamer's speech, such as his idioms and colloquialisms (for example lines 487, 489) and his excursion into learned language (lines 593, 596).

The maiden begins by welcoming what she takes to be the dreamer's change of heart and new attitude of humility. Unlike

Cleanness and *Patience*, *Pearl* does not refer explicitly to the beatitudes taught by Christ in the Sermon on the Mount, but the third
beatitude, 'Blessed are the meek: for they shall inherit the earth'
(Matthew 5. 5), nevertheless well expresses the import of her
words on the high value accorded meekness in heaven (lines
401–7). The maiden takes herself as an example of 'weak' earthly
meekness becoming 'strong' heavenly meekness when she tells
the dreamer of her marriage to Christ. As noted above, she says
she was *ful yong and tender of age*, i.e. an innocent child, when she
died (lines 411–12),[24] and yet (*Bot*, line 413) Christ married her
and crowned her queen in heaven (lines 414–15). The marriage
implies a bond between them (their innocence), and the crowning
a sharing of Christ's heavenly power. Her calling Christ 'the
Lamb' (lines 407, 413) evokes Christ's own meekness and innocence. The familiar yet strange title derives primarily from the
Book of Revelation and from John the Baptist's words in John
1.29: 'Behold the Lamb of God which taketh away the sin of the
world'.

The dreamer does not ask about the Lamb and her marriage
at this point, though he does later (lines 771–2). Instead he questions the maiden's claim to be a queen, thereby signalling that this
is what touches him most immediately:

> 'Blysful,' quoth I, 'may thys be trwe?
> Dyspleses not if I speke errour.
> Art thou the quene of hevenes blwe
> That al thys worlde schal do honour?' (lines 421–4)

['Dear,' I said, 'may this be true? Do not be displeased if I speak in
error. Are you the queen of the blue heavens, whom all this world
shall honour?']

He explains that his problem is that he knows that Mary is queen
of heaven, and he assumes, as line 423 indicates, that there can
only be one queen in heaven. He entertains the possibility that
Mary might lose her pre-eminence if someone better qualified in
some *favour* 'gracious attribute' were found (lines 427–8), thereby
revealing both his naiveté and his reductionist attitude to matters
of rank. His implicit question to the maiden is: are you claiming
to be that better-qualified person? His implicit point is that no one
better qualified ever will be found than Mary, who is unique, like
the phoenix:

> Now, for synglerty o her dousour,
> We calle hyr Fenix of Arraby,
> That freles flewe of hyr fasor,
> Lyk to the quen of cortaysye. (lines 429–32)

[Now, on account of the singularity of her gentleness, we call her the Phoenix of Arabia, that flew flawless from her creator, like the queen of courtesy (did).]

The dreamer speaks of his love for his pearl before and at the end of his dream using terms from *The Romance of the Rose*, and elsewhere he makes occasional use of the language of courtesy, though never as one who is at home with it: in this speech, he clumsily mixes a courteous phrase (line 422) with an endearment (line 421). In his previous speech he had contrasted himself with the maiden in his statement that while she was able to speak courteously, he was lacking in manners (lines 381–2). His interest in courtesy is always maiden-centred, as when, in line 422, he wants to forestall a negative response from her. Now he gives Mary the title *quen of cortaysye*, with *quen* in the sense 'chief exponent' as well as literally 'queen'. He uses a word from the register of courteous or courtly language, *dousour* (Modern French *douceur*), in a phrase which expresses the idea of Mary as uniquely sweet, gentle, and kind. His 'argument' is that, just as there is only one phoenix, so Mary is unique in her courtesy, and therefore can have no rival for the title of queen.

As a queen, he thinks, she must have a court, and for him a court means refinement and civilised behaviour, that is, *cortaysye*. Because he envisages heaven as like an earthly court, a place which values refinement above all else, he thinks of her purity in terms of refinement, and calls it courtesy. Middle English *cortaysye* includes 'refinement' as one of its meanings, and it is the word which, more than any other, sums up the courtly ideal. His emphasis on Mary's immaculateness may be because this is one area in which, as he sees it, the maiden cannot possibly compete with her for the title of queen of heaven.

The maiden's response to him is to echo him. She acknowledges that Mary is not only queen of heaven but empress of heaven, earth, and hell (lines 441–2), and that she *haldes the empyre over uus ful hyghe* 'holds supreme sway over us' (line 454). Her picture of heaven is more complex than the dreamer's, who

apparently follows the usual model of a hierarchy with God and
Mary at the top. She reconciles the apparent paradox by drawing
on Saint Paul's image of the church as the body of Christ, in
which all the parts relate harmoniously to each other and to the
central body, who is Christ himself (1 Corinthians 12. 12–31). She
picks up the dreamer's word *cortaysye*, and his idea of Mary as
quen of cortaysye, and develops them. She tells him that Paul says
that it is through *courtaysye* (the biblical word is 'spirit') that the
body and its parts hold together (lines 457–8). She explains
heaven as a court with a special property: the courtiers are *all*
kings or queens (lines 447–8). At the same time all in heaven
acknowledge Mary as supreme empress. So, to explain the paradox of the co-existence of hierarchy and equality in heaven, she
appeals to the dreamer's understanding of courtesy as a way of
speaking and behaving which unites all courtly ranks, enabling
one rank to communicate with another on an equal footing. In the
heavenly version of this courtesy, they all accept each other's
royal rank, and Mary's position of supreme empress, with goodwill and without rancour (lines 447–55), and Mary allows that all
have their title to the heavenly crown (line 443).

The dreamer defers to the maiden's explanation, but in an
offhand manner, as when he picks up her word *juel* earlier, which
suggests that he has neither understood it nor tried very hard to
do so:

> 'Cortaysé,' quoth I, 'I leve,
> And charyté grete, be yow among.' (lines 469–70)

['I accept,' I said. 'that courtesy and great charity are amongst you.']

This appears to mean no more than that he accepts that the
inhabitants of heaven behave with politeness and kindness
towards each other. There is no sign that he has advanced on his
earlier surface understanding of courtesy, or that he has engaged
with any of the points she has made.

The dreamer does not continue with Mary, but finds another
way to challenge the maiden's title of queen. With continuing cir-
cumspection (*Bot my speche that yow ne greve*, 'but may my speech
not offend you', line 471), he asserts that she presumes too much
in making herself a queen, given that she died so young (lines
473–4). When he complains that even the man who had lived a

long hard life in the hope of achieving heavenly bliss could expect
no more than to be crowned in heaven, a reward which she has
achieved without effort (lines 475–80), it looks as though he has
his own situation in mind. When he says that the maiden died
before the age of two without even knowing how to pray (lines
483–5), he implies that her reward would have been more acceptable had she had a chance at least to *begin* to practise the Christian faith. When he says that she was made queen on the first day
(line 486), his implication is that, given her poor credentials, she
ought at least to have been made to wait longer for her reward. He
offers a concession: countess or below would be acceptable, but
not queen (lines 489–92). His words confirm the hint (in lines
427–8) that he is obsessed by ideas of hierarchy, and that his ideas
of what constitutes an acceptable hierarchy are tied in with his
sense of justice. As he sees it, the highest status in heaven should
be reserved for those who have done most to deserve it. The
longer and harder people have worked for God, the greater their
heavenly reward should be.

Reward

In the second stage of her argument the maiden turns to parable
to show the dreamer that the heavenly reward is not earned but
given. She retells the parable of the labourers in the vineyard
(Matt. 20.1–16). In the Bible the workers who begin work in the
vineyard at different hours of the day are nevertheless paid the
same wages of one penny at the end of the day, the wages which
the vineyard owner agrees with all of them before they start. The
wages are the kingdom of heaven, the vineyard owner is God.
The retelling follows the Bible closely but supplies additional
detail which makes the point of the parable more emphatic. The
hard work of those who bear the heat and burden of the day is
graphically described (lines 511–12). At the point where the vineyard owner tells his steward 'Call the labourers, and give them
their hire' (Matt. 20.8), the poem extends the owner's speech:

> And fyrre, that non me may reprené,
> Set hem alle upon a rawe
> And gyf uchon inlyche a peny.
> Bygyn at the laste that standes lowe,
> Tyl to the fyrste that thou atteny. (lines 544–8)

[And further, so that no one may reproach me, put them all in a line, and give each one alike a penny. Begin with the last who stand low, till you reach the first.]

The addition spells out that all the workers are to be treated and paid equally, and it also indicates that treating them equally, the very thing that they complain of, is looked on by the vineyard owner as a way of forestalling complaint. As in the maiden's earlier account of the heavenly community, the poem brings out the difference between the earthly and the heavenly perspective. From the earthly point of view (the dreamer, the labourers in the vineyard), God's justice should ensure that all are rewarded according to what they deserve. From the heavenly point of view (the maiden, the vineyard owner), God's grace makes up for people's limitations and all are rewarded equally. The vineyard owner does not expect that what he regards as a generous arrangement will lead to trouble, because the labourers will see his generosity towards the last as injustice towards the first. In the Bible the steward is told to begin the payment 'from the last unto the first' (Matt. 20.8). *That standes lowe* is an added detail which works interpretation of the parable into the retelling. 'Low' seems to mean both 'low down in the order of the vineyard workers', that is, at the tail end of the queue for payment because last into the vineyard, and also 'humbly' or 'in poverty'.

In Matthew 20.12 the workers complain to the vineyard owner: 'Saying, These last have wrought but one hour, and thou hast made them equal unto us, which have borne the burden and heat of the day.' In the poem they elaborate their grievance at length:

> And sayden that thay hade travayled sore:
> 'These bot on oure hem con streny;
> Uus thynk uus oghe to take more.
> 'More haf we served, uus thynk so,
> That suffred han the dayes hete,
> Thenn thyse that wroght not houres two,
> And thou dos hem uus to counterfete.' (lines 550–6)

[And they said that they had toiled hard: 'These (others) have laboured for just one hour; we think we ought to get more. We have deserved more, so it seems to us, who have suffered the heat of the day, than these who did not do even two hours' work, and (yet) you make them equal to us.']

This aggrieved language recalls the dreamer's complaints to the maiden about what he sees as her undeservedly high status in heaven (lines 475–80), which prompted her to retell the parable in the first place. By having the workers speak like the dreamer, the maiden draws attention to the similarities in their attitudes.

The vineyard owner's reply brings out particularly the point that he does not see himself as being in any way unjust. His one question in the Bible, 'Didst not thou agree with me for a penny?' (Matt. 20.13), becomes three in the poem:

> And I hyred the for a peny agrete,
> Quy bygynnes thou now to threte?
> Was not a pené thy covenaunt thore?
> Fyrre then covenaunde is noght to plete.
> Wy schalte thou thenne ask more? (lines 560–4)

> [If I hired you for a penny in total, why are you now beginning to complain? Was not a penny what you agreed to then? It is not right to claim more than the agreement. Why should you then ask for more?]

These three questions are followed by a further two, taken from the Bible, which lead up to the ominous words that conclude the parable. In the Bible these are: 'So the last shall be first, and the first last: for many be called, but few chosen' (Matt. 20.16). In the poem the vineyard owner who responds severely to incomprehension and ingratitude is identified as Christ:

> 'Thus schal I,' quoth Kryst, 'hit skyfte:
> The laste schal be the fyrst that strykes,
> And the fyrst the laste, be he never so swyft;
> For mony ben called, thagh fewe ben mykes.' (lines 569–72)

> [Christ said, 'I shall arrange it (i.e. the giving of reward) as follows: the last shall be the first who comes, and the first the last, be he never so swift; for many are called, though few are chosen (ones).']

Because of the identification the reader is left in no doubt as to the general application of these words to all men and women, and the words are made all the more ominous in that they now, in the poem, announce a deliberate plan on Christ's part. This is not Christ the Lamb, more like the God of *Cleanness*, who becomes angry when his gifts are rejected.

The maiden continues her uncompromising presentation of the parable by glossing it. She first applies its meaning to *pore men* in general, signified in the parable by those labourers who *standes lowe* as they queue for their reward. They, she says, will always get their share, however little and however feeble their labour (lines 573–5). In another allegorical shift the *pore men* become herself, one who enjoys the highest bliss of heaven without having done any work in the world at all (lines 577–84). The crux of her comment on the parable is that God's mercy (line 576) determines heavenly reward, not his justice (line 580). In this way she refutes as misconceived the dreamer's criticism of her high status in heaven. In the heavenly perspective, the lowest and the poorest and those who spend least time in the world are the most highly regarded, because they have least chance of being corrupted by worldliness: 'Blessed are the meek'. Her gloss, like her retelling of the parable, ends on an ominous note, as she contrasts her own reception by Christ with the fate of others who have worked long and hard for their reward, those whom the dreamer thinks should get the most. Not only, she says, do they get no more than those who do little or no work; they may end up with nothing at all (lines 585–8). Her explanation squares with what the God of *Patience* tells Jonah, that few would prosper if he operated justice without mercy (*Patience*, lines 520–3). By means of the parable she both refutes the dreamer's criticism of her status in heaven and issues a covert warning to him to change his attitude.

In the parable the maiden takes work, the result of God's curse on Adam, as the defining human activity. She enhances the parable's emphasis on work's regulated and quantitative aspects: the contract between employer and employee, the division of work time into hours, the hourly rate of pay, the number of hours worked, the amount of work done, the size of the wage packet. In that it is hierarchical and divisive the world of work is like her previous model, the royal court. But whereas the maiden explained that the characteristic attribute of courts, courtesy, put the lowest on the same footing as the highest, the message she sees in the parable is more uncompromising and harder for the dreamer to accept. In heaven, the world's lowest are not merely on the same footing as the highest, but are ranked above them.

The dreamer does not give in. He thinks he sees a weakness in the maiden's position, and, eager now to win the argument, he abandons his deferential manner and speaks, as he says, *apert* 'plainly' (line 589). For the first and only time he attempts to appropriate the maiden's own territory of reason and reasoning. His voice becomes one of scholarly disputation: *'Me thynk thy tale unresounable'* (line 590). From the way he continues, he means by *unresounable* that the maiden's view of God flies in the face of both authority (the Bible) and logic. To demonstrate that the maiden's claims run counter to God's word he appeals to the Psalms:

> Goddes ryght is redy and evermore rert,
> Other holy wryt is bot a fable.
> In Sauter is sayd a verce overte
> That spekes a poynt determynable:
> 'Thou quytes uchon as hys desserte,
> Thou hyghe kyng ay pertermynable.' (lines 591–6)

[God's justice is prompt and always active, or holy writ is no more than a fable. In the Psalter is found a verse of unmistakable meaning, that makes an incontrovertible point: 'You reward everyone according to his deserts, you high king ever supreme in judgement.']

But he omits the reference to God's mercy in the original psalm.[25] Like Langland's Lady Meed and Chaucer's Wife of Bath, he quotes the Bible selectively, leaving out what does not favour his own position. He is similarly unconvincing when he turns to logic to show that the maiden's claims are absurd:

> Now he that stod the long day stable
> And thou to payment com hym byfore,
> Thenne the lasse in werke to take more able,
> And ever the lenger the lasse, the more. (lines 597–600)

[Now he who stood steadfast (in his work) the whole day long, if you came to receive payment ahead of him, then the less done in work the more able to take (payment), and always the greater the shortfall (in work) the greater (the payment).]

Against the maiden, the dreamer defends the position that God is just above all else. But in the quoted lines, which should drive home his argument, he seems to get tangled up in his own words, perhaps a sign of his indignation and exasperation. It is not difficult to see that his attempt at reasoning is, like all his speech, emotionally based. He wants to score a victory, and his Latinate words (*determynable, pertermynable*), more 'learned' than any of the maiden's, suggest a desire to impress. His learning turns out to be more show than substance, a disguise adopted by the will to further its self-regarding ends, and his ambitious defence of his position proves touchingly inept.

Grace

The dreamer's attempt at scholarly argument is repaid in kind and with interest. The maiden opposes his objection of unreasonableness by reference to the doctrines that lie behind the parable. She restates powerfully the central tenets of Christian belief. Her exposition, the third stage of her argument, comprises her longest speech, running without a break for twelve stanzas (lines 601–744). It is a commanding speech, all the more so because it avoids obscure learned words such as the narrator has just paraded.

The maiden picks up the dreamer's continuing preoccupation with ideas of 'more and less' with which he concludes his argument (lines 599–600). Such concepts do not apply in heaven, she says, for God's grace is limitless:

> He laves hys gyftes as water of dyche,
> Other gotes of golf that never charde. (lines 607–8)

[He pours out his gifts like water from a channel, or streams from a deep source that has never stopped flowing.]

Her simple similes here contrast with the dreamer's linguistic pretentiousness. She asserts her control over their dialogue when she succinctly sums up his attempt at argument, with a witty reference to the penny of the parable (lines 613–6).

She continues by extending her gloss on the parable. The heavenly reward is not earned but depends on the mercy which is made available to humanity through Christ's sacrifice, and those who die in infancy are in a better position to avail themselves of it than those who die later in life because they die without ever committing sin. For those who live beyond the age of innocence sin is inevitable, and they are only able to find salvation by God's grace. Initially the maiden keeps her speech in touch with her own situation, with the parable, and with the dreamer. She puts her points in the form of rhetorical questions to him. She challenges him to find an example of a man who never sinned (lines 617–20), and to deny that it is reasonable that those who have never sinned are well qualified for the heavenly reward (lines 634–6). But as before the maiden also restates and develops her points in a fuller and less argumentative way, as though to a wider audience. She relates her situation to the whole sweep of Christian history and doctrine. To explain the saving power of God's grace she begins with the Fall and the doctrine of original sin. She explains that all humanity forfeited the right to a place in heaven when Adam ate the forbidden fruit, and that Christ's blood then restored that right again. She charges her simple language with energy (*Ryche blod ran on rode so roghe* 'rich blood ran on the cruel cross', line 646). The crux of her exposition comes in the first stanza of the twelfth section (lines 661–72), where the maiden picks up on her first rhetorical question to the dreamer and her conclusion that as everyone sins so everyone needs God's grace to be saved (lines 617–24). She explains that the way for the sinner to avail himself of God's grace is through repentance.

Her main preoccupation, however, as throughout section twelve, is with the implications of her second question. She asserts that the innocent, having inherited God's grace through baptism, are saved as of right, and do not need further grace. She makes her categories of the righteous (who are only to be saved by grace), and the innocent (who are saved as of right), explicit:

> Ryght thus I knaw wel in this cas
> Two men to save is god by skylle.
> The ryghtwys man schal se hys face,
> The harmles hathel schal com hym tylle. (lines 673–6)

[Just so I know well in this matter that it is good according to reason to save two kinds of men. The righteous man shall see his face, the innocent man shall come to him.]

The ryghtwys man is here equated with the man in the Beatitudes who is clean of heart, whose reward is the beatific vision (compare *Cleanness* lines 27–8 etc., *Patience* lines 23–4). But in practice the righteous man, as the maiden has argued, can only achieve the necessary cleanness of heart through penance. It is only his penance which allows the maiden to put him on a par with *The harmles hathel*, so that he too may be allowed to enter heaven.

The dreamer, like Pertelote in *The Nun's Priest's Tale*,[26] had found only one 'authoritative' reference to back up his argument.

As Pertelote is out-referenced by Chauntecleer, so the dreamer is
by the maiden. She brings in three Old Testament passages, complete with ascriptions, two from the Psalms (lines 678–83,
699–700) and one from the Book of Wisdom (lines 689–94) to
support her own point of view. Her argument culminates when
she turns to the dreamer specifically again and brings the whole
weight of her exposition to bear on him:

> Forthy to corte quen thou schal com,
> Ther alle oure causes schal be tryed,
> Alegge the ryght, thou may be innome
> By thys ilke spech I have asspyed –
> Bot he on rode that blody dyed,
> Delfully thurgh hondes thryght,
> Gyve the to passe, when thou arte tryed,
> By innocens and not by ryghte. (lines 701–8)

[And so when you shall come to the court where all our causes shall
be tried, plead righteousness and you may be caught by these same
words (from the Psalms) which I have noted – unless he who died
bloody on the cross, grievously pierced through his hands, should
allow you to go free, when you are tried, through (your) innocence
and not (your) righteousness.]

Such trenchancy makes the dreamer's attempt at argument seem
pedantic by comparison.

Innocence

Having explained the crucial importance of innocence in the
scheme of salvation, the maiden now expounds its nature. She
connects it now not so much with childhood as with the state of
mind of a child. She has already alluded to the doctrine of
penance as the way forward for sinners (lines 661–72), and now
she illustrates what is necessary for a penitential state of mind.
She refers to the Bible again, to the New Testament story of
Christ's rebuke to the disciples who try to keep the children away
from him. She includes her version of Christ's warning: 'Verily I
say unto you, Whosoever shall not receive the kingdom of God as
a little child, he shall not enter therein' (Mark 10.15, compare
Luke 18.17). She links the story of the children to another parable, that of the pearl of great price, which tells of a merchant who

sells all his goods to buy for himself a single pearl, which is the kingdom of heaven (Matt. 13.45–6). In the poem's retelling he sells woollen and linen goods to buy the pearl (line 731), that is, he is a cloth-merchant. The maiden however calls him not a merchant but a jeweller (lines 730, 734). Her point is that in selling all his goods for a wonderful precious stone the merchant *becomes* a jeweller, acquiring the values of a true jeweller when he gives up his worldly goods for the sake of a beauty which is of another order. This recalls her first rebuke of the dreamer, when she accused him of not being a true jeweller because he was not prepared to surrender her, his most precious worldly good, to God.

The maiden twice calls the pearl of great price *mascelles* 'spotless' (lines 732, 744). From her use earlier in her speech of the corresponding noun *mascle* (she describes the innocent children as *Wythouten mote other mascle of sulpande synne* 'without stain or spot of polluting sin', line 726), she must mean that the *mascelles* pearl is a symbol of spiritual as well as physical spotlessness. Later she calls Christ *that maskeles mayster* (line 900). She identifies the pearl of great price with the pearl on her breast:

> Lo, even inmyddes my breste hit stode.
> My Lorde the Lombe, that schede hys blode,
> He pyght hit there in token of pes. (lines 740–2)

[Look, it stands right in the middle of my breast. My lord the Lamb, who shed his blood, he set it there as a sign of peace.]

The maiden has already explained that the Lamb has made humanity's peace with God for original sin. Now she explains that, as an innocent, she has been *given* the pearl of heaven by Christ. But when she ends her speech by speaking directly to the dreamer again, she tells him he will have to *buy* it:

> I rede the forsake the worlde wode
> And porchace thy perle maskelles. (lines 743–4)

[I advise you to forsake the mad world and purchase your spotless pearl.]

Like the merchant, sinners have to 'buy' the pearl (heaven) by selling all that they have (giving up the material world). She does not say here how this is to be done, but she has earlier made it clear that the way is through the *sorw and syt* 'sorrow and pain' of penance (line 663).

Though the maiden has expounded the meaning of innocence with great clarity and force, her third reply is harder on the
dreamer than her first two in two ways. Firstly, the theological
concept of innocence (unlike the story of Herod's massacre of
the innocents) was relatively unfamiliar and regarded as rather
abstruse.[27] She has moved into an area of abstraction and fine distinction which is intrinsically difficult. Secondly, as in the first
triad of questions and answers, the maiden's third answer, as well
being the most forceful, carries the most uncompromising message: that she, as an infant, is saved as of right, and he, unless he
changes his thinking, is likely not to be saved at all.

The Lamb

The maiden's exposition leaves the dreamer with no reply. He
abandons his attempt to take her on in argument. Perhaps disillu-
sioned with doctrine through his unsuccessful attempts to grapple with it, he now gets as far from the intellect as he can by asking
the most basic personal questions. When he picks up the maiden's
phrase *perle maskelles*, he applies it only to her (lines 745, 756), nor
does he ever use *maskelles* in an abstract sense but only with reference to her appearance (lines 745, 756, 769, 780). He ignores her
advice to make himself like the true jeweller of the parable.
Instead he continues to bear out the maiden's earlier accusation
that he is *no kynde jueler* (line 276). Because he treats her as a
material possession, *his* pearl does not liberate him from the
world, but anchors him to it. Unlike the jeweller in the parable, he
confuses the prize with what he needs to relinquish. He does not
see that in order to join her he must let her go.

His new questions are again three in number, and they and
the maiden's responses make up the last movement of the dialogue. Again the maiden answers the dreamer in kind, that is, she
replies to his personal questions in terms of her 'personal' relationship with Christ the Lamb. If he will not accept her doctrinal
explanations of the need for him to give her up, how it is that
though she died an infant she is no longer his little girl but a queen
in heaven, she will try to convince him by *showing* him that she
belongs to another. She moves from a largely thought-based to a
more visionary kind of teaching, beginning with graphic verbal
imagery and culminating in her obtaining for him (as she says) an

actual vision of the heavenly city. Her focus is now on Christ, not in his role in the scheme of salvation which she has just outlined, but as the strange figure of the Book of Revelation, Christ the Lamb, who is her beloved and her spouse. She tells him, in answer to his first question, which amounts to 'who made you so beautiful?' (a touch of purposeful flattery, perhaps), that she owes her power (*myght*) as well as her beauty to Christ (line 765). She explains her marriage to the Lamb, giving to Christ the language of the lover in the Song of Songs, the apocryphal book which was often understood as an allegory of Christ wooing the soul:

> He calde me to hys bonerté:
> 'Cum hyder to me, my lemman swete,
> For mote ne spot is non in the.' (lines 762–4)

> [He called me to his blessedness: 'Come here to me, my dear beloved, for there is no stain or spot in you.']

Christ's words here indicate that he calls her to him specifically because of her spotlessness, that is, her innocence. His further actions, as she describes them, indicate his desire to honour her for this. He washes her clothes, crowns her *clene in vergynté*, and adorns her with spotless pearls (lines 766–8).

The dreamer still does not respond. As far as he is concerned, he has been here before. When the maiden first told him that the Lamb had married her she told him also that he had made her a queen (line 415), and he at once challenged her right to this title. Now his prickliness returns. As her tone becomes more exalted, his becomes more reductive. Still obsessed with matters of rank, he now challenges her status as the Lamb's bride. He is astonished that the Lamb would think of marrying her, and, as he asks another question, seems almost to blame the Lamb for poor judgement:

> Quat kyn thyng may be that Lambe
> That the wolde wedde unto hys vyf? (lines 771–2)

> [What kind of thing might that Lamb be, who would wed you as his wife?]

He thinks about the maiden as the Lamb's wife in the same literal-minded way that he thought about her as a queen: the Lamb can have only one wife, and how unfair that it should be her. Again his sense of unfairness is triggered by the ease with which, as he sees it, she has achieved a high position compared with others who have served Christ for longer (such as, he no doubt thinks, himself). The maiden's teaching of more and less, effort and reward, righteousness and innocence, has passed him by. He imagines her pushing her way to the top:

> Over alle other so hygh thou clambe
> To lede wyth hym so ladyly lyf.
> So mony a comly anunnder cambe
> For Kryst han lyved in much stryf,
> And thou con alle tho dere out dryf
> And fro that maryag al other depres,
> Al only thyself so stout and styf,
> A makeles may and maskelles. (773–80)

[You climbed so high over all others to lead so queenly a life with him. So many lovely ladies have lived in great hardship for Christ, and you drove out all those worthy ones and excluded all others from that marriage, yourself the only one so firm and resolute, a peerless and spotless maiden.]

Lines 777–80 seem to carry more than a touch of sarcasm.

The maiden patiently corrects the dreamer's assumption that Christ in heaven is bound by the same laws against polygamy as men and women. She explains that she is one of a company of one hundred and forty thousand wives of the Lamb (lines 785–6).[28] After dealing with this mistake, she turns to the dreamer's question about the Lamb's nature (line 771). She explains the Lamb as an innocent like herself whose transformation from earthly weakness to heavenly strength is the model for her own. She finds patterns which imply that Christ the Lamb, and the innocence which he embodies, are the key to the whole of Christian history. She underlines the fact that Christ the Lamb in heaven was also Christ the Lamb on earth by quoting the famous allusions to the coming of the messiah by Isaiah ('He is brought as a lamb to the slaughter, and as a sheep before her shearers is dumb, so he openeth not his mouth', Isaiah 53.7), and John the Baptist ('Behold the Lamb of God, which taketh away the sin of the world', John 1.29). Her versions of these prophecies incorporate words of her own which bring out the guiltlessness/innocence of Christ. She expands the subject pronoun *he* in Isaiah 53.7 to two lines:

> That gloryous gyltles that mon con quelle
> Wythouten any sake of felonye,
> As a schep to the slaght ther lad was he. (lines 799–801)

[That glorious innocent who was killed without any charge of felony
(being proved against him) was led there like a sheep to the slaughter.]

She emphasises again in her own words Christ's sinlessness and
acceptance of his role:

> For synne he set hymself in vayn,
> That never hade non hymself to wolde . . .
> As meke as lomp that no playnt tolde,
> For uus he swalt in Jerusalem. (lines 811–12, 815–16)

[For sin he set himself at nought, he who never had any (sin) himself . . . as meek as a lamb that made no complaint, he died for us in
Jerusalem.]

To John the Baptist's words she adds the detail that he was *trwe
as ston* (line 822), with the same import. She explicitly connects
John's words with Isaiah's (*His wordes acorded to Ysaye* 'corre-
sponded to Isaiah's', line 819), thereby linking the Old Testament
to the New.

Finally, she extends and completes the design eschatologi-
cally, drawing attention to a threefold pattern:

> In Jerusalem thus my lemman swete
> Twyes for lombe was taken thare,
> By trw recorde of ayther prophete,
> For mode so meke and al hys fare.
> The thryde tyme is therto ful mete,
> In Apokalypes wryten ful yare.
> Inmydes the trone, there sayntes sete,
> The apostel John hym saw as bare,
> Lesande the boke with leves sware
> There seven syngnettes wern sette in seme.
> And at that syght uche douth con dare
> In helle, in erthe, and Jerusalem. (lines 829–40)

[And so there in Jerusalem my sweet lover was twice taken for a
lamb, by the true testimony of both prophets, because of his meek
appearance and his whole demeanour. The third time fully comple-
ments those (two), described (in writing) very clearly in the Apocalypse. In the midst of the throne, where saints sat, the apostle John

saw him most plainly, opening the book with square leaves where
seven seals were attached to the edge. And every host was in awe[29] of
that sight, in hell, in earth, and Jerusalem.]

The stanza reaffirms the historicity and significance of Christ the
Lamb by insisting on the authority of the written record of the
witnesses to the Lamb, that is, the *trw recorde* of Isaiah and John
the Baptist, and the writings of John of the Apocalypse (or Revelation).[30] Contrast helps create the sense of the fulfilment of
design. The two prophets give way to John of Revelation, the old
Jerusalem gives way to the new, and the figure of the Lamb led
meekly to the slaughter (the meekness is emphasised again in line
832) gives way to that of the Lamb on his heavenly throne, the
seat of judgement, opening the book with the seven seals. This
last image comes from the fifth chapter of Revelation, where it is
also stated that *only* the Lamb that was slain is able to open the
book with the seven seals. Like the poem, Revelation emphasises
the link between this eschatological image of the Lamb and the
suffering Lamb of the prophets; e.g. Revelation 5.9: 'Thou art
worthy to take the book, and to open the seals thereof: for thou
wast slain, and hast redeemed us to God by thy blood.' For the
maiden the Lamb is her lover, *my lemman swete*, the foundation of
her and her companions' happiness and that of all heaven. But as
he is now described he is a figure to inspire awe. Powerless in the
old Jerusalem, Christ's innocence is all-powerful in the new. The
sense of the biblical verses (Rev. 5.12–14) which record the worship of 'every creature which is in heaven, and on the earth, and
under the earth, and such as are in the sea, and all that are in them'
(Rev. 5.13) is conveyed even more forcefully in the last two lines
of the quoted stanza than in the Bible. For the maiden and the
poem the Book of Revelation is not only the last book of the Bible
but the climactic one. Only in Revelation does Christ the Lamb
come into his own.

   After she had explained Christ's calling her to be his bride in
the language of love, the maiden had left the dreamer in no doubt
as to her feelings for her husband. To her he is:

> My Lombe, my Lorde, my dere juelle,
> My joy, my blys, my lemman fre. (lines 795–6)

[My lamb, my lord, my dear jewel, my joy, my bliss, my noble
beloved.]

This outpouring of terms of affection follows her several earlier references to *my Lorde* and *my Lorde the Lombe*, beginning in line 285. He is hers and, as she has already said in so many words (line 418), she is his. Some of the terms of endearment which she uses (*my dere juelle, my joy, my blys*) are the same terms which the dreamer uses of her. But she never uses such language in speaking to the dreamer. His continuing use of this kind of language confirms that he feels the same love for his daughter in her transformed state that he felt for his earthly child. The maiden's use and non-use of it confirm that her feeling has moved away from the dreamer and is now focused on Christ. Christ uses the same language of her. He calls her *my lemman swete* (line 763), which is echoed by her *my lemman fre* (and again *my lemman*, line 805, *my lemman swete*, line 829). There is a crucial difference in the import of the *my* in the usages of the dreamer on the one hand, and of the maiden and Christ on the other. The dreamer's *my* indicates possessiveness and exclusivity; the maiden's and Christ's *my*, a love which is at once personal and beyond personality. The maiden has given her love to Christ in a relationship in which she willingly shares Christ with innumerable others.

The maiden explains this relationship which exists between Christ and every member of the company of the Lamb (that is, every innocent) as being of a mystical kind which none of the other inhabitants of heaven experience.[31] Because of his own spotlessness, the Lamb is attracted to all spotless (that is, innocent) souls and makes each one of them his wife (lines 841–6). By alluding to the Lamb's rich and abundant fleece of spotless white wool (line 844) she faces the dreamer (and the reader) in the most immediate way with the 'lambness' of her Christ, allowing no retreat into abstraction. She deals with the narrator's suggestion that she pushed other more deserving women out of the way in order to marry the Lamb in the same way that she answered his concerns about her place in the heavenly hierarchy. Just as all live in harmony in heaven as kings and queens, she says, so the band of innocents all live in harmony with each other as wives of the Lamb. She uses the same idiom in both passages to express the supernatural generosity and absence of self-regard of the inhabitants of heaven. In the earlier passage, each king and queen is glad of what the others have, *And wolde her corounes wern worthe tho fyve* 'and they wished that their crowns were worth five times as

much' (line 451). Similarly the wives have nothing but goodwill
for each other:

> And thagh uch day a store he feche,
> Among uus commes nouther strot ne stryf,
> Bot uchon enlé we wolde were fyf. (lines 847–9)

[And though each day he brings a (new) supply (of wives), neither
dispute nor strife comes amongst us, but (rather) we wish every single one (of us) were five.]

The maiden develops the point of the last line, explaining that not
only are the wives happy with each other, but, in contradistinction
to the 'natural' attitude, the more of them there are the happier
they are (lines 850–1). In a powerful summary of her argument
she returns to the privileged position of the wives of the Lamb
which she has touched on earlier (*The Lambes vyves in blysse we
bene* 'we are the wives of the Lamb who live in bliss', line 785)
and, by her use of the second person pronoun, brings the dreamer
and the earthly world into the picture:

> Althagh oure corses in clottes clynge,
> And ye remen for rauthe wythouten reste,
> We thurghoutly haven cnawyng;
> Of on dethe ful oure hope is drest.
> The Lombe uus glades, oure care is kest;
> He myrthes uus alle at uch a mes.
> Uchones blysse is breme and beste,
> And never ones honour yet never the les. (lines 857–64)

[Although our bodies decay in earth, and you (people on earth) cry
out in pain without rest, we have understanding in full; our trust is
entirely based on one death. The Lamb gladdens us, our care is
taken away; he rejoices us all at every feast. Everyone's happiness is
glorious and supreme, and no one's honour is less than another's.]

Her contrast between *ye* and *we* is dramatic. They, the innocents,
have not been made to wait for the Day of Judgement, but have
been plucked by the Lamb from the pain of the world to full
knowledge of the pleasures of heaven. Her point is that the innocents do not merely share in the general bliss of heaven, but are
looked after especially closely by Christ, their husband. The
wives of the Lamb, happy in him and in each other, are a select
group amongst the saved.

The maiden devotes the end of her speech to an attempt to communicate further to the dreamer the special nature of the relationship between the innocents and Christ. She turns to Revelation 14.1–4, which describes John's vision of the Lamb with the one hundred and forty four thousand who sing before the Lamb's throne a 'new song' which only they know. She has John speak her paraphrase of these biblical verses, which she expands to heighten the idea of the unique status of the Lamb's company. Thus the point of the verse 'and no man could learn that song but the hundred and forty and four thousand' (Rev. 14.3) is strengthened by particularly emphatic rhetoric:

> Nowthelese non was never so quoynt,
> For alle the craftes that ever thay knewe,
> That of that songe myght synge a poynt,
> Bot that meyny the Lombe that swe. (lines 889–92)

[Nevertheless there was none so skilful, for all the arts they ever knew, who might sing a single phrase of that song, except for that company that follow the Lamb.]

Other changes and additions to the biblical text bring it into line with the poem's interests. Revelation 14.4 explains that the company of the Lamb is made up of virgins (Vulgate *virgines*), and evidently envisages them as male, 'they which were not defiled with women'. In the poem they are *maydennes* (line 869), who, as the maiden has explained, are all married to the Lamb, which the 'virgins' who make up the company of the Lamb in the Bible are not.[32] In the Bible the one hundred and forty four thousand are said to have the name of the Lamb's father written on their foreheads (Rev. 14.1). In the poem, no doubt because of their marriage, their foreheads bear the Lamb's name as well as his father's. The Bible describes the 'new song' as like 'the voice of many waters, and as the voice of a great thunder' (Rev. 14.2).[33] But in the poem these descriptive details are applied to a sound which is called a *hue* 'shout' (line 873) and a *ledden loude* 'loud sound' (line 878). In the poem John is made to differentiate this sound from the more melodious 'new song' of the *maydennes*:

> A note ful nwe I herde hem warpe,
> To lysten that was ful lufly dere.
> As harpores harpen in her harpe,
> That nwe song thay songen ful cler,

> In sounande notes a gentyl carpe.
> Ful fayre the modes thay fonge in fere. (lines 879–84)

[I heard them sing a new note that was most delightful to listen to. As harpers harp with their harps, they sang that new song most clearly, a noble song in sonorous notes. They sang the melodies together most beautifully.]

There is no trace of these 'gentle' adjectives and adverbs in the Bible. The poem makes the song more appropriate to a feminine chorus and more expressive of meekness and innocence. The maiden diverges from the Bible again to reiterate her point that she and her companions, the only ones able to sing the 'new song', are uniquely and eternally joined to the Lamb by their spotlessness:

> For thay arn boght, fro the urthe aloynte,
> As newe fryt to God ful due,
> And to the gentyl Lombe hit arn anjoynt,
> As lyk to hymself of lote and hwe . . .
> That moteles meyny may never remwe
> Fro that maskeles mayster, never the les. (lines 893–6,
> 899–900)

[For they are redeemed, taken away from the earth, as new fruit due to God, and they are joined to the gentle Lamb, as those who are like him in manner and appearance . . . That spotless company may not be parted from that spotless Lord in any circumstances.]

Newe fryt is for Vulgate *primitiae* 'first fruits' (so Douay and Authorised Version, Rev. 14.4). The phrase establishes a verbal link with the *note ful nwe* and *nwe song* of the previous stanza. The singers are as *new* ('new, fresh, pure') as their song.

Redirection (2)

The dreamer's three-stanza reply marks a watershed in the dialogue, just as his earlier three-stanza reply did. Both indicate his acceptance (but not his understanding) of the maiden's situation as she has just explained it. In the first reply he accepts that he cannot join her in heaven, and in the second, after her long exposition, he says he accepts her high status in heaven as one who is *To Krystes chambre . . . ichose* 'chosen for Christ's bridal chamber' (line 904). But her explanation of the meaning of her marriage is beyond him. His concerns are still personal and practical. He sees her by the bank of the stream; does she not have a house to live in (lines 917–18)? He picks up her references to Jerusalem, and wonders if this is where she lives; but in his literal-minded way he cannot see how Jerusalem can be her home because that city, he firmly points out, is in Judea. He fails to appreciate that she has been talking about two cities, not one. The only city he can understand is one that can be located on a map. The maiden has already criticised him for being unable to accept more than he can see with his own eyes (line 308). Now he seems uncertain whether to believe her story that there are many brides of the Lamb. His frequent switching between *thou* and *ye* in the stanza beginning line 913 perhaps indicates that he is unsure whether his words should be directed to the maiden alone or to the maiden and her companion brides.

As in his first three-stanza speech, the dreamer is at once challenging and tactful with the maiden. As before he is elaborately courteous and contrasts her high state with his lowly one: compare line 382 (*I am bot mol and maneres mysse* 'I am but dust and lack (good) manners') with line 905 (*I am bot mokke and mul among* 'I am only muck and dust mixed together'). His posture of deference makes him long-winded. It is no accident that his two longest speeches come when he is most anxious to be tactful.

In the stanza which concludes his speech he refers somewhat disparagingly and perhaps ironically to the company of thousands which the maiden has spoken of (*so gret a route* 'so great a crowd', line 926; *So cumly a pakke of joly juele* 'so excellent a collection of beautiful jewels', line 929). And where is the city, he asks, they would need to live in? They can hardly sleep out of doors, but he sees no building in front of him (lines 927–8, 932). He ends by putting it to the maiden that, despite what she has said, she lives on her own by the stream (lines 933–4), which is where he sees her. So, again as in his first three-stanza speech, his words and attitudes seem confused, as though his accepting words do not match his feelings. His attempts at tact sit oddly with his implied accusation that she is not telling the truth. He is, presumably, not seriously accusing her of lying, but trying to provoke her into doing what he wants by challenging her to prove him wrong:

> If thou has other bygynges stoute,
> Now tech me to that myry mote. (lines 935–6)

[If you have fine buildings somewhere else, direct me now to that splendid city.]

His choice of verb is itself tactful. Line 936 may mean either 'instruct me where that splendid city is', or 'instruct me regarding that splendid city', or 'bring me to that splendid city'. He leaves it to the maiden to interpret his request as she wishes.

The maiden ignores the third possibility. In her reply she still operates at the rational level, meeting the dreamer's misunderstanding by explaining the distinction between the old and the new Jerusalem. She echoes her explanation of the earthly and the heavenly Lamb by presenting the heavenly city as the fulfilment of the promise of the earthly one. In the one, she says, Christ made our peace with God (lines 953–4), and in the other eternal peace is to be found (lines 955–6). She has more to say about the New Jerusalem. It is the final destination of all who, cleansed of sin, will join the spotless company after the Day of Judgement:

> That is the borgh that we to pres
> Fro that oure flesch be layd to rote,
> Ther glory and blysse schal ever encres
> To the meyny that is wythouten mote. (lines 957–60)[34]

[That is the city we hasten to after our flesh is laid (in the earth) to rot, where glory and bliss shall ever increase for the company that is without spot].

The *we* in line 957, following the *oure* in line 953, can hardly be taken to refer to the maiden and her company alone. Implicitly, she looks forward to the expansion of her heavenly company to include, after the Day of Judgement, *all* who are innocent, including those made innocent again by penance. In telling of the joys of heaven as she experiences them, the maiden tells the dreamer, if he will listen, what awaits him if he too dies in a state of grace.

From the maiden's point of view, these are fitting words to conclude the third triad of questions and answers. By now, however, the dreamer has only one thing on his mind. Ignoring what she has just told him about the need to be spotless in order to enter the city of heaven, he now asks unambiguously to be allowed in to see where she lives (lines 963–4). She has to tell him that he may not enter the city because he is not *clene wythouten mote* (line 972). Their dialogue ends where it started, with the dreamer asking for too much and the maiden correcting his presumption.

Nevertheless the maiden makes a concession to his weakness. She accepts that he, like all people, is first a creature of the physical body and the senses, only secondarily of the mind. At the beginning the garden and the paradise landscape impress themselves on him through his senses of sound, smell, and above all sight. After the maiden's reproaches, when he appears to accept that he can never be with her again, he says that the sight of her in bliss leaves him with both positive and negative sensations (lines 377, 385–8). He is very conscious of her appearance, as when he first sees her and again when he asks her who made her so beautiful (lines 745–56). Now he says he believes she has nowhere to live because he can *see* no building, and, if she is to prove him wrong, he demands to *see* the New Jerusalem. By contrast the maiden has little interest in the visual as such. Long visual descriptions are not for her. When she uses visual detail it is as a pointer to underlying meaning: for instance, when she evokes the beauty of the rose it is as a metaphor for transience (lines 269–70), and when she refers to the spotless whiteness of the Lamb's fleece she uses the words *pechche, mot, masklle*, with their double meaning 'blemish' and 'sin', in order to bring out his innocence (lines 841–4).

When the dreamer had first wanted to join her the maiden had reproached him for trusting too much in the power of sight (lines 295–6, 307–8). But now she tells him that she has obtained special dispensation from Christ for him to see the heavenly city from the outside (lines 967–70). Just as in her early efforts to persuade him not to try to join her across the stream she abandoned her metaphorical style of speech for a bluntly homiletic one, so now, after so signally failing to satisfy his doubts by her words, she abandons her verbal style of teaching in an effort to get through to him by working with his most basic bodily faculties. She wants the sight of heaven and its inhabitants to convince him of the truth of what she has said. She is about to deploy her strongest weapon. Unfortunately for her intentions and his desires, it turns out to be a two-edged weapon.[35]

Heaven

The city is the culmination of the bejewelled landscape which
takes up the far side of the stream. The circumstances in which the
dreamer finds himself when he sees the city parallel those of John
when he describes how he sees the city in Revelation. Like John,
he describes himself as on a hill, from which he observes the city
come down out of heaven (lines 979–81; compare Rev. 21.10). The
maiden, as guide, parallels John's guiding angel (Rev. 21.9). The
dreamer is doubly blessed, being granted a vision within a vision.

His description of the city divides into two parts. In the first
part (sections 17–18, lines 985–1092) the city appears to him, as to
John, as a static tableau, and his description closely follows Revelation 21.11 to 22.5. In the second part (lines 1093–1152) the city
comes to life and the description becomes less dependent on Revelation.

The first part retains many of John's details and his objective
method of description. It may seem that the dreamer adds little to
John's account. However, he selects and re-orders, not only to
make the description more coherent,[36] but to bring out the brightness of the heavenly city even more than the original does. He
retains and heightens the biblical emphasis on the jewels and precious metals which give the city its radiance by filling out details,
so that the city is presented to an even greater degree than in the
Bible as a place of dazzling light, clarity, and purity, with the
colours white and gold, the colours of the pearl and pearl-maiden,
particularly prominent. The dreamer focuses on the twelve layers
of the foundation to the city wall, each consisting of a particular
precious stone, the twelve gates in the wall, and the glass-like
transparency and brightness of the place. The first two lines of
the description come from part of Revelation 21.18, 'and the city
was pure gold, like unto clear glass'. To the biblical nouns the
poem adds a verb and adjectives conveying brightness:

> The borgh was al of brende golde bryght,
> As glemande glas burnist broun. (lines 989–90)

[The city was all of pure bright gold, burnished bright like gleaming glass.]

Later in the description, part of Revelation 21.21: 'and the street
of the city was pure gold, as it were transparent glass' appears as

The stretes of golde as glasse al bare 'the streets of gold like clear glass' (line 1025). This is echoed in the second part of the description when the dreamer describes the virgins in the company of the Lamb as walking together *On golden gates that glent as glasse* 'on golden streets that shone like glass' (line 1106).

The precious stones which make up the twelve layers of the foundations of the city wall are merely enumerated in the Bible (Rev. 21.19–20), but they have more presence in the poem. Each is given at least one line to itself, and salient descriptive detail, sometimes drawing attention to their brightness, is added: thus the jasper in the lowest layer of the foundation *glente grene* 'glinted green' (line 1001), and the chalcedony in the third layer *con purly pale* 'shone purely and palely' (line 1004). The biblical wall of jasper (Rev. 21.18) shines like gleaming glass (line 1018), and like *glayr* 'white of egg', as used in manuscript illumination (line 1026). The poem adds the detail that the buildings of the city were adorned with all kinds of precious stones (lines 1027–8). The lustre of the twelve biblical gates of pearl is heightened: each consists of *A parfyt perle that never fates* 'fades' (line 1038), and to the gates are added portals *pyked of* ['adorned with'] *rych plates* (lines 1036–8). There is emphasis on the light gleaming in all the streets (line 1043), on the transparency of the walls and buildings, enabling the narrator to look straight through them (lines 1049–50), and on the brightness (line 1056) and purity (line 1060) of the river which flows from the throne of God. The biblical tree of life becomes *tres ful schym* 'bright trees' (line 1077). To the biblical statement that the city had no need of sun or moon because it was lit by the light of God and the Lamb (lines 1045–8, from Rev. 21.23) the dreamer adds two statements of his own, the second lengthy, to the effect that the light of the sun, moon, and planets could not compare with the radiance of the heavenly river (lines 1057–8, 1069–76).

The dreamer makes reiterated acknowledgement of John or Revelation as the source for his description. The maiden too had referred her account of Christ and his company to Revelation and had used John's words. Her use is purposeful, as she explains:

> Lest les thou leve my tale farande,
> In Appocalyppece is wryten in wro:
> 'I seghe,' says John, 'the Loumbe hym stande
> On the mount of Syon, ful thryven and thro.' (lines 865–6).

[In case you think my fine words false, it is written in a passage in the Apocalypse: 'I saw,', says John, 'the Lamb standing on the mount of Syon, most splendid and noble.']

The maiden shows that she thinks that the dreamer is likely to respect the authority of John where he will not respect hers. She sees that, for him, she does not validate the Bible, but that the Bible validates her.

Unlike the maiden, the dreamer does not give his reasons for his deference to Revelation, but the context suggests that there may be two reasons. Just as the maiden wants to validate the truth of what she says for the dreamer, so the dreamer wants to validate the truth of his description for his reader. His second reason is so that he can acknowledge the extent to which he is dependent on Revelation for words to describe what he sees. In Section 2 of the poem, though hard put to it to describe the paradise landscape, he found his own words nonetheless. But the city of heaven is of a different order, and this time he does not try to compose a description himself but turns for help to Revelation. So the plethora of 'earthly' comparisons found in Section 2, a sign of his struggle to communicate what he saw, is not repeated now. Almost without exception, the few simple similes he uses are from the Bible.[37] The poem almost asks the reader to imagine the dreamer sitting down apprehensively to write up this part of his dream-experience and looking with relief to Revelation to perform the task for him.

But the dreamer is not the poet, who, I think, has another purpose in drawing attention so overtly to the Book of Revelation at this climactic moment of the dream. The dreamer simply enumerates the different features of the heavenly city in the manner of Revelation, steadily and objectively, with minimal input from himself. Whereas at the beginning of the dream he had communicated his pleasure in the beauty of the paradise landscape, he now concentrates on recording the pearl-like brightness of the heavenly city without any mention of his own response to it. Although he is presumably not aware of this, this is the one occasion when his language rises to match the maiden's in *gravitas*. The poet has the maiden and the dreamer share his recasting of the words of Revelation, allowing the reader to see that differing significances are implicit in their respective uses of this language.

Only in the last stanza of Section 18 (lines 1081–92) does the dreamer attempt to communicate his reaction to his vision. In a kind of ultimate extension of the inexpressibility topos he used at the beginning of the dream he says that the heavenly city was beyond human powers of endurance, so that no one 'in the body' could have survived his experience. When he says that he felt *nawther reste ne travayle* 'neither rest nor exertion' (line 1087), and that he was *ravyste wyth glymme pure* 'ravished by the pure radiance' (line 1088), he appears to mean that he was overcome to the extent that he had lost all bodily sensation, that is, to use John's phrases, he was 'in the spirit' (e.g. Rev. 160) or 'out of the body'. He compares himself to a stunned quail:

> I stod as stylle as dased quayle
> For ferly of that frech fygure. (lines 1085–6)

[I stood as still as a dazed quail, in amazement at that vivid vision.]

These lines strikingly recall his comparison of himself to a hawk standing stock-still in the hall on his first sight of the maiden (lines 182–4). Both similes convey the dreamer's amazement, but there is a significant difference in their import. The hawk is a powerful, active bird, which, indoors, has to be made (by hooding) to curb its instinct to be active. The hawk simile suggests that the dreamer too has strength, and that he remains still because he too curbs his instinct to do something, fearful that if he gives way to his desire to call out to the maiden he will lose her. By contrast the quail is a weak creature, and the quail image is banal and comic. It conveys the dreamer's view of himself not as frustrated but as drained of all power, transfixed like a quail blinded by bright light, and this image, combined with his struggling language in the rest of the stanza, confirms how insufficient his own resources are to express the nature of his vision and his response to it. In accordance with the Christian paradox, however, the dreamer's moment of greatest weakness is also his moment of apotheosis. The vision of the heavenly city does what the maiden's words had been unable to do. For the first time his voice transcends emotion. With the steady accumulation of descriptive detail punctuated by the references to John, it takes on an incantatory quality, expressive of the state of trance to which the dreamer refers in the quail stanza. He is, for the moment, purged

of all sense of self by the immensity of his vision. But because the
moment of apotheosis is achieved only by the neutralisation of his
body, his will, his humanity, it is not really his voice.

The dreamer's transcendental state does not last. The quail
stanza marks the transition between the first and second sections
of the description, in which consciousness returns to him and his
old self comes flooding back. He sees movement in the city, the
procession of virgins. Suddenly the inanimate tableau changes to
a scene which participates in the processes of life. There is a sense
of release, as for the first time the dreamer begins to relate to the
city directly instead of through the medium of the Bible. As the
city comes to life, so does he. With the reactivation of his will and
the energy this gives him he begins to appropriate his vision of the
city to his own experience, as he had done with all that had gone
before – the paradise landscape, his first sight of the maiden, and
the maiden's teaching. Following his John-inspired references to
the sun and the moon, the dreamer now introduces a conventional
sun and moon image of his own:

> Ryght as the maynful mone con rys
> Er thenne the day-glem dryve al doun,
> So sodanly on a wonder wyse
> I was war of a prosessyoun.
> This noble cité of ryche enpryse
> Was sodanly ful wythouten sommoun
> Of such vergynes in the same gyse
> That was my blysful anunder croun. (lines 1093–100)

[Just as the resplendent moon rises before the light of day fully sub-
sides, so suddenly in a marvellous manner I was aware of a procession. This noble city of rich splendour was suddenly, without
summons, full of virgins of the same appearance as my beautiful one
with her crown.]

Though the sudden appearance of the band of virgins is preter-
natural, the effect of light materialising within light is something
for which the dreamer is able to supply an analogy from the
human world. He finds his own words once more, and as before
his words reflect the simplicity of his attitudes. The magnificent
language of his Revelation-based description of the city is re-
placed by more pedestrian wording (line 1097). The most exotic
details of the appearance of the virgins and Christ are merely

noted (lines 1101–4, 1111–12). A conventional statement of difficulty, reminiscent of the descriptions of the landscape and the
maiden at the beginning of the vision, appears: *Tor to knaw the
gladdest chere* 'it was hard to know who (amongst the maidens) had
the happiest demeanour' (line 1109).

The dreamer's former concerns and attitudes thrust themselves forward. The first thing he notices about the procession is
that all those who take part in it look like his pearl-maiden (lines
1099–1104). The phrase he uses to refer to her, *my blysful anunder
croun,* shows that his feeling for her is the same as ever. Whereas
the maiden had instructed him in the specially exalted status of the
band of virgins, and he notes the exotic details of their appearance
(lines 1101–4), he still sees them in terms of an ordinary situation,
a group of young women at a church service (line 1115). Similarly,
though he describes Christ at the head of the procession as the
strange figure from Revelation, the Lamb with seven horns of gold
(line 1111), and adds the further exotic detail that his clothes are
(like the maidens'), of precious pearls (line 1112), he coalesces this
unfamiliar image with the familiar one of a man with white robes,
gentle looks, and a wound in his side. Christ is nowhere described
like this in Revelation. This is Christ as he was widely portrayed
in the so-called 'affective' works of later medieval religious literature and art which aimed to inspire devotion by generating in their
audience an emotional response to Christ's suffering, and it is this
image of Christ which takes precedence for the dreamer. Heaven
appears to him no longer as of another order, entirely beyond his
reach. He has found an image of humanity to which he can relate.
The Lamb with the seven horns and the pearly clothes belongs to
the maiden; this is *his* Christ:

> So worthly whyt wern wedes hys,
> His lokes symple, hymself so gent.
> Bot a wounde ful wyde and weete con wyse
> Anende hys hert, thurgh hyde torente;
> Of his quyte syde his blod outsprent. (lines 1133–7)[38]

[So gloriously white were his clothes, his looks mild, himself so gracious. But a wide wet wound showed near his heart, through the torn
skin; his blood gushed out from his white side.]

The familiarity of the image is matched by the ordinariness, not
to say banality, of the dreamer's language. The dreamer is moved

immediately to pity and wonder – not so much wonder at the sight
of the wounded Christ, as at the cruelty of those who were able to
inflict such a wound on one so gentle, as though he knows nothing of the Crucifixion story:

> Alas, thoght I, who did that spyt?
> Ani breste for bale aght haf forbrent
> Er he therto hade had delyt. (lines 1138–40)

[Alas, I thought, who did that evil deed? Any (man's) breast ought
to have burnt up for sorrow before he took pleasure in that.]

He shows no sign of being conscious of the significance of
Christ's wound in God's design for salvation as the maiden had
expounded that significance (lines 649–56). His utter artlessness
is moving. It is as though no knowledge comes between him and
what he sees. His response to Christ – immediate, warm, compas-
sionate – is of the kind which affective writing and art was looking for, but stripped of all reflection so that there is nothing there
but bare emotion. Such a response supports a view of the dreamer
in the dream as a creature of the will – well-meaning, vulnerable,
spontaneous, and also naïve, superficial, thoughtless. It is one of
the poem's triumphs that the dreamer's 'naïve' language, whether
in dialogue or narrative, can be as powerful as the maiden's most
sublime expressions.

The reawakening of the dreamer's will is well indicated by his
changing usage through section 19 of the link-word, *delyt*. To
begin with it is used only in its primary sense, 'delight', and only
of the inhabitants of heaven. As such it indicates that the dreamer
sees heaven as a place of joy. The procession of maidens moves
through heaven *wyth gret delyt* 'with great delight, most joyfully'
(lines 1105, 1116), the inhabitants of heaven show *delyt* at the
approach of the Lamb (line 1117), and no one doubts the Lamb's
delyt, despite his wound (lines 1141–4). But when the dreamer
uses the word of himself (lines 1128, 1129, 1152, 1153), it takes
on the sense of 'desire' as well as 'delight'. He first uses the word
of himself after he has described the joy of heaven's song of
praise to the Lamb:

> To love the Lombe his meyny in melle
> Iwysse I laght a gret delyt. (lines 1127–8)

[Indeed *I* took a great delight in praising/felt a great desire to praise the Lamb among his retinue.]

Whatever the precise shade of meaning of these lines, it is clear that the dreamer is no longer content merely to observe but wants to join in the praise of the Lamb. The city is no longer still and silent, but a place of celebration which draws him in. This is another key moment.[39] As when he walked through the paradise landscape, his delight in what he sees leads to desire for still greater delight. He is in the grip of *more and more* again.

Thus the dreamer is in no state to take a detached view of the maiden when he recognises her as one of those in the heavenly procession. Again he calls her *my* own child. He will not allow her identity to be submerged in the company of virgins. His ambiguous phrase *my lyttel quene*, line 1147 (*quene* means 'girl', 'woman', and 'queen') suggests that he sees her now in just the way he first saw her in the dream, as a little girl rather than an adult, or as the two together. As before he wants to be with her. The word that he uses for his desire is *luf-longyng* 'love-longing' (line 1152), which recalls the similar compound *luf-daungere* 'power of love' (line 11) which he used for his pre-dream state of frustrated desire. This suggests that he still sees his love for her only in the worldly terms of *The Romance of the Rose*. His use of the words *luf-longyng* and *delyt* together in line 1152 confirms that the sight of her still elicits from him a primitive emotional response in which joy and desire are inextricably mixed.

By securing the supreme vision for the dreamer the maiden has short-circuited the painful business of trying to communicate through language, but in doing so she has released the power of the dreamer's sense responses to an unprecedented and over-whelming degree. Though the vision at first takes him completely out of his bodily self, the appearance of the band of maidens, of Christ, and finally of his own pearl-maiden, opens the floodgates of his will. Within a moment, it seems, he goes from spiritual to physical ecstasy, and, as he has done before, instead of bowing to heaven's ways he tries to make heaven bow to his. The new development is that he now forces the issue by taking action.

It is as though the maiden's teaching has never been. Despite all she has done to try to educate him, the dreamer is now irresistibly drawn to cross the dividing stream. His rush to do so

shows that nothing he has heard or seen in heaven acts on him
with the same force as his need to be with his daughter. More generally it asserts that there is an irresolvable conflict between
human nature and the tenets of Christian doctrine, a conflict
which, when it comes to a head in situations of extreme stress,
human nature will win.

Earth (2)

The last section of the poem moves through four stages. The first
is the dreamer's account of his waking from his dream (lines
1153–73), the second his reflections immediately on waking (lines
1174–88), the third his final conclusions about the significance
of his experience (the fourth stanza, lines 1189–1200), and the
fourth his statement of where he now is in relation to God and
his dead daughter (the fifth and final stanza, lines 1201–12). The
most significant development of the dreamer's attitude is marked
by the change of verb tense from past in the first three stanzas to
present in the last two.

The section boundary is marked by a change of tone. The
dreamer, as he continues with his narration, begins to pass judgement on himself and to draw negative conclusions. In the first two
lines of the last section he states that he was moved to madness
(*My manes mynde to maddyng malte*, line 1154) by the delight
which poured into him through his senses (*in yye and ere*, line
1153). His use of the phrase *manes mynde* indicates that he recognises that his earthly sense of self had returned to him by the end
of his dream. He in effect accuses himself of arrogance: *I thoght
that nothyng myght me dere* 'I thought that nothing might hinder
me' (line 1157). His language (*astraye*, line 1162; *so mad arayde* 'in
a state of frenzy', line 1166; *rasch and ronk* 'rash and arrogant',
line 1167) continues to emphasise his view of his attempt as an act
of wilful folly. The narrative conveys the impetuousness of his
attempt by a number of words which denote swift action: *start*
'start forward' (lines 1159, 1162), *flonc* 'flung myself' (line 1165),
raas 'rushing forward' (line 1167), *sparred* 'ran' (line 1169),
braththe 'impetuous action' (line 1170). The phrases containing
these words loosely alternate with others, which convey the
abruptness with which his dash to cross the stream is thwarted.
He is 'shaken out of' (*of ... bitalt*, line 1161) and 'called away

from' (*Out of ... bycalt*, line 1163) his purpose. He is 'quickly checked' (*rapely ... restayed*, line 1168), and then 'startled' (*brayed,* line 1170) out of his dream. The verbal pattern conveys a sense of the clash between human and divine wills, a clash which the dreamer acknowledges when he ascribes his failure to the fact that his attempt to cross the stream *was not at my Prynces paye* 'was not to my prince's (i.e. Christ's) liking' (line 1164).

The dreamer's waking brings him back to the garden where he had lost his pearl. His first words are words of acceptance: *Now al be to that Prynces paye* 'now may everything be to that Prince's pleasure' (line 1176). But, as he indicates, his words go with consternation (line 1174) and sighing (line 1175), and they are followed by his statement of his distress at being flung out of *that fayre regioun* (line 1178) and deprived of all its sights (line 1179). His next words, he says, arose out of his distress:

> A longeyng hevy me strok in swone,
> And rewfully thenne I con to reme:
> 'O perle,' quoth I, 'of rych renoun,
> So was hit me dere that thou con deme
> In this veray avysyoun.
> If hit be veray and soth sermoun
> That thou so stykes in garlande gay,
> So wel is me in thys doel-doungoun
> That thou art to that Prynses paye.' (lines 1180–8)

[A heavy longing overcame me, and sorrowfully then I cried out: 'O pearl,' I said, 'of noble splendour, how precious it was to me, what you spoke of in this true vision. If it is a true and correct statement (of your situation) that you are thus set in a bright garland, then it is well with me in this dungeon of sorrow that you give pleasure to that prince.']

In this passage he seems to acknowledge both that his vision was a true one (that is, in the tradition of scriptural visions, one that revealed divine truths), and that, whereas his dream-self had constantly challenged what the maiden said, he now accepts it as true. In particular, he seems to accept that she now belongs to Christ and not to him. But the *veray* of line 1184 is immediately qualified by his *If hit be veray* in the next line, which suggests that he is not fully sure of the truth of his vision. If her words are now precious to him, it is perhaps because she spoke them rather than because he believes them.

The next and last two stanzas, in which the narrative ceases to be retrospective, make up the last phase of the concluding section. The dreamer summarises the state in which he now finds himself. He considers in a more distanced way his mistake in trying to cross the stream. He sees his mistake as a matter of his wanting more than God had given him, a mistake shared with all humanity (lines 1189–96). His attitude – the 'natural' human attitude – had been that in losing his daughter so young he had suffered at the hands of a cruel fate (line 249). But he has moved on; his dream-experience has given him a new perspective. For the first time he takes responsibility for the part he had played in creating his own pain. His conclusion brings him into line with the maiden's teaching at the end of their first dream-dialogue (lines 337–60). He refers to this teaching (*As the perle me prayed that was so thryven* 'as the pearl that was so lovely had urged me', line 1192), and sums it up with his own generalisation:

> Lorde, mad hit arn that agayn the stryven,
> Other proferen the oght agayn thy paye. (lines 1199–200)

[Lord, they are mad who strive against you, or offer you anything contrary to your pleasure.]

He has come round to an attitude of resigned acceptance of God's will. There is a suggestion that he has at last freed himself from the tyranny of the senses. His regret on waking was that he had lost the marvellous sights of heaven (line 1179), but he now talks of his throwing away the chance to be near to God and his *mysterys* (lines 1193–4).

The final stanza implies that God and the church have taken over the space left in the dreamer's life by the death of his daughter. He says that he is now a *god Krystyin* who finds comfort at all times in Christ (lines 1202–4). He reduces his dream to an episode in the ongoing life of a Christian (lines 1205–6), and formally gives up his daughter to God (lines 1207–8). The last four lines of the poem turn a conventional closing formula into a significant statement.[40] They suggest that the dreamer gives more attention than before to the church and its rituals as the mainstay of his faith. Until this moment he had seemed to be locked in a private, self-absorbed struggle, as expressed in the last stanza of the first section, when, in the isolation of the garden, his reason struggled with his will. Now, for the first time, he looks beyond himself and his daughter and becomes aware of the church as a community, and himself (and the reader) as part of that community. The shift is marked very simply by his pronominal usage. The priest, he says, shows Christ to *us* (line 1210), and his final prayer is for *us*, not for himself alone:

> He gef uus to be his homly hyne
> Ande precious perles unto his pay. (lines 1211–12)

[May he grant us to be his lowly servants (*and* servants in his household) and precious pearls to his liking.]

This brief prayer, as well as fulfilling the formulaic role of concluding the poem, attends to another aspect of the maiden's teaching: that, through the sacraments, all Christians have the potential to find salvation. The last two lines of the poem contain his only prayer, and his only use of the word *perle* to mean others besides his daughter. His words indicate that he is now able to see not only beyond the bodily, but also beyond the literal.

But there is a sub-text in these two last stanzas which pulls against a sense of resolution. His words imply that he wants to put his dream-experience and the loss of his daughter behind him and move on (lines 1205–8). But he is still acutely aware that, through the human folly of wanting more than his due, he has lost all the joy that his dream brought him (lines 1197–8). The fact that he feels the loss of his dream keenly is borne out by the subdued language of the last stanza, and the fact that he is not cured of his heartache over the loss of his daughter is indicated by the formula of blessing which he uses as he commits her to God. This confirms that he is her father,[41] but it does so only indirectly, like his indications of their relationship in the dream. The continued obliquity of his identification suggests that his loss is still too painful for him to be able to confront it fully.

The dreamer's claim that pleasing Christ is easy is also suspect:

> To pay the Prince other sete saghte
> Hit is ful ethe to the god Krystyin;
> For I haf founden hym, bothe day and naghte,
> A God, a Lorde, a frende ful fyin. (lines 1201–6)[42]

[To please the prince or be reconciled (to him) is very easy for the good Christian; for I have found him, at all times, a God, a lord, a most excellent friend.]

The difficulty in taking this statement at face value is that it makes it all sound *too* easy. Implied in the quoted lines is the dreamer's claim that since he has stopped struggling against the will of God and become a 'good Christian', all is well. But there is no sign that he *feels* being a 'good Christian' in the same way that he feels the death of his daughter. There is a sense of his taking on a role – the role of the 'good Christian' – and going through the motions. He commits his dead daughter to God, takes communion, utters a prayer. He does not seem to have embraced his new life with any zest but rather to have fallen back on the accepted attitudes and routines of piety as a support to help him get through his days. The fact that the indication of his apparent new direction is confined to the last few lines of the poem is significant; it is articulated too sketchily to make it entirely convincing.

Conclusion

How then is the reader to interpret the dreamer's state of mind? Is his calm that of a man who is now at peace with himself, who has found that his dream-experience has confirmed the promises of his faith and set him on the right road? Or is it a calm brought about by a sad acceptance that what must be must be, a making the best of it in which the hurt still shows through? His final prayer, in which he asks God to permit him and his fellow Christians to become his *homly hyne* as well as his *precious perles* (whether on earth or in heaven is not clear), indicates his new humility. But is the humility brought about by new insight or by a sense of defeat? Is his equation of *homly hyne* and *precious perles* a positive perception, or does it point to a still limited outlook which attends to the *doel-doungoun* more than to the promise of heaven? There are no final answers, but the dreamer does not behave as one who is overjoyed that his daughter has found her place in heaven. He is obviously better off than before his dream in that his pain is no longer acute, but it seems to be not entirely gone. It may be that he still has nagging doubts of the truth of his dream, as when he first woke from it. But his underlying difficulty remains that, whether or not his daughter is in heaven, she is not with him. In this regard his faith's answers to death, even after the confirmations of his vision, still seem empty. The life to come cannot compete with the here and now. If the dreamer is to be taken as a representative figure for all humanity then the poem demonstrates that the ways of God can never be justified to men, for the distance between God and man is too great to be bridged.

Notes

1   See *Piers Plowman*, B, Passus 1.
2   Helen Barr, '*Pearl* – or the jeweller's tale,' *Medium Ævum* 69 (2000), 59–79, argues the contrary, that the fourteenth-century context is highly relevant. She sees the dreamer as a fourteenth-century jeweller with mercantile values and uncertain of his social position, and the poem as both timeless and 'a map of late fourteenth century cultural processes' (73). The case is very well argued, but I still do not see any sustained level of fourteenth-century cultural meaning, and it runs counter to what I see as the nature of the poem's metaphorical mode, in which the metaphorical is given primacy over the literal. There is no clear evidence that the dreamer is to be understood literally as a jeweller, and the poem generally steers clear of any such confining specificity.
3   Ballade-type stanzas were much used by English poets in the latter part of the fourteenth century. Many other stanza forms similar to that of *Pearl* are to be found, but none precisely like it. S. G. Fein, 'The twelve-line stanza forms in Middle English and the date of *Pearl*', *Speculum* 72 (1997), 367–98, concludes that *Pearl* may be the earliest refrain poem in a twelve line-stanza to survive (371). She thinks that its antecedents are probably biblical narratives in alliterated twelve-line stanzas written in the west or north-west of England (393).
4   In the first part of the central dialogue the dreamer tells the maiden, in three separate speeches, how much he misses her and wants to join her. In the second part, in one plus three speeches, he asks four questions about her life in heaven and argues with her. In the third part, in three plus one speeches, he puts four further questions and requests to the maiden, this time without argument, culminating in his request that she show him where she lives. The vision of the heavenly city follows. The dreamer's speeches are normally one stanza long, but the 'plus one' requests are shorter (3–4 lines), and two longer three-stanza speeches, of different character from the others, separate the three parts. The maiden replies to all of the dreamer's questions/requests as he puts them, in speeches of variable length, the longest of thirteen stanzas.
5   Quotations from the *Gawain*-poems are from J. J. Anderson, ed., *Sir Gawain and the Green Knight, Pearl, Cleanness, Patience* (London: Dent, 1996).
6   The *Middle English Dictionary* under *perl(e)* gives a fourteenth-century example of this usage from Trevisa's translation of Higden's *Polychronicon*: 'Kyng Egelrede wedded Emme, the perle and the precious stone of Nor-

manes.' In *Sir Gawain and the Green Knight* the Green Knight calls Gawain
a pearl amongst knights: 'As perle bi the quite pese is of prys more, / So is
Gawayn, in god fayth, bi other gay knyghtes.' (*Gawain* 2364–5) [As the pearl
beside the white pea is of greater value, so is Gawain, upon my word, beside
other good knights.]

7   A similar point is made by Putter, *Introduction*, pp. 182–3. Putter follows
David Aers, 'The self mourning: reflections on *Pearl*', *Speculum* 68 (1993),
54–73, in further suggesting that the dreamer 'takes comfort in metaphors
and tropes which prolong her existence in his mind'.

8   *The Book of the Duchess*, line 1309.

9   For simplicity the Bible is normally referred to and quoted in the Authorised
Version. Discrepancies between it and the Vulgate Latin text, which was
the authoritative text in the fourteenth century, are noted when they are significant; sometimes the Douay translation of the Vulgate is cited and/or
quoted.

10   By extension the harvesting of grain into barns was taken to signify the har-
vesting of Christian souls into the church or heaven, as in the image of Holy
Church as a barn for the housing of Piers's sheaves in *Piers Plowman*
B.19.319–30, 345.

11   This is the sense which applies in *Piers Plowman* B.5.11 ff., where the allegorical figure of Reason preaches to the people as to how they should mend
their sinful lives.

12   The opposition between will and reason, and the idea that the human will
should be subject to reason, are commonplace in medieval religious writing.
A good instance is found in the twelfth-century homily *Sawles Warde*, in
which man is allegorised as a house in the charge of Wit ('Reason'), the master of the house, who has to discipline his unruly wife Wil (ed. J. A. W. Bennett and G. V. Smithers, *Early Middle English Verse and Prose*, London:
Oxford University Press, 1966, pp. 246–61).

13   The details of the paradise landscape suggest particularly descriptions of the
earthly paradise in the Alexander romances and (in the same tradition) *Mandeville's Travels*. See the chapter on 'The earthly paradise' in Kean, *The
Pearl*, pp. 89–113.

14   The use of the 'inexpressibility topos' in *Pearl* as compared with some oher
works of medieval literature is discussed by Ann Chambers Watts, '*Pearl*,
inexpressibility, and poems of human loss', *PMLA* 99:1 (1984), 26–40.

15   By *ble of Ynde* 'indigo blue' (line 76) the poet probably means an intense blue
used in manuscript illumination and other decoration. Compare *Cleanness*
1411: *And al in asure and ynde enaumayld ryche* 'and all richly enamelled in
azure and indigo' (of the dish covers at Belshazzar's feast).

16   The quoted lines bring to mind the first two lines in lyric no. 9 in G. L.
Brook's edition of *The Harley Lyrics*, 3rd edn (Manchester University Press,
1964), p. 40: 'A wayle whyt ase whalles bon, / A grein in golde that godly
shon.' [A lovely girl as white as whale's bone, a precious stone set in gold that
shone beautifully.]

17   See the discussion of the maiden's dress in Ian Bishop, *Pearl in its Setting*
(Oxford: Blackwell, 1968), pp. 114–21.

18   Putter, *Introduction* (p. 178), notes that the dreamer's and the maiden's dif-

fering use of the first person plural pronoun is indicative of the contrast between the dreamer's desire to be with her and the maiden's aloofness. When the dreamer uses it (we, our, us) he always means himself and the maiden. When the maiden uses it, she always means herself and her companions in heaven, never herself and the dreamer.

19 The words and attitudes of dreamer and maiden here recall Joseph and Mary's finding the missing boy Jesus preaching in the temple. Mary says: 'Son, why hast thou thus dealt with us? behold thy father and I have sought thee sorrowing', and Jesus replies: 'How is it that ye sought me? Wist ye not that I must be about my Father's business?' (Luke 2.48–9). Both encounters show human feeling foundering on the rock of divine alterity, and bring out the gulf between human and divine ways. Luke 2.50 continues: 'And they understood not the saying which he spake unto them.'

20 This property of pearls is noted in *Cleanness*: 'And wax ho ever in the world in weryng so olde, / Yet the perle payres not whyle ho in pyese lasttes.' (lines 1123–4) [And however long it may be worn (in the world), yet the pearl does not deteriorate during its lifetime.]

21 The idea of the pearl as an image of cleanness or purity is also found in *Cleanness*, where, for example, the reader is urged to purify himself with penance until he becomes a pearl (*Cleanness*, line 1116).

22 A study which emphasises the importance of the jewel/jeweller metaphor in *Pearl* and relates it to contemporary attitudes to jewels and jewellers is Felicity Riddy, 'Jewels in *Pearl*', in Brewer and Gibson, *Companion*, pp. 43–55.

23 Compare especially *Pearl*, line 344, *Who nedes schal thole be not so thro* 'Let him who must endure be not so impatient', with *Patience*, line 6, *And quo for thro may noght thole, the thikker he sufferes* 'And he who may not endure, on account of his impatience, suffers the more'.

24 Later (line 483), the dreamer indicates that she died before the age of two, which would make her technically an innocent in the eyes of the church. The significance of the age of two comes from Herod's killing of all male children 'two years old and under', Matt. 2.16.

25 Vulgate Psalm 61.12–13 (in Authorised Version, 62.11–12) has: *Semel locutus est Deus; duo haec audivi: quia potestas Dei est, et tibi, Domine, misericordia; quia tu reddes unicuique iuxta opera sua.* 'God hath spoken once, these two things have I heard, that power belongeth to God, and mercy to thee, O Lord; for thou wilt render to every man according to his works' (Douay).

26 In *The Canterbury Tales*, VII, 2940–1, Pertelote quotes briefly from Cato in support of her argument that Chauntecleer should pay no attention to his dream.

27 The early Middle English work entitled by its editor *Vices and Virtues* (ed. F. Holthausen, 2 vols, EETS 89, 159, London, 1888, 1920) has a brief discussion of *innocencia*, which it translates as 'uneilindnesse' (p. 133), literally 'harmlessness'. It laments that too few men are concerned to possess this virtue.

28 The number in Revelation 14.1 is one hundred and forty-four thousand, as in *Pearl* lines 869–70. The number in *Pearl*, line 1107, is one hundred thousand.

29 The verb *dare* may carry the stronger meaning 'tremble (for fear), cower' which is very usual in Middle English; this is the meaning in *Gawain*, lines 315, 2258.

30   The last book of the Bible is called Apocalypse in the Vulgate, Revelation in the Authorised Version. The Vulgate ascribes the book (incorrectly) to John the apostle, and this was the accepted medieval view of its authorship (see line 836).

31   In Revelation the other inhabitants of heaven are the four beasts, the twenty-four elders (e.g. Rev. 5.8), and 'many angels' (Rev. 5.11).

32   It is not altogether clear that the company of the Lamb in *Pearl* is made up entirely of females. In Middle English the word *maiden* could mean a male virgin, and male as well as female virgins and innocents were considered to be married to Christ in heaven.

33   The Vulgate, and the Douay translation which follows it, make it clearer than the Authorised Version that the 'new song' is the same as the 'voice of many waters', etc.

34   *We* in line 957 and *oure* in line 958 evidently refer to humanity in general, not only the brides of the Lamb. The pronouns follow on from line 953: *In that on oure pes was mad at ene* 'in the one (city) [i.e. the old Jerusalem] our peace was made secure'.

35   Andrew and Waldron note in their edition that the first word of the last stanza of section 16, *Moteles* (line 961) has a decorated initial *M*. They regard this as a scribal error, as the decorated initial elsewhere in *Pearl* is reserved for the initial of the first word of the first stanza in a section. But it is more likely that the initial is meant to draw attention to the importance of the stanza in the poem's development. It begins the last exchange between the dreamer and the maiden, one which is extra to the established 3–3–3 pattern, and it marks the beginning of the high point of the dreamer's dream-experience, his vision of the New Jerusalem. See further Condren, *Numerical Universe*, pp. 71–2.

36   Sarah Stanbury, *Seeing the Gawain-Poet* (Philadelphia: Pennsylvania University Press), 1991, p. 33, sees the city as more visually coherent in the poem than in Revelation. She refers to Theodore Bogdanos in noting that 'the dreamer's spatialized city contrasts to John's sequential and spatially incoherent perception'. She suggests that 'for his description of a city with a complex topography, the poet seems to be drawing . . . on the pictorial traditions of Apocalypse illustrations that depict a city in both projection and elevation'.

37   The one exception is the comparison of the shining wall of jasper to egg-white (as used in manuscript illumination), line 1026. This comparison is the dreamer's own. It follows the style of the preceding line, which has the biblical comparison of the streets of gold to clear glass.

38   Some illustrated Apocalypse manuscripts show a wounded Lamb (the slain Lamb of Rev. 5.6, 12), but taken together the details in lines 1133–7 suggest the traditional iconography of the human Christ.

39   Prior, *Fayre Formez*, p. 45, sees a similar (though more sudden) shift in the dreamer's attitude, again with lines 1127–8 as pivotal: 'The dreamer's glimpse of divine love, the wholly transcendent love that the Pearl Maiden has been trying to explain to him since the beginning of the dream, is only a

vision of the heavenly joy, not the joy itself. The last line of the stanza quoted above [line 1128] suddenly and radically shifts the perspective from the heavenly response back to the earthly one of the dreamer . . . who "catches" the joy from the blessed. The dreamer's subsequent rash behaviour, when he attempts to cross the river, reveals that he does not understand that the heavenly joy, the *gret delyt* verbalized in the *canticum novum*, cannot be his, any more than the Pearl's love can be his.'

40 A concluding formula is also made into a significant statement in *Gawain*, lines 2529–30. See below, p. 244.

41 'In Christ's blessing and mine' seems to have been a formula usually, though not exclusively, used by fathers to bless their children (at the end of letters, etc.). See N. Davis, 'A note on *Pearl*', in John Conley, ed., *The Middle English Pearl: Critical Essays* (Indiana: Notre Dame University Press, 1970), pp. 325–34.

42 His attitude is reminiscent of Piers when he first talks to the folk and announces that he knows God 'as kyndely ["naturally, intimately"] as clerc doth his bokes' (*Piers Plowman*, B.5.538). Piers too says he finds it easy to serve God (5.549–53). The difference is that Piers's confidence is absolute, though it turns out to be misplaced, and the dreamer's uncertain.

2

Cleanness: the wages of sin

Introduction

Cleanness combines discussion of a religious virtue with retelling of stories from the Bible. Its three main stories (at the end of the poem the narrator refers to the *thrynne wyses* in which he has dealt with his theme) are from the Old Testament. They centre on Noah, Sodom and Gomorrah, and Belshazzar's feast. All three have a number of episodes. The story of Noah includes God's anger with the corruption of the world, his command to Noah to build the Ark, the Flood, and God's covenant with Noah never to destroy the whole world again. The story of Sodom and Gomorrah begins with the appearance of God to Abraham in the form of three men, and Sarah's laughter when God tells Abraham that she will become pregnant. Other episodes are Abraham's pleading with God to spare the cities, the visit of the angels to Lot, his offer of his daughters to the men of Sodom, and the flight of Lot, whose wife is turned into a pillar of salt when she looks back at the burning city. The story of Belshazzar's feast is taken back to Nebuchadnezzar's sacking of Jerusalem and the bringing of the Temple vessels to Babylon. The episode of the feast itself includes Daniel's exposition of Nebuchadnezzar's fall from grace. Some material of non-biblical origin is attached to the stories, including the description of the Dead Sea as all that is left of Sodom, Gomorrah, and the other three cities of the plain, and the description of the elaborate decoration of the Temple vessels at Belshazzar's feast. Summary accounts of the fall of the angels and the fall of man preface the story of Noah, and these two episodes are preceded by a version of Christ's parable of the wedding feast from the New Testament.

The stories take up most of the poem, but they are set in passages of discussion, the function of which is to link the stories to the idea of cleanness/uncleanness and to each other. The stories are all offered as illustrations of the proposition, advanced in the opening lines and constantly reiterated, that God loves cleanness and hates uncleanness. This is made into a threatening proposition: 'be clean or else'. The emphasis, in both the stories and the discussion passages, is on the negative side of the proposition, on the dire consequences of uncleanness. The word 'cleanness' used in a religious context had two different groups of senses in Middle English, both abstract: the more general one of 'freedom from sin' and the more particular one of 'chastity'.[1] Both senses were widely current. The sacrament of penance, which was so important in the practice of the faith in the later middle ages, made the former sense universally understood through the idea that the penitent is made clean of sin. The latter sense is the one which is found if one looks up 'cleanness' in treatises on morality such as handbooks for priests, where it is regularly opposed to the sin of lechery. Both senses apply in the poem, but it is the former which is fundamental to it; the latter is used to illustrate the former.

The poem works metaphorically. In the first two discussions and stories homosexuality, which medieval religious treatises consider to be, along with other kinds of deviance from the heterosexual norm, the worst of the branches of the deadly sin of lechery, is given great prominence. In the third story the same prominence is given to sacrilege, regarded as spiritual sodomy: just as, according to the poem, the inhabitants of Noah's world and Sodom and Gomorrah violate the human body, which is figuratively God's temple (1 Cor. 3.16–17), so Belshazzar violates the holy vessels of the literal Temple of Jerusalem. Such extreme sins rouse God immediately to destructive fury. But the poem is not mounting a crusade against homosexuality or sacrilege, against any other extreme sin, or against any particular sin. Its crusade is against *all* sin, and it takes the sins of homosexuality and sacrilege as extreme examples of sin in general. It sees cleanness and uncleanness in absolute terms: one is either entirely clean or not clean at all. In the words of the poem, a single *spec of a spote* (line 551) is sufficient to turn cleanness into uncleanness. As such cleanness is an unrealistic and inhuman virtue for, as

Pearl teaches, spotlessness is in practice not within a fallen human being's reach. The absolutist logic of *Cleanness* is, firstly, that God in justice must punish all human beings, because, in practice if not in theory, all are sinners (with a few excepted categories, such as the innocents of *Pearl*), and sin must in justice be punished. Secondly, God's punishment must be to send all human beings to hell, because on Judgement Day he makes only the one distinction, between the saved and the damned; the kind and degree of sin are therefore irrelevant. Thus, unless it goes against its own absolutist position, the poem's distinction between sin and extreme sin must be rhetorical only. Its final lines, which cut across this distinction, confirm that this is so. The idea of a God of strict justice, combined with that of human beings as inevitably sinful, leads to the conclusion that God and his virtue of cleanness are both inhuman, in the sense that both set impossibly high standards which pay no attention to human limitations.

As in *Patience*, the first word and the first statement are the central focus of the poem. But whereas *Patience* seeks to enlarge on its opening by exhibiting different approaches to patience in such a way as to prompt the reader to think about them, *Cleanness*, despite being over three times the length of *Patience*, is less generative.[2] It goes round the same ideas, as attested by the recurrence of the same language and imagery. The use of logical connectives (*for, forthy, then, thus*), the making of distinctions, and the general contrastive movement of the whole narrative, may create the impression of a developing argument. But the poem in fact does not argue a case. Unlike *Patience*, which wants to inspire reflection, *Cleanness* wants to make an impact, and to this end it is not logical, but works by repeated assertion, albeit disguised as argument. The purpose of the discussions and illustrative stories is not so much to enlarge perspectives on the nature of cleanness as to give reinforcement to the assertions. The poem is in the business of rhetoric rather than exposition, and it may be regarded as, in essence, one long rhetorical flourish based on its opening proposition.

The discussions and the stories which follow them are closely connected. The opening asserts that God is so clean himself that he cannot tolerate any uncleanness in those who come near him, whether they be priests who handle his body in the bread of holy communion or souls who seek entry to heaven. The attendant *exemplum*, the parable of the wedding feast, is retold in such a way as to demonstrate this, and the poem prefaces the parable with an 'earthly' version of it to make the point that God is even harder on uncleanness than an earthly prince would be. After the narrator has brought the parable to a close and explained it, he goes on to distinguish between 'ordinary' sins and the sin which God hates most of all, *fylthe of the flesch*. Again the attendant *exemplum* supports the discussion, by contrasting the falls of Lucifer and Adam with the fall of the pre-Flood world into sexual depravity. The point made by the *exemplum* is that God punishes Lucifer and Adam in moderation for their 'moderate' falls, whereas he destroys the whole world in the Flood on account of the widespread practice of *fylthe of the flesch*. The leading idea of the next discussion is that it is pointless to try to hide uncleanness from God because he will always find it out, and this is well exemplified in the story of Sodom and Gomorrah when he sends his spies into Sodom to verify what he has heard about the practices of the Sodomites (line 780), and when he becomes instantly aware of the disrespect shown him by Sarah and again by Lot's wife. The last linking discussion points to penance as the way out of sin, and the following *exemplum* holds up Nebuchadnezzar as an example of penance.

Various ways of looking at sin are considered – as rebellion against God, as disrespect for God, as *untrawthe* (that is the breaking of the covenantal bonds of faith and obedience which bind man to God), and as 'unkindness' (*unkyndely*, line 208), that is the breaking of the bonds of *kynde* which bind man to God's natural order.[3] But the idea of virtue as cleanness and sin as uncleanness always remains central. It is a sign of this centrality that the words *clene*, *unclene* and their derivatives and synonyms are constantly reiterated. There are indeed whole vocabularies of cleanness and uncleanness. The vocabulary of cleanness spans the range of moral and physical, as *honest, pure, puryté* (used only once, of the Virgin Birth, line 1074), *fetys* 'neat', *frely* 'fair', *fresch, gay, schene* 'bright'. Uncleanness is expressed by a mostly physical vocabulary, with words which mean dirt of one kind or another, and which communicate thereby the unpleasantness of sin: *fylthe* (*frothande fylthe*, line 1721), *gore, glette* 'slime', *souly* 'filthy', *fenny* 'muddy', *myre*.

The vocabulary draws notably on the courtly register. Courtesy, which amongst other things manifests the concern of courtly society to distance itself from vulgarity, metaphorically indicates the desire of God and the good to keep clear of the defilement of sin. God in heaven is imaged as a king *clene in his courte* (line 17). The poem's emphasis on God's fastidiousness or squeamishness, his cultivated distaste for dirt and indecency, helps make the link between his cleanness and courtliness; three times he is described as *scoymus* 'squeamish, fastidious, disdainful' (lines 21, 598, 1148). God in response to Noah's sacrifice speaks to him *In comly comfort ful clos and cortays wordes* 'full of seemly cheer and courteous words' (line 510). Lot is made part of the same discourse: as the narrator explains, he hopes to chasten the homosexual lechers of Sodom by his *hendelayk* 'courtesy' (line 860), and he uses the language of courtesy in speaking to them. Christ's cleanness too is expressed in terms of courtesy (lines 1089–1100): thus he heals the sick with *hynde speche* 'courteous speech' (line 1098), and the detail that he broke bread with his hands as cleanly as though it had been cut with a knife, found in the mystery plays, is here made a mark of his courtesy by the use of courtly language (lines 1105–8). Less often, words from the negative side of the courtly register are used (*vylanye* 'discourtesy, disgrace'). The reader is never called upon to take account of the possibility of ironic use of this language. Thus the narrator makes it clear that Lot's courteous address to the lechers is without irony, despite the context. In accordance with its monologic method. *Cleanness* makes no use of irony whatsoever.

Movement between positive and negative, as in the opening statements, is fundamental to the way the poem works, and this is evident at all levels, from the larger conceptual and structural framework down to minor linguistic detail. It is noticeable that adversative connectives are used frequently at the beginning of a sentence or clause as a means of moving the poem forward: *bot, yet, thagh, wheder, and* (in the sense of *bot*), *and yet, bot thagh.*

Cleanness is, then, a poem of extremes. Issues are polarised, morality is a matter of black and white, the middle ground is eliminated. Although at times the poem may seem to argue otherwise, its underlying idea is that in the eye of its God there are no degrees of sin and no degrees of punishment of sin: virtue is virtue and sin is sin, and 'the wages of sin is death' (Rom. 6.23). This position, as expressed in the poem, is radically different from that of *Pearl* and *Patience*, in which human beings are a mix-

ture of good and bad. In these poems the divine side is also different, more tolerant of human weakness, and the two sides,
despite a gap of understanding, at least try to communicate
through dialogue. In the scheme of *Cleanness* the human beings
are either sinners or not sinners (both by turns in the case of Nebuchadnezzar), and there is no true dialogue between even the virtuous and God. Such exchanges as there are are one-sided: Noah,
Abraham, and Lot speak to God only with exaggerated deference,
God in his turn speaks condescendingly, and there is no conversation or debate.[4]

A few passages seem to invite sympathy: the descriptions of
the fleeing Flood victims[5] and the about-to-be-engulfed
Sodomites, and the details of the wedding guest hanging his head
in shame and Belshazzar behaving honourably towards Daniel.
On the other side God may seem unacceptably out of control,
changeable of mood and given to fits of extreme anger. But the
narrator's depiction of God as fierce and vengeful dramatises the
point that he is not to be trifled with. Shocking as it may be, this
is the way God is, and any human judgement of him, for or
against, is irrelevant. The depiction keeps within range of the
biblical God, in the sense that the germ at least of all God's
thoughts and actions, his regrets and changes of mind, is in the
biblical texts.

The narrator's voice is flat and bluntly didactic. He addresses
his audience directly from time to time, always from a position of
unassailable authority. He leaves them in no doubt of his view of
the spiritual state of the world: *Nou ar we sore and synful and souly
uchone* 'now we are vile and sinful and filthy, each one of us' (line
1111). For the most part (though not in the line just quoted) he
maintains a clear boundary between himself and his audience or
reader, frequently using the imperative and the second-person
pronoun, usually the singular pronoun. The reader has the sense
of being preached at in a way that allows for no argument. A striking feature of the narrator's preaching style is the question put to
the reader (*Wich arn thenne thy wedes* ['clothes'] . . .?, line 169)),
and then immediately answered (*Hit arn thy werkes* . . ., line 171),
so that the reader is given no chance to reflect or respond.[6]

The overarching structure of the poem is based on the pattern of alternating passages of discussion and narrative. The
opening discussion and the first narrative (the parable of the wed-

ding feast, the only New Testament narrative) set the agenda and
claim Christ's seal of approval for the ideas of the whole poem.
The discussions not only link the narratives to each other and reiterate the importance of cleanness; each also draws attention to a
particular aspect of cleanness which the story it introduces highlights. A linear pattern is superimposed on the alternating one:
God's attitude to his creation becomes more complex from one
story to another (as in the Bible), in step with the increasing complexity of human society as it evolves. Correspondingly, the stories and the discussions get progressively longer and more
complex.[7] Superimposed on both of these patterns is one of contrasts, both large-scale and small-scale, which expresses the
poem's polarised attitudes. But, though the poem is carefully
worked out from beginning to end, the poet evidently wanted to
give the impression of a certain freedom of construction. The
movement from one element to another tends to be associative,
and ideas may be linked to other ideas and to stories in what seems
an *ad hoc* fashion. Discussion or exposition flows into narrative,
then the narrative leads back to further discussion, which in turn
leads into narrative again, and so on. The poem seems designed to
read as a homiletic outpouring, with the fluid but far from hap-
hazard structure contributing to the sense of urgency which it
generates.

The stories are apocalyptic,[8] the God who acts in them is
frightening, and the poet enlarges on the violent episodes he finds
in his sources. They are inhuman in scale, content, and the way in
which they are told, with few humanising touches[9] of the kind
found in *Patience*. Indeed there is little in the poem to engage the
reader on the human level. In contrast to the other three *Gawain*-
poems there is no central figure and no one who is human enough
for the reader to empathise with. Instead there is an unremitting
focus on the transcendental, on God, heaven, and epic events, so
that, except for special effects, ordinary life is excluded.

The idea that sin is a perversion, abhorrent in itself and
abhorrent to God, is at the core of the poem. Because God cannot
tolerate it, sin of whatever kind means damnation for the sinner.
Cleanness has no interest in ambiguity of any kind. On the contrary, the narrator seems determined to remove all possibility of
ambiguity. No gap between poet and narrator is visible, so the
reader is never allowed to rest from the message or find a way of

moderating it. The narratorial stance is that of a preacher dominated by an idea and prepared to bend all his materials to the service of that idea. Rather than simply accept a story, interpretation,
or tradition as he finds it, he is prepared to wrench it into the
shape he wants. Hence, to pick out just two examples, he demotes
the falls of Lucifer and Adam to minor episodes preceding the
Flood, and ignores the cynicism of the *Romance of the Rose* context from which he derives his idea of imitating Christ. He gives
his all to making his point about the need for cleanness as strongly
as possible. Stories, ideas, and arguments are presented in the
most heightened, not to say strident, way. The poem does not so
much ignore the dialogic approaches of its companion poems as
face them down, denying the possibility of alternatives.

Thus the poem itself models the uncompromising nature of
God's justice. In a sense the process of reading gives a taste of
what it feels like to be the recipient of God's hostility; as God is
hard on sinners, so the poem is hard on its readers. With its reit-
erations, including its reiterated scenes of violence, and its insis-
tent rhetoric, it seems remorseless. Its length, compared to
Patience, only makes it seem more so. To move on from *Cleanness*
to *Patience*, which restores the human dimension of the Christian
faith, is to experience a sense of release.

The beginning

The first lines of the poem at once establish its proposition in contrastive terms:

> Clannesse who-so kyndly cowthe comende,
> And rekken up alle the resouns that ho by right askes,
> Fayre formes myght he fynde in fortering his speche,
> And in the contraré kark and combraunce huge.
>
> For wonder wroth is the wyy that wroght alle thinges
> Wyth the freke that in fylthe folwes hym after. (lines 1–6)

[Whoever was able to praise cleanness appropriately, and reckon up
all the justifications that are hers as of right, might expect to find
excellent patterns to help him in his discourse, and in doing the contrary great trouble and difficulty. For the one who made all things is
very angry with the man who serves him in a state of filth.]

The meaning of these lines may not be entirely clear,[10] but there is no doubt of the oppositional patterning, and in particular the opposition of *clannesse* and *fylthe*. The subsequent discussion restates this fundamental opposition several times. In the first thirty-two lines the words *clannesse* and *clene* each occur six times in all (*clannes(sse)* three times and *clene* three times), and there are four occurrences of *unclannesse* and its synonym *fylthe* (*unclannesse* once and *fylthe* three times). In line 7 the narrative refers to priests as an example of men who serve God in a state of filth (that is in a state of sin, see line 15) and thereby attract his anger. It emphasises that priests in the nature of their role are on intimate terms with God, charged with administering his sacraments: *Thay hondel ther his aune body, and usen hit bothe* 'they handle there (i.e. at the altar) his own body, and partake of it also' (line 11). Again there is a polarised contrast. Clean priests are said to win great reward (line 12), and unclean priests, those who are *inwith alle fylthes* (line 14), are said to drive God to anger because they are not only sinful in themselves but also defile *Bothe God and his gere* (line 16), that is God and the sacraments. Unclean priests are also contrasted with the angels, steeped in *alle that is clene* (line 19), who serve God in his heavenly court as the priests have the role of serving him on earth. Priests' uncleanness is further referred to a strongly-expressed contrast between their outward appearance and inner nature (*honest utwyth and inwith alle fylthes*, line 14), and the same inner-outer dichotomy is used to point up the contrast between the unclean priests and the angels, who are clean *bothe withinne and withouten* (line 20), and therefore have inner and outer nature in harmony. It is indicated that God is surrounded by so much cleanness in Heaven that it would be surprising if he were prepared to tolerate uncleanness (lines 17–22). As always in the discussions and the examples, the negative predominates.

Having asserted his proposition, that God loves cleanness and hates uncleanness, the narrator looks to biblical authority to back it up. He chooses as his two defining biblical texts the sixth beatitude and the parable of the wedding feast. He refers to the biblical authority of Matthew's gospel when he introduces his text of the beatitude (*as Mathew recordes*, line 25) and his text of the parable: *As Mathew meles in his masse* 'as Matthew speaks in his gospel (read at mass)', line 51. But his appeal is primarily to the authority of Christ himself. He draws attention to the fact that both the beatitude (*Kryst kydde hit hymself in a carp ones* 'Christ made it clear himself in a speech once', line 23)) and the parable (*Thus comparisunes Kryst the kyndom of heven*, line 161) are Christ's own words. The narrator thus finds the highest possible authority to support his proposition.

The parable narrative carries the same message as the biblical stories which follow and it may be said to define their parameters. It elaborates the Bible in similar ways to the stories, depicting a God who is benign and angry by turns, and bringing out the fierceness of his reaction to the unclean and the terror he inspires in them. All the stories are linked to the sixth beatitude, but the parable is linked to it more immediately than the other stories because it pictures directly the reward/punishment for clean-ness/uncleanness promised by the poem's two-sided version of the beatitude.

Thus the opening discussion, the beatitude, and the parable are closely connected. In terms of narrative linkages the beatitude is linked to the discussion by line 23 (quoted above), and the beat-itude to the parable by a linking line which looks forward to the clothing imagery of the parable: *Forthy hyy not to heven in hateres totorne* 'and so do not hasten to heaven in torn clothes' (line 33). The parable's clothing imagery is taken back to the beatitude itself (the wording *That any unclannesse has on*, line 30, suggests that uncleanness is thought of as being worn like a garment), and to the earlier discussion, in the detail that the angels who sur-round God wear clean clothes (*wedes ful bryght*, line 20). At the same time the beatitude and the parable are managed so as to bring their message into line with the opening proposition. In the Bible the beatitude is positive and the parable is negative in emphasis. In the poem a positive-negative contrast is established in both. Thus the beatitude is first quoted in its positive biblical form (Matthew 5.8 has: 'Blessed are the pure in heart; for they shall see God'):

> The hathel clene of his hert hapenes ful fayre,
> For he schal loke on oure Lorde with a loue chere. (lines 27–8)

[The man clean of heart gains good fortune, for he shall look on our lord with a humble countenance.]

This is followed immediately by the non-biblical negative form, which is given greater weight than the positive by a further statement of God's intolerance of uncleanness:

> As so says, to that syght seche schal he never
> That any unclannesse has on, auwhere aboute;
> For he that flemus uch fylthe fer fro his hert
> May not byde that burre, that hit his body neghe. (lines 29–32)

[For he who drives all filth far from his heart may not endure the shock of its coming near his person. That is to say that the man who has any uncleanness on him, anywhere about him, shall never come to that sight.]

The narrator then supplies an *exemplum* which links beatitude to parable, and continues the negative emphasis. It consists of a parable of the parable, for which there is no basis in the Bible:

> Forthy hyy not to heven in hateres totorne,
> Ne in the harlates hod and handes unwaschen.
> For what urthly hathel that hygh honour haldes
> Wolde lyke if a ladde come lytherly attyred,
>
> When he were sette solempnely in a sete ryche,
> Abof dukes on dece, with dayntys served?
> Then the harlot with haste helded to the table
> With rent cokres at the kne, and his clutte trasches,
>
> And his tabarde totorne, and his totes oute,
> Other ani on of alle thyse, he schulde be halden utter,
> With mony blame ful bygge, a boffet peraunter,
> Hurled to the halle dore and harde theroute schowved,
>
> And be forboden that borghe, to bowe thider never,
> On payne of enprysonment and puttyng in stokkes;
> And thus schal he be schent for his schrowde feble,
> Thagh never in talle ne in tuch he trespas more. (lines 33–48)

[Therefore do not hasten to heaven in torn clothes, nor in the beggar's hood and with unwashed hands. For what earthly man who holds high rank would be pleased if a fellow came badly attired, when he was solemnly seated on a rich throne, above dukes on the dais, served with dainties? If then the beggar hurried to the table with leggings torn at the knee, and his patched old shoes, and his tabard torn, and the toes of his shoes out of shape, or any one of all these, he should be thrown out, with many a sharp rebuke, perhaps a blow, pushed to the hall door and violently thrust outside, and be

forbidden to go to that great house ever again, on pain of imprisonment and being put in the stocks. And so he shall be punished for his
poor clothes, though he should never again offend either in general
appearance or detail of dress.]

The introduction of this preliminary parable enables a new contrast to be developed, which draws a distinction between men's
attitude to uncleanness and God's. It puts the feast in charge of an
earthly lord, and it is entirely concerned with the guest at the feast
and the lord's response to him, giving graphic details of the
guest's ragged clothes and of his punishment. It both prepares the
reader for the main focus of the parable proper as it is retold in the
poem (that is, on the guest in ragged clothes and his punishment),
and allows the poem to remark again God's extreme hatred of
uncleanness. The two lines which link the two versions of the
parable, and which transfer the guest in ragged clothes from one
version to the other, make the distinction between the earthly and
heavenly reception of uncleanness explicit:

> And if unwelcum he were to a worthlych prynce,
> Yet hym is the hyghe kyng harder in heven. (lines 49–50)[11]

[And if he were unwelcome to a noble prince, the high king in
heaven is still harder on him.]

The fate of the guest in the two parable narratives bears out this
statement. In the preliminary one the disgraced guest is thrown
out from the feast, banned forever from returning to the lord's
house, and threatened with imprisonment if he does return. In
the parable proper the lord (i.e. God) goes further, ordering the
guest to be imprisoned at once in a dungeon and tortured (lines
153–60). But the difference between the two does not affect the
overall meaning of the parable, or of the poem. The preliminary
parable appears to be included to add weight to the main point of
the biblical one, that God punishes the guest in dirty clothes
severely. It provides a lead-in to the parable proper and heightens
its impact.

The parable

The narrative of the parable proper is shaped to bring out the
contrast between the lord's treatment of the guest in dirty clothes
and his treatment of the other invitees and guests. The parable is

thus reworked to bring out the distinction, formally made in the discussion section which follows, which shapes the 'argument': that between a greater and a lesser kind of sin. The shaping involves altering the version in Matthew 22.1–14, which is announced as the source of the story, and conflating it with the version in Luke 14.16–24. Apart from the details of the lord's preparations for the feast in lines 55–60, which extend the details in Matthew 22.4, the first part of the retelling largely follows Luke. There is one significant added detail, found in neither Matthew nor Luke, which prepares for the end of the parable and identifies its main point of interest for the poem: Matthew is reported as saying (which he does not) that the lord invited the guests to come *in comly quoyntis* 'in comely attire' (line 54).

As in Luke, the invited guests make their various excuses, the lord is angry with them, he sends his servants out into the streets of the city to bring in all the people they can find of whatever condition, and when they do this and he sees there is still room he sends them out once more, this time into the countryside beyond the city, to find more people to fill his house. Finally he announces that none of those who were invited and who refused should ever taste his supper. The poem makes the point that the lord feels that the guests who have refused have shown him no respect: *And denounced me noght now at this tyme* 'and [they] did not honour me at this time' (line 106). In Matthew some prospective guests refuse while others revile and kill the king's servants, and the episode ends apocalyptically: 'the king . . . was wroth; and he sent forth his armies, and destroyed those murderers, and burned up their city' (Matt.22.7). In the poem this episode is omitted. The lord's violence is reserved for the guest in dirty clothes. For God to show greater violence towards others would cloud the main point of the parable as the poem sees it.

In Matthew the servants go out only once more, not twice as they do in Luke and the poem, and they bring back 'all that they found, both bad and good' (Matt. 22.10). The main episode of the guest without a wedding garment is taken from Matthew 22.11–13 (there is no equivalent in Luke), and the contrastive phrase 'both bad and good' is expanded from Matthew 22.10 by other contrastive phrases which describe the guests: some are *worthy* and some *wers* (line 113), nobles sit on the high dais and others sit below (lines 115–16), and good service is given to all whether they are of high or low status (lines 119–20). The lord's commands to his servants to go out and find guests to replace those who have refused his invitation are also expressed in the poem in terms of contrasts. The first command contains three contrastive pairings: he orders the servants to approach people *on fote and on hors, / Bothe burnes and burdes* [men and women], *the better and the wers* (lines 79–80). The servants bring back squires on horses and men on foot, bondmen and freemen (lines 87–8). In Luke the lord asks his servants to bring back only the disadvantaged: 'the poor, and the maimed, and the halt, and the blind' (Luke 14.21). In the poem this verse becomes the lord's second command, and, though the emphasis is still on the guests being disadvantaged, contrast between them is again introduced:

> Be thay fers, be thay feble, forlotes none,
> Be thay hol, be thay halt, be thay on-yyed,
> And thagh thay ben bothe blynde and balterande cruppeles.
> (lines 101–3)

> [Be they bold, be they timid, overlook none, be they sound, be they lame, be they one-eyed, and though they be both blind and hobbling cripples.]

The guests are thus established as a motley collection, but alike in that they are all at least more or less respectably dressed: *And ay a segge soberly semed by her wedes* (line 117). This is the point of contrast between the guest who is singled out for blame and the other guests. They, though they may be far from perfect, are on the right side of the dividing line, and he is not. The contrast of reward is made extreme: *served to the fulle* (line 120) on the one hand, and thrown into a dungeon on the other.

The episode of the guest in unsatisfactory clothes is expanded from three biblical verses to twenty-eight lines. The lord's anger, evident in what he says, is confirmed by the narrator both before his first speech (*And gremed* ['was angry'] *therwith the grete lorde, and greve* ['injure, punish'] *hym he thoght,* line 138), and after it, when his words are described as *brothe* 'angry' (line 149). Lines 153–60, in which the lord orders the guest to be cast out, are based on Matthew 22.13: 'Then said the king to the servants, Bind him hand and foot, and take him away, and cast him into outer darkness; there shall be weeping and gnashing of teeth'. As well as

enlarging on the biblical punishments to which the guest is condemned, the poem supplies another narratorial indication of the
lord's fury (*Then the lorde wonder loude laled* ['spoke'] *and cryed*,
line 153). As with the guests who refused, the detail indicates that
the lord's anger comes particularly from his sense that he has not
been treated with the respect due to him: *Thou praysed me and my
place ful pover and ful nede* 'you set a very poor and meagre value
on me and my house' (line 146). There is a final addition in which
the lord makes explicit the purpose of the punishments: *to teche
hym be quoynt* ['well-dressed'] (line 160), recalling his desire when
he first sends out his servants that the guests should come to the
feast *in comly quoyntis.*

The poem thus begins and ends the parable with the point
about the need for clean clothes, and sharpens the focus of the
Matthean version on the lord's anger with the guest in unclean
clothes. It further constructs contrasts which are not present in
the Bible: between the well-dressed company and the one poorly-
dressed guest, and between the friendly attitude of the lord
towards the well-dressed guests and his anger with the badly-
dressed one. The narrative makes this latter contrast dramatic by
elaborating the biblical text in such a way as to bring out the sud-
denness of the change in the lord's mood. At one moment he is the
amiable host, mingling with his guests and engaging in cheerful
small talk (lines 129–32), the next he is furious at the sight of the
guest's poor clothes. The emphasis on his anger is continued with
the series of angry questions to the guest, put with a *felle chere*
'grim countenance' (line 139). Also significant in pointing up the
lord's anger is the description of the guest's fearful response (lines
149–52). In the Bible there is no response at all.

The passage of explanation and exhortation which follows
the parable spells out its meaning in the most explicit terms, referring to Christ's own biblical comparison of the feast to the kingdom of heaven. It restates the assertions of the poem's opening,
with similar backwards and forwards movement between positive
and negative. It picks up the first part of the concluding verse of
the parable in Matthew – 'For many are called . . .' (Matt. 22.14)
– when it refers to *this frelych feste that fele arn to called* 'this splendid feast to which many are called' (line 162). It explains that this
means that all baptised Christians are invited to the feast (lines

163–4). The second part of the biblical verse, '. . . but few are chosen', is omitted, no doubt because the sense conflicts with the poem's point that *all* will be welcomed by God, so long as they are clean.

The passage focuses on the idea that clean clothes are absolutely necessary if one is to be admitted to heaven. It explains further that one's clothes are one's actions (*werkes*), and that, to be accepted in heaven, they must not only be *fayr* 'attractive' (line 174) but *lyned with the lykyng that lyye in thyn hert* 'lined with the good disposition of your heart' (line 172). This detail is crucial. For a man to see God he must be clean/attractive inwardly, whole and honest of heart (lines 593–4). So Lucifer has the *fayre wedes* (line 217), but not the good disposition, and he is cast into hell. Again and again the poem indicates that a sinner may appear to be clean, but it also leaves the reader in no doubt that God always sees through superficial cleanness to the reality underneath (see below, pp. 101–2).

The discussions

The discussions which link the parable to the story of the Flood, the Flood to Sodom and Gomorrah, and Sodom and Gomorrah to Belshazzar's feast, all make the sixth beatitude their base point, alluding to it, indirectly, twice or three times in each case. But there is no interest in exploring what it means to be 'pure of heart'. The long list of sins which follows the exposition of the parable begins with a brief allusion to the negative formulation of the beatitude in terms of sin (lines 177–8), and ends with another such allusion, which simply repeats the first in more emphatic terms (lines 189–92).

The list of sins itself is miscellaneous, with sins of different orders lumped together. Some are vague (*colwarde* 'villainy, baseness', *croked dedes*, *mayntnaunce of schrewes* 'supporting evildoers'). Others are traditionally categorised as deadly (*slauthe, pryde, covetyse*), or as associated with the deadly sins (*mensclaght, roborrye, traysoun, to much drynk*). Others, though they obviously represent sinful behaviour, are not usually identified as specific sins at all (*dysheriete and depryve dowrie of wydoes* 'misappropriating and stealing widows' dowers', *fals famacions and fayned lawes* 'false rumours and spurious laws'). The list gives the

impression of being put together at random and not in any way
considered. It is plain from its miscellaneousness that the reader
is not meant to attach significance to any particular named sin.
Rather it enforces the general point, made in the negative formu-
lations of the sixth beatitude which frame the list, that all sin
attracts God's punishment.

In context, the list has another function. It fills out the 'ordinary' side of the distinction, foreshadowed in the parable and now
elaborately developed, between 'ordinary' sin and an extreme
kind of sin which is especially hateful to God. The statement is
best punctuated as a single long sentence (this is the practice of
most recent editions) which, with its succession of unresolved
negative clauses, builds up a considerable momentum:

> Bot I have herkned and herde of mony hyghe clerkes,
> And als in resounes of ryght red hit myselven,
> That that ilk proper prynce that Paradys weldes,
> Is displesed at uch a poynt that plyes to scathe;
>
> Bot never yet in no boke breved I herde
> That ever he wrek so wytherly on werk that he made,
> Ne venged for no vilté of vice ne synne,
> Ne so hastyfly was hot for hatel of his wylle,
>
> Ne never so sodenly soght unsoundely to weng,
> As for fylthe of the flesch that foles han used;
> For, as I fynde, ther he foryet alle his fre thewes,
> And wex wod for the wrache for wrathe at his hert. (lines
> 193–204)

[But I have heard from many great scholars, and also read it myself
in true writings, that that same excellent prince who rules paradise is
displeased at everything that has to do with sin; but I have not yet
found written down in any book that he ever punished his creation
so fiercely, or extracted retribution (so fiercely) for any abomination
of vice or sin, or was so precipitately violent for the hatred in his
mind, or was ever so abruptly concerned to take drastic vengeance,
as for filth of the flesh that fools have indulged in; for I find that then
he abandoned all his gracious ways, and became furious for revenge
on account of the anger in his heart.]

The differentiating characteristic of this especially odious kind of
sin, here called *fylthe of the flesche*, is that it rouses God to
destructive fury. The distinction is maintained through the two

following linking passages. In anticipating his second main story (of Sodom and Gomorrah) the narrator refers to the difference in God's response to different kinds of uncleanness in a sentence which is a condensed version of the sentence just quoted:

> Thus alle illes he hate as helle that stynkkes;
> Bot non nuyes hym, on naght ne never upon dayes,
> As harlottrye unhonest, hethyng of selven;
> That schames for no schrewedschyp, schent mot he worthe!
> (lines 577–80)

[Thus he hates all evils as stinking hell, but none angers him, neither by night nor by day, so much as unclean lewdness, contempt for one's person; he who is ashamed of no depravity, let him be destroyed!]

In leading in to this second story the narrator again contrasts the way God punishes 'ordinary' sin (by keeping the sinner out of heaven, line 596), with his punishment of extreme uncleanness:

> Bot of the dome of the douthe for dedes of schame,
> He is so skoymos of that skathe he scarres bylyve;
> He may not dryye to draw allyt bot drepes in hast. (lines
> 597–9)

[But concerning the punishment of men for deeds of shame, he is so revolted by that sin that he takes alarm at once; he cannot bear to hold back but kills in haste.]

Line 599 indicates once more that the consequence of the sin of extreme uncleanness is that God, when faced with it, loses control. His punishment becomes a matter not of considered judgement but of furious reaction. At the end of the final linking passage, between the stories of Sodom and Gomorrah and Belshazzar's feast, the distinction is maintained in terms of spiritual rather than physical uncleanness, anticipating the story to come: any defilement of what is sacred to God, whether it is a repentant soul or a holy vessel, rouses him to anger as surely as sodomy does, for God cannot bear that what once belonged to him should be unclean again (line 1144).

All three of the linking passages discussed here refer to God's haste to take vengeance. To lines 200, 201, and 598–9, quoted above, should be added line 1150, with its detail that vengeance overtook Belshazzar *hastyly sone* 'very speedily'. The effect of

God's precipitate revenge is that doing penance, which offers, as
the final linking passage explains, a theoretical remedy for all sin,
is effectively not available for the extreme sins of physical and
spiritual *fylthe*. There is simply no time for it. It is thus not God's
anger alone which is so damaging, but the speed with which his
anger leads him to act. The stories bear this out. The people of
Noah's world and of Sodom and Gomorrah cry to God for mercy,
but neither they nor the other sinners in the poem who incur
God's anger have time to repent of their ways. On the other hand
God is 'moderate' in punishing Lucifer, Adam, and Nebuchadnezzar, and they are given time to repent. Nebuchadnezzar does
so, Lucifer throws away his chance, as the poem notes (lines
230–4), and Christ takes Adam's repentance upon himself.

It is hard to take seriously a distinction between sins which
God *hates as helle that stynkkes* (line 577), and others which he
hates even more. It is harder still to take the distinction seriously
when the narrator chooses to exemplify it, as soon as he has made
it, by prefacing his first major biblical narrative, the story of the
Flood, with accounts of the Fall of the Angels and the Fall of
Man as examples of 'lesser' sins. These episodes are universally
recognised in Christian tradition as the primary events which
bring evil into the world and the primary examples of the severity of God's punishment of sin. The distinction is created by
comment which manifestly involves distortion. The poem states
that the Fall of Satan and the Angels was in accordance with the
moderation of God's nature (*In the mesure of his mode,* line 215),
and that though it was 'a fearful calamity and a mighty vengeance'
(*a brem brest and a byge wrache,* line 229), yet God did not become
angry (*And yet wrathed not the wyy,* line 230). Similarly, in the Fall
of Man, God's vengeance showed moderation (*Al in mesure and
methe was mad the vengiaunce* 'the vengeance was taken in all
measure and moderation', line 247), and a reference to the doctrine of the Fortunate Fall is brought in to support this statement
(*And efte amended with a mayden that make had never* 'and afterwards mitigated by a maiden who was without peer', line 248). In
the Flood, by contrast, God showed *malys mercyles and mawgré
much* 'merciless anger and great hostility' (line 250). In a general
way the cumulative structure of the Fall-Fall-Flood narrative
sequence mirrors the structure of the sentence in which the distinction is first announced.

It appears then that this elaborate distinction, like that between the *urthely hathel* and the heavenly lord in the two versions of the parable, is made primarily for rhetorical effect. The distinction not only is against common understanding but, like the parable distinction, it adds little to the poem's meaning. Its purpose seems to be not so much to help the narrator to argue a serious point about God's attitude to uncleanness as to create the *appearance* of an argument. Making and applying the distinction adds interest to the multiplying of examples of uncleanness, and gives the poem its chance to make its point about the disgusting nature of *all* sin, and God's loathing of it, in the most graphic terms.

The link from the Flood to Sodom and Gomorrah contains two exhortations to the reader to avoid uncleanness and practise cleanness, both of which contain uncompromising negative/positive allusions to the beatitude. The first warns against being found in *fylthe of the flesch* which cannot be washed clean, and emphasises the absolutism of God's attitude: concerning *synne that syttes unclene* (probably, in the light of line 548, 'sin that remains uncleansed'), the narrator urges that *On spec of a spote* (line 551) will be enough to deprive a man of the beatific vision. To achieve the vision he needs to be as clean as a polished beryl or perfect pearl (lines 553–6).

The second exhortation enlarges on the idea that uncleanness cannot be hidden from God. It paraphrases verses from the Psalms (also used in *Patience*) to the effect that one who lives foolishly (that is, sinfully) must expect the creator of all eyes and ears to see, hear, and know everything: 'Understand, ye brutish among the people: and ye fools, when will ye be wise? He that planted the ear, shall he not hear? He that formed the eye, shall he not see?' (Psalm 94.8–9). The idea of a deceptive outer beauty or cleanness is first brought into the poem with the example of the false priests who are *honest utwyth and inwith alle fylthes* (line 14). As already noticed, it is found in the examples of Lucifer the rebel angel (lines 209, 217–18), and the descendants of Adam who lived before the Flood (lines 253, 262). The prominence of the idea in this particular linking discussion relates to the next story. In accordance with tradition, Sodom is said, at the end of the story, to have been *an erde of erthe the swettest* 'the most pleasant place

on earth' (line 1006), and its inhabitants exceptionally good-look-
ing (*so fayr a folk*, line 1014). Especially prominent is the description of the fruit growing beside the Dead Sea, *so red and so ripe
and rychely hwed*, which is nothing but *wyndowande askes* 'swirling
ashes' inside (lines 1041–8). The strange fruit is one of the Dead
Sea's *teches and tokenes* 'signs and tokens' (line 1049) of the city,
its people, and its fate.

The conclusion that God is the *gropande* ['searching'] *God*,
who probes one's innermost being (lines 591–2), leads to the second positive/negative allusion to the beatitude (lines 593–6). In
between the two exhortations, as the narrator looks backwards to
the story of the Flood and forwards to the story of Sodom and
Gomorrah, he refers once more to the *vycios fylthe* which so
defiles a man's soul that he is deprived of the sight of God (lines
574–6).

If this link warns the reader to beware of *fylthe* and of trying
to hide it, the next takes a seemingly more positive stance. The
switch from negative to positive comes in the last line of the
account of the Dead Sea, which states that all may understand
from the *teches and tokenes* that God loves cleanness (line 1052).
Only the positive formulation of the beatitude is alluded to: to see
Christ, the sinner must make himself clean (lines 1053–6). As in
the parable of the wedding feast a secular example prefaces a
sacred one, in order to clarify and emphasise the sacred meaning:
in lines 1057–64 there is a quotation from *Clopyngnel* (Jean de
Meun) and *his clene Rose* (*The Romance of the Rose*), in which the
lover who wants to impress his mistress is advised to imitate her
ways. Then comes the application:

> If thou wyl dele drwrye wyth Dryghtyn thenne,
> And lelly lovy thy Lorde and his leef worthe,
> Thenne confourme the to Kryst, and the clene make,
> That ever is polyced als playn als the perle selven. (lines
> 1065–8)

> [If then you will have love-dealings with the Lord, and love your
> Lord truly and be his dear one, then be like Christ, who is always
> polished as smooth as the pearl itself, and make yourself clean.]

This use of *The Romance of the Rose* suggests the narrator's willingness to plunder whatever he can find to make his point, for the
clene Rose is not clean at all but a knowing *exposé* of the worldly

mores of courtly society. In the passage quoted in *Cleanness*, one critic observes, 'Jean ironically relishes the polished deceptions of love service'.[12] *Cleanness* entirely overrides the original context of the passage, and forces it into the narrator's own mould.

The idea of Christ as like a polished pearl is developed by reference to the perfect cleanness of his incarnation, birth, and ministry. But this again makes for a difficulty. In the two versions of the parable the heavenly lord's standards are more demanding than those of the secular lord, and now imitating Christ is presented as more demanding than imitating a mistress. The problem for the sinner to whom the exhortation to be clean is directed is that the greater the heightening of Christ's cleanness and his desire to have everything clean around him, the more intimidating the task of imitating him becomes. The account of Christ's life focuses on the incarnation, birth, and ministry as miracles which turn uncleanness into cleanness. Thus Mary is not deflowered but made cleaner by becoming pregnant with Christ, the cowshed becomes a place of beauty, and the pain of childbirth is changed to joy (lines 1069–80). At the birth there is no sign of Joseph, or the shepherds and kings (as there is, say, in the mystery plays), only the miraculous worship of the angels, the ox, and the ass. There is no interest in the individual stories of Christ's healing the sick. Instead the emphasis is on the healing power of his perfect cleanness, symbolised by the fact that he broke bread as cleanly as though he had cut it with a knife (lines 1105–8). Christ is presented as a fastidious aristocrat who heals more out of distaste for uncleanness than out of compassion. Moreover, the account of Christ's life ends with the ministry. The poem has nothing to say about the events of the passion, in which Christ's humanity is most in evidence. The passage rises to sublimity of expression, but it delivers only difficult, abstract meaning. Christ's humanity, the point of contact between man and God, is entirely written out.

The narrator apparently identifies the difficulty. *How* may we sinners make ourselves clean like Christ? Again he uses the language of the sixth beatitude:

> Nou ar we sore and synful and souly uchone,
> How schulde we se, then may we say, that Syre upon throne?
> (lines 1111–12)

[Since we are vile and sinful and filthy, each one of us, how should
we see, then may we say, that lord on his throne?]

In answering his question the narrator for the first time states that
God is merciful, and then identifies the sacrament of penance as
the way for the sinner to restore himself to a state of cleanness.
The previous linking discussion had introduced the subject of
penance indirectly by transferring from the world to the individual the idea of being washed clean of sin (line 548), and coupling
this with the statement that the individual needed to be as clean
as a beryl or pearl if he was to appear in heaven (lines 553–6). Now
imagery of pearls, beryls, washing and polishing is explicitly associated with penance. The reader is urged to *pure the with penaunce
tyl thou a perle worthe* ' purify yourself with penance till you
become a pearl' (line 1116), and to polish himself brighter than
the beryl or pearl by taking penance from the priest (lines
1131–2). As the pearl may be restored to its original brightness
by being washed in wine (lines 1125–8), so the unclean soul
may be restored to its original state of cleanness by being *waschen
wyth water of schryfte* (line 1133). Christ himself has just been
described as polished as smooth as the pearl (line 1068), so
penance is held out to the sinner as offering the possibility of perfect cleanness on a par with Christ's. But the discussion continues
to ride above the human level. It gives the reader no understanding of how penance works – how and why it brings about so
apparently miraculous a transformation, or what may be involved
in taking the sacrament, including the probability, if it is properly
administered and taken, of difficulty and pain. The narrator
implies that penance is not difficult: *Nobot wasch hir wyth
wourchyp in wyn* 'all you have to do is to wash it [the pearl which
has lost its lustre] reverently in wine' (line 1127). But it is nowhere
demonstrated that penance is easy, just as it is nowhere demonstrated that imitating Christ is easy. This is a theoretical view of
penance which is hard to engage with.[13]
   Significantly, the discussion ends by drawing attention to the
danger inherent in penance. It asserts that it is worse to commit
sin after penance than not to take the sacrament at all. As the
poem puts it, such a relapse leads God, in line 1138, *wel hatter to
hate then hade thou not waschen* 'to hate much more hotly than had
you not washed (in the water of penance)', and the unfortunate

penitent is warned to expect the dire retribution which is God's reponse to extreme uncleanness: *War the thenne for the wrake, his wrath is achaufed* 'look out then for vengeance, his anger is kindled' (line 1143). The germ of this idea is a commonplace of didactic religious writing,[14] but this is a uniquely harsh version of it. The narrator makes God's fierce justice a part even of his sacrament of mercy. Thus the final focus of this linking discussion is not on Christ as merciful and on penance as a solution to sin. Hope is held out and then taken away again. God's attitude to penance becomes another example of his uncompromising standards, and the message to the sinner is still 'Beware!'

The stories (1): contrast

Positive-negative contrast is a principal determinant in the shaping of the illustrative stories as it is of the discussions. It operates in both small-scale and large-scale ways. Numerous local contrasts are made throughout the narratives. At the level of verbal detail, God is indicated as one who *al spedes and spylles* 'makes and mars everything' (line 511), a phrase which is apt to his characterisation in the poem. Daniel indicates Nebuchadnezzar's power in similar terms, but more expansively:

> Who-so wolde wel do, wel hym bityde,
> And quos deth so he dezyre he dreped als fast;
>
> Who-so hym lyked to lyft, on lofte was he sone,
> And quo-so hym lyked to lay was lowed bylyve. (lines
> 1647–50)

[Whoever he wished to do well, good fortune befell him, and the man whose death he desired he killed immediately; whoever it pleased him to lift up was soon on high, and whoever it pleased him to lay low was quickly brought down.]

Noah contrasts the raven and the dove when he speaks to the dove before sending it out to look for dry land: *Thagh that fowle be false, fre* ['true'] *be thou ever* (line 474). When the dove returns with the olive branch the narrative notes the change of mood in the Ark from an attitude of grim endurance to joy: *Then was ther joy in that gyn, where jumpred er dryyed* 'then there was joy in that vessel, where the motley company (literally those jumbled

together) had suffered before' (line 491). After the destruction of
the cities Sodom's present and former states are contrasted (lines
1006–12). In the story of Belshazzar's feast, God's use of Nebuchadnezzar to punish the erring Jews is summed up in a striking
chiasmus:

> . . . he fylsened the faythful in the falce lawe
> To forfare the falce in the faythe trwe (lines 1167–8)

[. . . he helped the faithful in the false religion to destroy the false in
the true faith.]

The contrast between a former high state and a present fallen
state, indicative of God's punishment of pride, is made with
respect to the Jews of Jerusalem (lines 1257–60), Nebuchadnezzar (lines 1330–2, and line 1685: *Thus he countes hym a kow, that
was a kyng ryche*), and Belshazzar (lines 1791–2). There is contrast
between the former state of the sacred vessels, solemnly conse-
crated to God's use in the Temple, and their use in the hands of
Belshazzar. The contrast is made in two separate passages (lines
1445–50 and 1496–1500), and it emphasises the enormity of Belshazzar's sacrilege. What had formerly served God is now made
to serve Satan (line 1459). All the contrasts work towards the one
great contrast, between cleanness and uncleanness.

Sometimes the narrator's desire to make the cleanness/
uncleanness contrast as sharp as possible drives him to take up
unorthodox positions, as in the passage on the Fall of the Angels
and the Fall of Man which prefaces the Noah story (discussed
above, p. 100). When God speaks to Abraham about the hateful
practices of the Sodomites, he contrasts their *usage unclene* (line
710) with the joys of heterosexual lovemaking:

> I compast hem a kynde crafte and kende hit hem derne,
> And amed hit in myn ordenaunce oddely dere,
> And dyght drwry therinne, doole alther-swettest;
> And the play of paramores I portrayed myselven,
>
> And made therto a maner myriest of other.
> When two true togeder had tyyed hemselven,
> Bytwene a male and his make such merthe schulde come,
> Welnyghe pure Paradys moght preve no better.
>
> Elles thay moght honestly ayther other welde,
> At a stylle stollen steven unstered wyth syght,

Luf-lowe hem bytwene lasched so hote
That alle the meschefes on mold moght hit not sleke. (lines
697–708)

[I devised for them a natural skill and taught it to them privately, and
valued it exceptionally highly in my plan of creation, establishing
love, the sweetest of all gifts, in that skill; and I devised the dalliance
of lovers, and contrived in that regard the most pleasant practice of
all. Whenever two virtuous people joined themselves together,
between a man and his mate such pleasure should come that paradise itself might scarcely prove any better. As long as they used each
other decently, at a quiet private meeting with none to look on, the
fire of love might flare up between them so hotly that all the misfor-
tunes in the world would be unable to extinguish it.]

The implication of this extra-biblical passage is that God sees the
joys of his gift of heterosexual sex as so great that his fury at
men's meddling with his gift is understandable. If 'clean' sex is
like paradise, then who would bother with 'unclean' sex, unless to
insult the Creator? But the narrator puts ideas and language into
the mouth of God which the poet's clerical contemporaries would
have more readily associated with uncleanness (in the sense of
sexual immorality) than cleanness.[15] Similarly, when Lot offers his
daughters to the men of Sodom in an attempt to take their attention away from the angels (in the shape of young men) who are his
guests, he is made to do so with an enthusiasm which goes far
beyond the restrained language of the biblical verse: 'Behold now,
I have two daughters which have not known man' (Gen. 19.8). He
emphasises their heterosexual desirability:

In Sodamas, thagh I hit say, non semloker burdes.
Hit arn ronk, hit arn rype, and redy to manne. (lines 868–9)

[In Sodom, though I say it myself, there are no prettier women; they
are grown, they are ripe, and ready to be mastered.]

Lot is made to seem so concerned to protect his angel guests and
to draw a distinction between the practice of the Sodomites (he
accuses them of degrading themselves, lines 863–4) and the *crafte
that is better* (line 865) that he loses sight of the fact that he is pros-
tituting his daughters, an issue of some sensitivity in patristic
commentary.[16] The explanation is that the narrator is anxious to
make the distinction between 'good' heterosexual pleasure and
'bad' homosexual pleasure as dramatic as possible. Given his pur-

pose, he is not interested in making moral distinctions (or in having God make such distinctions) between one kind of heterosexual sex and another. So the narrator attaches no blame to Lot, who
remains firmly on the side of cleanness. Thus the angel who later
urges Lot to flee the coming destruction is given a speech, without equivalent in the Bible, in which he differentiates Lot's cleanness from the filth of the Sodomites which is all around him (*For
thou art oddely thyn one out of this fylthe* 'for you are absolutely the
only one untouched by this filth', line 923), and tells him that
because of his cleanness God has *highly hevened thi hele fro hem
that arn combred* 'specially exalted your safety above those who are
overwhelmed' (line 920).

Nebuchadnezzar is another figure whose virtue is made
greater in the poem than it normally is in scriptural tradition in
order to create a contrast. The main point of the long first part of
Daniel's speech in which he interprets the writing on the wall, in
the poem as in the Bible, is that Belshazzar has failed to learn from
the example of Nebuchadnezzar, his father. God had humbled the
pride of the father, and now the son has shown a similar pride in
defiling the sacred vessels. In the poem however Belshazzar had
always *(ay,* line 1711) lifted up his heart against God, *With
bobaunce and with blasfamye bost at hym kest* 'hurled defiance at
him with arrogance and blasphemy' (line 1712). In lines which
have no parallel in the Bible Nebuchadnezzar by contrast is said
to have respected God:

> For of the hyghest he hade a hope in his hert
> That uche pouer past out of that prynce even. (lines 1653–4)

> [For he had a belief in his heart about the most high (God), that
> every power came directly from that prince.]

The poem takes this contrast back to an earlier stage of the story
in a passage (lines 1309–28) which again has no biblical authority.
It emphasises that Nebuchadnezzar, from the moment that he
sees the magnificence of the temple vessels, is in awe of them and
treats them and the God they represent with respect (lines
1313–14). He comes to accept Daniel's teaching about God (lines
1325–7), and learns humility from it: *And ofte hit mekned his
mynde, his maysterful werkkes* 'and often it softened his purpose,
his imperious actions' (line 1328).

A narratorial comment looks forward darkly to Belshazzar's very different attitude to the temple vessels and the price he will pay for it:

> And ther he wroght as the wyse, as ye may wyt hereafter,
> For hade he let of hem lyght hym moght haf lumpen worse.
> (lines 1319–20)

> [And in this he (Nebuchadnezzar) acted like a wise man, as you will see later, for had he set little store by them he might have fared worse.]

Thus Nebuchadnezzar honoured the true God, but Belshazzar did not, devoting himself to idols instead (lines 1340–1). Nebuchadnezzar learned humility, but Belshazzar ruled *in pryde and olipraunce* 'in pride and arrogance' (line 1349). When Belshazzar becomes active in the story a few lines later it is in terms which reinforce the negative contrast with Nebuchadnezzar: another reference to Nebuchadnezzar's respectful treatment of the vessels (lines 1429–32) is followed immediately by Belshazzar's command that the vessels be brought to him for his women to drink from. The long description of the elaborate decoration of the vessels (lines 1456–88) relates to this contrast. It establishes the vessels as objects of great richness and beauty which might be expected to inspire respect. The description of the drinking brings out the indignity done to the vessels by the heedless way in which they are used (lines 1509–20). The narrator's purpose is to magnify the biblical difference between the two kings of Babylon, so as to justify putting one on the right side of the line between cleanness and uncleanness and the other on the wrong side. Indeed he may be said to create the difference, as some medieval authors make no distinction between them, at least as far as their attitudes to the temple vessels are concerned.[17]

The stories (2): progression

In passing from the Flood to Sodom and Gomorrah to Belshazzar's feast, the reader is aware of the growing length and complexity of the stories. In the first narrative, as in the Bible, there is only the one story line: God's anger, Noah's building of the ark, the flood, God's covenant with Noah. The only dialogue is given to God and Noah. In the second narrative, again as in the Bible, there is more incident around the main episode (the destruction of the cities). The third has still more complexity, partly because different biblical narratives are put together. There are other progressions. From story to story the world becomes less primitive and takes on religious, social, and political dimensions. There is a growing emphasis on human individuality. The victims of God's wrath in the first story are the whole human and animal creation. In the second the principal victims are the anonymous populations of the cities which are wiped out *en masse*. Lot's wife is the one individual victim. In the third the principal victim is Belshazzar, an individual, and the Jews of Jerusalem are not exterminated *en masse* but meet a variety of deaths at the hands of Nebuzaradan and his army. God targets his vengeance more precisely by using human agents. Thus Nebuchadnezzar is 'raised up' (*wakned*) by God as an enemy to Zedekiah specifically for the purpose of punishing the idolatrous Israelites (line 1175).[18]

Sin, too, becomes less physical and more complex. In the poem Noah's world is destroyed for its sodomy alone. In the story of Sodom and Gomorrah the emphasis is on the same sin, but there is also the spiritual *untrawthe* of Lot's wife. In the story of Belshazzar the world has moved on to the era of the law and the prophets. Religion now dominates the biblical scene, and, at the time of the Babylonian Captivity, the true faith is under threat from pagans. It is appropriate that the poem's exemplary sin should now be not the bodily sin of the first two stories but the spiritual sin of sacrilege, and that the third story should exemplify a whole range of interconnected, mainly spiritual, sins.

As in the Bible, God himself shares in this developmental process. He destroys all living things, then makes an agreement with his surviving creation never to do so again, then makes another agreement with his chosen people that he will favour them over others. He talks to Noah as God the father or creator, to Abraham as the Trinity, and to Lot not in his own person but through his embassy of two angels. In the first two stories he himself carries out his punishments. In the story of Belshazzar he operates from a greater distance, communicating through his prophet Daniel and punishing through the agency of Nebuchadnezzar, Nebuzaradan, and Darius.

In his first vengeance God is portrayed as still so close to his creation that he feels personally betrayed by it, and in his anger punishes guilty and innocent indiscriminately. The poet seizes on anthropomorphic biblical detail and develops it considerably so that the force of God's wrath is communicated in the most immediate way. As he contemplates the sin of Noah's world God is said to be moved to fierce anger (line 283) and a promise of vengeance, like a man (*As wyye*) anguished inwardly (line 284). The words he speaks to Noah are described as wild and vengeful (*Wylde wrakful wordes*, line 302). This is a considerable extension of the biblical 'and it grieved him at his heart' (Genesis 6.6). His actual speech to Noah, in which he twice announces his intention to destroy all life, is indeed *wylde* and *wrakful*. The beginning (lines 303–4) matches the wording of part of Gen.6.13 ('the end of all flesh is come before me'). But there is no biblical equivalent for the next two lines, which bring out the strength of God's feeling:

> With her unworthelych werk me wlates withinne;
> The gore therof me has greved and the glette nwyed. (lines
> 305–6)

[In my heart I am disgusted with their shameful behaviour; the vileness of it has angered me and the filth has distressed me.]

The point of the lengthy and spectacular extension of the biblical description of the Flood is to communicate to the reader the horror of the situation, especially of God's attitude. As the rain from the heavens causes seas and rivers to burst their banks (lines 363–72), the description of the irresistible force of the water conveys a sense of God's power. The passage gathers momentum as it depicts rising floodwaters and rising panic in a scene which is not in the Bible at all, the flight of people and animals to high ground. The emphasis is on their terror (they flee *for ferde of the wrake* 'for fear of the vengeance', line 385) and God's heedlessness:

> And alle cryed for care to the kyng of heven;
> Recoverer of the Creator thay cryed uchone.
> That amounted the mase, his mercy was passed,
> And alle his pyté departed fro peple that he hated. (lines
> 393–6)

[And all cried in distress to the king of heaven; each one cried to the Creator for relief. That was pointless, his mercy was no more, and all his pity (was) gone from the people that he hated.]

The passage heightens the sense of God's implacability by showing the recipients of his vengeance to be not the vicious men who
according to the Bible had filled the earth (Gen. 6.11–13; compare
lines 273–82 in the poem), but hapless women, children, and animals. Moreover the narrative presents the people and animals
caught up in the Flood in such a way as to bring out the pathos of
their plight. The animals stare to the heavens and *Rwly wyth a
loud rurd rored for drede* 'pitifully with a loud noise roared for fear'
(lines 389–90). Women are forced to flee their houses with their
children (line 378), friends embrace each other before they die
(lines 399–400), and lovers make their final farewells:

> Luf lokes to luf, and his leve takes,
> For to end alle at ones and for ever twynne. (lines 401–2)

[Lover looks to lover and takes his leave, to end all at once and part
for ever.]

It is a harrowing and affecting picture. God is depicted as so infu-
riated by uncleanness that his desire for vengeance leads him to
punish the innocent along with the guilty.[19] In *Patience* it is God's
thought that there are women and children, innocent people, and
animals in Nineveh that leads him to abandon his promised
vengeance on the city.

After the Flood God effectively admits that he has not done
well. When he makes his covenant with Noah never to kill all living things again, the narrator states (as the Bible does not) that
God's heart was touched not only by grievous sorrow at what he
had done (*the swemande sorwe soght to his hert*, line 563), but by
regret:

> Hym rwed that he hem uprerde and raght hem lyflode,
> And efte that he hem undyd, hard hit hym thoght. (lines
> 561–2)

[He regretted that he had raised them up and given them sustenance,
but afterwards it seemed to him hard that he had destroyed them.]

One attitude is directly opposed to the other. God moves from
violent behaviour (*felly he venged*, line 559) to courteous (*He knyt
a covenaunde cortaysly with monkynde there*, line 564). The poem
gives God not only strong feelings but changeable feelings. Noah
makes his sacrifice of clean beasts, and God's mood changes to

one of benignity. He promises never again to destroy the whole world, and he bids all on the Ark to go forth and multiply.

In the second story God is less precipitate and also less emotional. Whereas in the Noah story he decides to destroy all living things as soon as he hears about mankind's corrupt ways, with Sodom and Gomorrah he determines to ascertain for himself, by going to the cities, whether or not the citizens are guilty (lines 691–2). In speaking to Noah God simply reiterates his disgust and his intention to destroy, but in speaking to Abraham he offers an explanation and justification of his proposed action, spelling out the nature of the sin which gives him such offence (lines 695–6). He agrees to each request in Abraham's long-winded plea which culminates in his request that he should spare the cities if as few as ten good men were to be found in them. For the first time he responds to the plea of a human being, modifying his attitude and indicating a new reluctance to destroy the innocent along with the guilty. He gives no sign to Abraham that he has heard his plea for Lot's safety, but later the angels who are guiding Lot and his family out of Gomorrah explain to Lot that God had made special provision for him, for two reasons: firstly that he was the only innocent man in the city, and secondly that Abraham had asked it of God (lines 919–24).

In this story, as in the story of Noah, God's anger is mentioned where the Bible is silent. In the Bible God, in speaking to Abraham, refers to the grievous sin of the cities (Gen. 18.20), but in the poem he states that their sin *gares me to wrath* 'drives me to anger' (line 690), and announces his intention of punishing them so severely that they will be an example to others for evermore (lines 711–12). In the Bible the destruction of the cities begins without comment: 'Then the Lord rained upon Sodom and upon Gomorrah brimstone and fire' (Gen. 19.24). In the poem God acts *in his greme* ['anger'] (line 947). When Lot's wife puts salt in her guests' food, the narrator comments: *Ho wrathed oure Lorde* (line 828).

The destruction of Sodom and Gomorrah, like the Flood, is elaborated in dramatic detail. It too conveys the awesome power of God in his anger, manifested through his control of the elements. Its function in the poem is the same as the story of the Flood: to flesh out the message that God hates uncleanness in a dramatic narrative which elicits from the reader an emotional response of pity and fear. As the people and animals of Noah's world are caught between springs gushing from the earth and rain from above, so the cities are envisaged as caught between fiery rain and the sudden opening up of the ground beneath them. The poem paints a picture of ruin on a grand scale (lines 961–8). Again there is a focus, though a less detailed and affecting one, on the victims and their despairing appeals to a God who does not respond:

> Rydelles wern tho grete rowtes of renkkes withinne,
> When thay wern war of the wrake that no wyye achaped;
> Such a yomerly yarm of yellyng ther rysed,
> Therof clatered the cloudes, that Kryst myght haf rawthe.
> (lines 969–72)

[The great crowds of people in those places were in despair, when they became aware of the vengeance that no man might escape; such a doleful clamour of yelling rose up there that the clouds resounded with it, that Christ might have pity.]

There is no hint this time of a repeat of God's emotional reaction to his first act of destruction, and indeed no mention of God at all. Instead the poem follows the tradition of attaching a description of the Dead Sea to the story. At the end of the extensive account of the sea's unpleasant properties (lines 1015–48), attention is drawn to their symbolic significance. They are *teches* ['signs'], *tokenes,* and *wittnesse* of both the evil of the cities and the vengeance which overtook them (lines 1049–51). They are unnatural as well as unpleasant, symbolising the unnaturalness of the sin which so angered God. The beautiful flowers and fruits which grow on the trees round the sea symbolise the handsomeness of the people of the cities (*so fayr a folk,* line 1014), and their foul natures are symbolised by the fact that inside the fruit is nothing but ashes (lines 1047–8). The narrator links the passage, by way of his quotation from *The Romance of the Rose,* to his account of the Incarnation. He emphasises the miraculous in both, but the miracles are of contrasting kinds. Whereas God's anger with mankind turns beauty to corruption, his love for mankind turns corruption to beauty (lines 1073–80).

In the third story God never speaks in his own person, except by report of Daniel. In the age of the prophets, he has chosen Daniel as one of his prophets to act as his permanent channel of communication with mankind. He is more discriminatory in his punishment of sin, and, for the first time, is seen to be prepared to give sinners a chance to mend their ways. This is evident in the episode of Nebuchadnezzar's madness. As noted above, the poem contrasts Nebuchadnezzar's behaviour with the *fylthe* of the apostate Jews of Jerusalem and Belshazzar. Daniel explains that when Nebuchadnezzar falls victim to pride by putting himself on a par with God, he does not turn to idol worship, as the Jews do, or to any of the other extreme sins which make God angry. The Jews are ruthlessly and gruesomely put to death,[20] but not Nebuchadnezzar, who is cast out from Babylon and turned into a strange animal instead. In this the poem implicitly parallels him with Lucifer, who likewise falls victim to pride by claiming to be God's equal, and is similarly not destroyed but cast out of heaven and changed from the most beautiful of the angels to the blackest devil. Nebuchadnezzar's exile brings him to his senses, he acknowledges God again, and his high position is restored.

Nebuchadnezzar is sometimes seen as a primary model for the Christian sacrament of penance,[21] and *Cleanness* highlights the 'penitential' episode in his life. But the poem makes him a very imperfect exemplar of penance. It focuses on the grotesqueness of his animal form, emphasising his humiliation by God much more than his repentance and restoration,[22] and there is no indication that he ever sees himself as a penitent. *Cleanness* offers only an abstract discussion of penance, and a shadowy instance of it in action, showing it not as forestalling God's punishment but following it. For a full realisation of penance in action, and a demonstration and explanation of its saving powers, the reader must turn to *Patience*.

In the story of Belshazzar's feast God's punishments are directed first against the Jews of Jerusalem and later against Belshazzar. He is more selective in his punishment than in the first two stories, but his anger is no less, and again there is emphasis on the fear and despair of the victims. The narrative states that the idolatry of the Jews *wakned his wrath and wrast hit so hyghe* 'wakened his anger and worked it up so high' (line 1166). The besieged Jews endure the agonies of famine (lines 1194–6). Their despair is indicated by language similar to that used for the inhabitants of Sodom and Gomorrah who are caught in the destruction of the cities (compare line 969, *Rydelles wern tho grete rowtes of renkkes withinne*, with line 1197, *Thenne wern tho rowtes redles in tho ryche wones* 'then the crowds in that great city were in despair'). God's revulsion at the sin of uncleanness is suggested in this story by the brutal ways in which the unclean are despatched and by the gruesome detail of the killings. Some of the detail is biblical. An example is Nebuchadnezzar's treatment of Zedekiah and his sons, in which he kills the sons in front of their father and then gouges out the father's eyes (lines 1221–4). But the account of Nebuzaradan's pitiless treatment of the women, children, and priests of Jerusalem is new in the poem:

> Nabizardan noght forthy nolde not spare,
> Bot bede al to the bronde under bare egge.
> Thay slowen of swettest semlych burdes,
> Bathed barnes in blod and her brayn spylled,
>
> Prestes and prelates thay presed to dethe,
> Wyves and wenches her wombes tocorven
> That her boweles outborst aboute the diches,
> And al was carfully kylde that thay cach myght. (lines 1245–52)

[Nebuzaradan would not by any means spare them on that account, but ordered everyone to be put to the bare blade of the sword. They killed there the sweetest of fair ladies, bathed children in blood and spilled out their brains, pressed priests and prelates to death, cut open the stomachs of women and girls so that their bowels burst out over the ditches, and all whom they might catch were ignominiously killed.]

The description makes the most of the horror of the event. More violent non-biblical detail accompanies the account of Nebuzaradan's killing of priests and women in the Temple when he goes to fetch the vessels:

> Pulden prestes bi the polle and plat of her hedes,
> Dighten dekenes to dethe, dungen doun clerkkes,
> And alle the maydenes of the munster maghtyly hokyllen
> Wyth the swayf of the sworde that swolwed hem alle. (lines 1265–8)

[They pulled priests by the crown and struck off their heads, put deacons to death, struck down clerics, and ruthlessly mowed down all the maidens of the temple, with the sweep of the sword that devoured them all.]

The fearsomeness of God in his anger is manifested most clearly with Belshazzar hinself. The hand that writes the mysterious letters is made more frightening (*grysly and gret*, line 1534) than in the Bible, and Belshazzar's terror is heightened (lines 1538–43). The biblical account of Belshazzar's reaction to the writing is elaborated to make the point that his former arrogance is now entirely reversed. The biblical detail that 'his knees smote one against another' (Dan. 5.6) is kept (line 1541), and the detail that he bellowed like a frightened bull roaring for fear is added (line 1543). The Bible records his response to the inability of his learned men to interpret the writing: 'Then was king Belshazzar greatly troubled, and his countenance was changed in him, and his lords were astonied' (Dan. 5.9). The poem elaborates this to show a Belshazzar beside himself with fear and impotent fury:

> Thenne cryes the kyng and kerves his wedes;
> What! He corsed his clerkes and calde hem chorles.
> To henge the harlotes he heyed ful ofte;
> So was the wyye wytles he wed wel ner. (lines 1582–5)

[Then the king cries out and tears his clothes; look! He cursed his clerks and called them churls. Again and again he threatened to hang the villains; the man was so distracted he was almost mad.]

The Bible devotes only two verses to Belshazzar's death and Darius's taking of the kingdom (Dan. 5.30–1). The poem enlarges considerably on this, creating a sense of climax, and bringing out the idea of retribution. Much is made of the coming of night after the feasting. Ominous references to the darkening of the skies and worsening of the weather (lines 1759–60) are matched by doom-laden statements anticipating Belshazzar's fate (lines 1753–6, 1765–6). A picture of ordinary people making their way home at the end of the day and eating a simple supper is unexpectedly worked into the account (lines 1761–3), to highlight the drunken excess of the feasting at the palace. When retribution comes, in the shape of Darius and his allies, it comes with ruthless swiftness (lines 1779, 1786). The savagery of Belshazzar's death is brought out by yet more ugly detail:

> Baltazar in his bed was beten to dethe,
> That bothe his blod and his brayn blende on the clothes.

> The kyng in his cortyn was kaght bi the heles,
> Feryed out bi the fet and fowle dispysed,
> That was so doghty that day and drank of the vessayl;
> Now is a dogge also dere that in a dych lygges. (lines 1787–92)

[Belshazzar was beaten to death in his bed, so that his blood and his brains mingled on the bedclothes. The king in his bedcurtain was taken by the heels, brought out by the feet and foully maltreated, he who had been so bold that day and had drunk of the vessels; now a dog lying in a ditch is as precious.]

The insistence in the third story on the gruesomeness of the several killings demonstrates that, though God's methods of avenging himself have changed when compared with the first two stories, his angry response to uncleanness has not. Throughout the poem, the vividly realised death and destruction, in the style of apocalyptic writings, suggest the terror of God the judge in his wrath.

God's anger is presented as such that it frightens even those whom he selects for salvation. As soon as he receives God's command Noah hastens to build the Ark *In dryy dred and daunger, that durst do non other* 'in great fear and dread, not daring to do otherwise' (line 342), a detail which is not in the Bible. Abraham's response to God's angry words is also one of fear: *Thenne arwed* ['was frightened'] *Abraham, and alle his mod chaunged* (line 713). The subsequent passage, in which Abraham first asks God to spare Sodom if fifty inhabitants can be found who keep his law, then forty-five, then forty, and so on down to five, takes up fifty lines (lines 715–65), and expands Genesis 18.23–32 considerably. The point of the expansion is twofold: to portray Abraham as entirely abject in his pleading with God (which he is not in the Bible), and to portray God as condescending and conscious of his magnanimity in acceding to Abraham's requests, when in the Bible he answers Abraham briefly and directly. God offers no answer to Abraham's extra-biblical plea to him to temper his ire so that Lot should be spared, leaving Abraham to return home in a state of anxiety, *wepande for care* and *mornande for sorewe* (lines 777–9).

The biblical account of Lot's escape from Sodom is extensively reworked so that it becomes a more alarming experience for Lot. The Bible notes both God's mercy to Lot ('the Lord being merciful unto him', Gen. 19.16), and Lot's acknowledgement of his mercy ('thou hast magnified thy mercy, which thou hast shewed unto me in saving my life', Gen. 19.19). When Lot pleads to be allowed to escape to Zoar (Segor in the poem), he receives an accepting answer: 'And he said unto him, See, I have accepted thee concerning this thing also, that I will not overthrow this city, for the which thou hast spoken' (Gen. 19.21). The poem removes all reference to God's mercy and acceptance. In the poem, but not in the Bible, the angels rouse Lot *glopnedly* 'in alarming fashion' (line 896), and Lot responds *ful ferd at his hert* (line 897). When the angels tell him to flee because of the coming vengeance, Lot, in an extra-biblical addition, expresses his fear that he will not be able to find a place to hide from the *fooschip* 'enmity' (line 918) of his creator. In the Bible the angels 'hastened' Lot and his wife and daughters on their way (Gen. 19.15). In the poem they do so with menaces:

> The aungeles hasted thise other and awly hem thratten,
> And enforsed alle fawre forth at the yates. (lines 937–8)

[The angels hastened the others and fearsomely threatened them, and drove all four out at the gates.]

God may have 'highly honoured' Lot, but the language of these two lines suggests that he and his family are herded out like cattle.

It is true that, though the God of *Cleanness* is pre-eminently a God of terror, he has his *in bono* moments in the first two stories. His benignity, like his anger, is enhanced in the poem when compared with the Bible. He is said to speak to Noah with cheerfulness and courtesy (*In comly comfort ful clos and cortays wordes*, line 512), and he uses a formula of courteous speech to wish the survivors well: *and menske yow bytyde* 'and may good fortune come to you' (line 522). At the beginning of the second story, he responds positively to Abraham's invitation to eat with him (lines 641–2). God is benign also in the episode of Sarah's denial of her laughter. The narrative refers to Sarah as *Sare the madde* (line 654), and makes it clear that Sarah laughs in scorn (*busmar*, line 653) at God's announcement that she will bear a son from whom will come God's chosen people. It might seem that Sarah's scorn of God is not so different from that of Lot's wife, who is also referred to as mad (*wod*, line 828) when in line 827 she *scelt hem in scorne* 'scorned them [God's embassy of two angels]' by salting their food. But the narrative, no doubt because Lot's wife is *wil-*

fully scornful in that she deliberately goes against Lot's wishes, puts them on opposite sides of the cleanness-uncleanness dividing line. The failings of Lot's wife (summed up as *mistrauthe* 'faithlessness', line 996) make God angry (*Ho wrathed oure Lorde*, line 828), and she is turned into a pillar of salt. God corrects Sarah, but does not become angry with her.

But even at his most benign, the God of *Cleanness* remains the great lord, keeping a distance between himself and his creation. When Sarah laughs at God, and then denies it, he does not show any understanding of her reason for laughing or say he forgives her, but, after correcting her, confines himself to the cold *bot let we hit one* 'but let it pass' (line 670). When in the parable of the wedding feast the lord greets his guests, he does not do so as they arrive, but comes down from his chamber later. He begins with *the best on the bench* (line 130), and then goes round the room making polite conversation. The scene suggests a formal reception in which the host acts not out of a desire to welcome his guests but to conform to protocol. Such small details testify to the poem's, and its God's, devaluation of the human.

The ending

With great explicitness an eight-line conclusion relates all the stories back to the opening proposition. Again the two sides of the proposition are flatly opposed to each other. First the negative is put:

> Thus upon thrynne wyses I haf yow thro schewed
> That unclannes tocleves in corage dere
> Of that wynnelych Lorde that wonyes in heven,
> Entyses hym to be tene, telled up his wrake. (lines 1805–8)

[Thus in three ways I have shown you clearly that uncleanness sticks in the noble heart of that gracious Lord who dwells in heaven, incites him to be angry, his hostility aroused.]

The earlier distinction between a lesser and a greater uncleanness, never made meaningful, is here collapsed. The reader is now told that simple *unclannes*, that is, presumably, *all* sins, not only extreme sins like those of Noah's world, Sodom and Gomorrah, and Belshazzar, make God angry. The positive side of the proposition is put in the last four lines:

Ande clannes is his comfort, and coyntyse he lovyes,
And those that seme arn and swete schyn se his face.
That we gon gay in oure gere that grace he uus sende,
That we may serve in his syght ther solace never blynnes.
(lines 1809–12)

[But cleanness is his delight, and he loves refinement, and those that
are seemly and pleasant shall see his face. May he send us the grace
to be well dressed, so that we may serve in his sight where bliss never
ends.]

Here again are the imagery of the sixth beatitude and the parable
of the wedding feast. Though there is no first line–last line repe-
tition, as in the other three poems, the ending of *Cleanness* obviously recalls the poem's beginning in its ideas and language. But
whereas in the other three poems the reader reads the last line differently from the first because it is informed by all that comes
between, *Cleanness* uses its considerable length not to develop its
opening message, examine it, or move on from it, but, as argued
above, to drive it home. The reader, having got as far as the conclusion, perhaps entertains the faint hope that at the last moment
Cleanness will find something new to say about God's justice. But
of course it does not. For that, the reader needs to turn to the next
poem in the manuscript.

Notes

1   *MED*, under *clennesse*, notes this distinction as sense 2.a, 'moral purity, sin-
     lessness, innocence; uprightness, integrity', and sense 2.b, 'chastity, conti-
     nence; celibacy, virginity; also, self-restraint in marital relations'.
2   David Wallace, '*Cleanness* and the terms of terror', in Robert J. Blanch,
     Miriam Youngerman Miller, and Julian N. Wasserman, eds, *Text and Mat-
     ter: New Critical Perspectives of the Pearl-Poet* (Troy, New York: Whitston,
     1991), pp. 93–104, argues that the narrative of the poem is dominated by the
     question 'What must I do to be clean?', a question which he sees as 'restated
     and reformulated with increasing urgency as the narrative advances' (p. 94).
     For him the answer which the poem gives has to do with 'the struggle to be
     righteous' (p. 100). But *Cleanness* is not concerned with elucidating such
     questions in the way that, say, *Piers Plowman* is. The narrator does raise Wal-
     lace's question explicitly in lines 1110–12, but the answer he gives is no real
     answer (see below, pp. 104–5). Contrast its pat quality with the involved
     exposition of truth and love which Lady Holy Church gives Will in answer
     to his question 'How shall I save my soul?' (*Piers Plowman*, B-text, Passus 1).
3   Examples of studies which focus on such aspects are Michael W. Twomey,

and J. A. Glenn, 'Dislocation of *kynde* in 'The sin of *untrawthe* in *Cleanness*', in Blanch, *Text and Matter*, pp. 117–45, *Cleanness*', *Chaucer Review*, 18 (1984), 77–91.

4 The point is best made by the passage in which Abraham begs God to spare the city of Sodom. See below, p. 118.

5 See below, pp. 111–12.

6 Another prime example of this technique occurs in lines 1109–16.

7 I take the story of the Flood as running from line 249–544 (296 lines), Sodom and Gomorrah from line 601–1052 (452 lines), and Belshazzar's feast from line 1157–1804 (648 lines). I take the discussion between the Flood and Sodom and Gomorrah as running from line 545–600 (56 lines), and that between Sodom and Gomorrah and Belshazzar's feast as running from line 1053–156 (104 lines).

8 Several studies of *Cleanness* have read the poem as eschatological, concerned with the Last Judgement, pointing out that the parable of the wedding feast and the three main stories were all taken as types or figures of the Last Judgement, and drawing attention to the apcalyptic context of 2 Peter, which may have suggested part of the narrative framework of *Cleanness* (2 Peter 2.5–7 links the stories of Noah, Sodom and Gomorrah, and Lot). See, for example, S. L. Clark and Julian N. Wasserman, '*Purity*: the cities of the raven and the dove', *American Benedictine Review*, 29 (1978), 285–6, and Charlotte C. Morse, *The Pattern of Judgment in the Queste and Cleanness* (Columbia: Missouri University Press), 1978, pp. 131–3; also her 'The image of the vessel in *Cleanness*', *University of Toronto Quarterly*, 40 (1971), 202. But to me the poem's complex verbal surface suggests that any eschatological sense must serve the literal one, not the other way round. The poem does not want to take the reader off to the end of time, but to make him aware of the severity of God's judgement of uncleanness in the here and now. If the reader makes the eschatological connection, it serves to heighten his sense of the intensity of God's anger against uncleanness by associating it with the *dies irae*.

9 The most striking such touch comes with an unexpectedly colloquial comment on the efforts of Belshzzar's men of learning to read the writing on the wall: . . . *as lewed thay were/As thay had loked in the lether of my lyft bote* '. . . they were as unenlightened as if they had looked on the leather of my left boot' (lines 1580–1).

10 I take 'in doing the contrary' to mean denigrating cleanness, as do Andrew and Waldron in their edition. Menner in his edition takes it to mean praising uncleanness. Prior, *Fayre Formez*, p. 10, agrees with Vantuono in his edition that the meaning is the condemning of uncleanness, which is the task the poet undertakes.

11 MS *worthlych* makes reasonable sense, but the poet may have written *wordlych* 'worldly, earthly', which is better for the contrast. Andrew and Waldron in their edition emend the text to *wordlych*.

12 Keiser, *Courtly Desire*, p. 172.

13 The maiden in *Pearl* is less remote in her explanation of penance than the narrator of *Cleanness*. She identifies *sorw and syt* 'sorrow and grief' (*Pearl*,

line 663) as a constituent of penance. Most medieval didactic religious works approach the subject of penance from the point of view of the sinner, that is, they do not minimise its difficulty, and at the same time they give encouragement. I take as typical the section on penance in *Barlam and Iosaphat*, ed. John C. Hirsh, EETS OS 290 (London: Oxford University Press, 1986), and quote from pp. 47–8: 'Whan we falle in eny synne after oure bapteem, we must clense it ayen by grete penaunce, and sorow of herte, and wepynge of eye. . . . Penaunce . . . nedith grete sorowe and laboure. . . . Who may numbre the mercy of God, that is so infenyte? For sothe, no man. Than syth that synne is numerable and may be mesured, how may synne ouercome the grete mercy of God that is uinnumerable and may nat be mesured? Therfor we sholde neuere be in dispeyre for oure synne. For Cryst shedde his precious blode to foryeue us oure synne. In many placis of holy wrytte we haue founde the vertu of penaunce, and moste by the precepte of oure lorde, Jesu Cryst. For Cryst hymself taught and seide: "Do ye penaunce. The kyngdom of heuene shal neghe vnto you."'

14 The usual expression of the idea is that for good penance the penitent should not return to his sins, as in, e.g., the section on penance in the sermon for Easter Sunday in *Speculum Sacerdotale*, ed. E. H. Weatherly, EETS OS 200 (London: Oxford University Press, 1936), p. 121. *Barlam and Iosaphat* states that the penitent must be careful not to fall again into sin because he may never have the power to rise again, may never have the grace to do penance again, or may die before he has the chance to do penance. But he is advised, should he 'casualy' fall into sin again, to do further penance: 'For God seith: "Turne ye to me, and Y shal turne to you"' (pp. 49–50).

15 Putter, *Introduction*, pp. 207–8, takes a different view. He argues that 'the poet's association of marital sex and paradise is not, as it might first appear, unothodox or daring', noting that the association is made by theologians and other writers on the grounds that marriage was first ordained by God in Eden. He quotes from *Piers Plowman*, B-text (ed. Schmidt), 9.117–18: 'And thus was wedlok ywroght and God hymself hit made; / In erthe the heuene is; hymself was the witnesse.' The *Cleanness* poet may have been aware of this tradition, though the association of extra-marital and courtly love with paradise was more usual in medieval literature. It is not certain that the passage refers to sex in marriage. The word *make* might mean mistress or lover as well as marriage partner (*mach* is used to mean homosexual partner in line 695), and some of the terms used (*drwry, play of paramores*) belong to the language of courtly love. *Honestly* probably means not 'made honest by marriage' but 'in a straightforward, unperverted way', maintaining the contrast with what the poem sees as the perversion of the inhabitants of Sodom. The language of lines 706–7 moves into the register of sexual desire and lust. Malory uses such language of the love between Sir Gareth and Dame Lyonesse, which he calls *hoote love* and *hoote lustis*, for example: 'And so they brente bothe in hoote love that they were acorded to abate their lustys secretly' (Thomas Malory, *Works*, ed. Eugene Vinaver, 2nd edn, Oxford: Oxford University Press, 1977, p. 205). Even if the passage is taken to refer to marriage it does not square with the advocacy of sexual restraint in marriage which was the clerical norm. So in Chaucer's *Parson's Tale* sex is per-

mitted between husband and wife for three purposes: engendering children, paying each other the debt of their bodies, and to avoid *leccherye and vileynye*; the third purpose is classed as venial sin. But 'if they assemble oonly for amorous love and for noon of the forseyde causes, but for to accomplice thilke brennynge delit, they rekke nevere how ofte, soothly it is deedly synne' (*Canterbury Tales*, X, 942). For Reginald Pecock, *clennes of matrymonye* requires a husband and wife not to go to bed together except in the hope of engendering a child (Reginald Pecock, *Reule of Crysten Religion*, ed. W. C. Greet, EETS OS 171, London: Oxford University Press, 1927, p. 356).

16   Putter, *Introduction*, pp. 205–7, notes that Augustine warned his readers that Lot's conduct was not to be imitated. (In this he was followed by other commentators.) Putter comments that in the Bible Lot is primarily concerned with protecting his guests and not with 'the relative merits of homosexual or heterosexual sex', as he is in the poem.

17   The *Gawain*-poet's treatment of Nebuchadnezzar, in holding him up as a 'positive' contrast to Belshazzar, is unusual and complex. Gower, *Confessio Amantis* 5.6995–7025 (in *The English Works of John Gower*, ed. G. C. Macaulay, 2 vols, EETS ES 81, 82, London: Oxford University Press, 1900, 1901) makes no distinction between Nebuchadnezzar and Belshazzar in the way they treat the Temple vessels, seeing both as guilty of sacrilege. In homiletic writing Nebuchadnezzar is often a type of pride, e.g. in his story as retold in the exemplum against the sin of pride in Gower, *Confessio Amantis* 1.2785–3066. Twomey, '*Untrawthe*', p. 143, notes that 'in much medieval commentary, Nabuchodonoser is antitypally the devil as king of the Earthly City'.

18   Other possible evolutionary significances have been noticed. On a more symbolic level, Stanbury, *Seeing*, p. 50, develops an argument that the Old Testament episodes 'dramatize a process of intuitive change through history, in which God's chosen are increasingly given visual signs and are expected to interpret and respond to them'.

19   Malcolm Andrew, 'The realizing imagination in late medieval English narrative', *English Studies* 76 (1995), 113–28, concerned with the application and effect of the poet's 'realising imagination', suggests that the presentation of ordinary people as victims in the Flood scene creates 'a sense of the world as morally complex and of judgment as problematic' (115–17).

20   Though women and children are killed (see quotations below, p. 116), no sympathy is generated for them, and they are not to be taken as innocent, as in the Noah story. The killing is not a sign that God has reverted to killing the innocent, but a sign of his ruthlessness towards the guilty. The women and children are part of the apostasy of the whole community, whereas in the Noah story the crimes against God are committed only by men.

21   Gary A. Anderson, *The Genesis of Perfection: Adam and Eve in Jewish and Christian Imagination* (Louisville: Westminster John Knox, 2001), pp. 141–3, refers to the third-century Christian theologian Tertullian's *On Penance* to show that Tertullian held up Nebuchadnezzar as a model of penance responded to by God. 'The Christian model for penance comes from a surprising person: King Nebuchadnezzar (Daniel 4) who is driven out of Babylon and becomes like a beast of the field. In the Greek versions of the

story, the evil king repents, confesses God, and is restored. Tertullian lifts up Nebuchadnezzar's penance as exemplary, for if this terrible person could be saved, then no one would be beyond God's mercy.'

22 In detailing Nebuchadnezzar's animal characteristics (lines 1673–1700) the episode conflates Daniel 5.21 (Daniel's speech to Belshazzar) with Daniel 4.25 (Daniel's interpretation of Nebuchadnezzar's dream), Daniel 4.32 (the voice from heaven) and Daniel 4.33 (the fulfilment of Daniel's interpretation). It also adds details of its own to the Bible's. At the same time the poem compresses the detail in Daniel 4.34–7, which it turns to for its account of Nebuchadnezzar's restoration (lines 1701–8).

3

Patience: the Lord hath given, the Lord hath taken away

Introduction

Patience is a poem of the same kind as *Cleanness* in that it too combines discussion of a moral quality with biblical narrative – in the case of *Patience*, one narrative only, the story of Jonah. In both poems human beings are at odds with God, but the outcomes are very different. *Cleanness* has a God who subordinates his mercy to his justice, *Patience* a God who subordinates justice to mercy. Death threatens, but no one dies.

Cleanness is cosmic in scale and uncompromising in its message and its rhetoric: *On spec of a spote* (*Cleanness*, line 551) is enough to exclude the sinner from heaven. *Patience* is less extreme in every way, small-scale, personal, moderate in tone, which is in itself a comment on its view of patience. Whereas *Cleanness* offers very few concessions to its reader, *Patience* is reader-friendly and engaging. Like the *Pearl*-dreamer, Jonah may be taken as a representative of 'natural' humanity, full of error, not evil, whose thoughts and feelings the reader can simultaneously criticise and identify with. God has affinities with the maiden in *Pearl*, not terrifying but firm in the way a father is with his children. There is an ongoing dialogue and a relationship between God and Jonah, and it is on this relationship that the theme of patience is centred. Jonah is impatient with God, and God in return is patient with Jonah. *Cleanness* discourages the reader from relating to either God or man, or for that matter the narrator, but *Patience* asks him to relate to all three.

It is significant that, unlike *Cleanness*, *Patience* sets out to explore the meaning of the virtue of its title. It is little interested in the dominant view of medieval religious writers that patience is a virtue of strength, taught by misfortune and enabling one to bear misfortune, and often associated with the cardinal virtue of *fortitudo*.[1] It remains apart from the tradition of vices and virtues literature in which patience, like other virtues and vices, tends to be linked to the same set of characteristics, texts, and examples from one work to the other. It chooses Jonah instead of the usual Job as its exemplar. It also goes beyond the usual modern view of patience as meaning biding one's time, holding on, putting up with something unpleasant. Its approach is subtle and layered, refusing to allow the concept of patience to be pinned down to a single fixed meaning or set of meanings.

The narrator associates patience with the Beatitudes preached by Christ in his Sermon on the Mount, which advocate humility as a way of life. The narrator sees patience, the virtue of the eighth beatitude, as especially important, and he sees it as a practical necessity. His idea that experience necessarily leads one to an attitude of patient acceptance is one to which all can relate. But his practical view goes with scornful criticism of those who are unwilling or unable to learn this lesson, like Jonah. Through its God, the poem exemplifies and explains a more spiritual view of patience which the narrator gives no sign of understanding.[2] The dialogic approach, which puts different possibilities in front of the reader, is one which the poet favours generally. But it is especially appropriate to *Patience*, as it helps establish the poet's view of the many-sidedness of patience and its connection with all the other virtues of the Beatitudes, which he sees as its key characteristic.

The prologue

Like *Cleanness*, *Patience* begins with a statement about the virtue it celebrates:

> Pacience is a poynt, thagh hit displese ofte.
> When hevy herttes ben hurt wyth hethyng other elles,
> Suffrauance may aswagen hem and the swelme lethe,
> For ho quelles uche a qued and quenches malyce. (lines 1–4)[3]

[Patience is a virtue, though it often displeases. When heavy hearts are hurt by scorn or anything else, patience may soothe them and lessen the bitterness, for it subdues every evil and extinguishes malice.]

By comparison with *Cleanness* one is struck by the relaxed approach. The message of these lines is reassuring, and the positive note which the narrator sounds here, through the idea that patience enables difficulties to be overcome, is one he maintains throughout the poem. The narratorial voice is low-key. The prologue has no intensifying adjectives and adverbs of the kind found in the first lines of *Cleanness*, and little use is made of contrast. There is for instance no sign of a clear-cut verbal opposition between *pacience* and its opposite equivalent to that between *clanness* and *unclannesse/fylthe* in the opening lines of *Cleanness*.

Where patience and impatience *are* contrasted, the contrast is managed with a light touch:

> For quo-so suffer cowthe syt, sele wolde folwe,
> And quo for thro may noght thole, the thikker he sufferes.
> Then is better to abyde the bur umbestoundes
> Then ay throw forth my thro, thagh me thynk ylle. (lines 5–8)

[Prosperity follows for whoever is able to put up with misfortune, but whoever may not endure, on account of impatience, only suffers the more. And so it is better for me to accept the blow when it falls than to be always giving vent to my impatience, though I may not like it.]

There is something of the contrastive rhetoric of *Cleanness* here, but the sharp edges of the contrast are made less sharp by the comparatives (*thikker* and *better* imply relative values rather than the absolute values of *Cleanness*), and by an element of witty word-play (on *thro* and *throw*; also *suffer* means both 'put up with' and 'suffer pain').[4] The shift to the first person in line 8 contributes to an engaging personal tone. Relative expressions are used again in line 34, where the narrator states that though it is good to have one of the virtues of the beatitudes it is better to have them all, and again in lines 47–8, where he concludes that it is better or easier *(lyghtloker)* for him to like poverty and patience than to resist and so have *the wers*.

Cleanness makes the sixth beatitude, 'Blessed are the pure in heart', its authoritative 'text'. *Patience* invokes the authority of the whole set of beatitudes. It quotes in more or less straightforward paraphrase the text of Matthew 5.3–10 until the eighth and final beatitude is reached. Here it departs considerably from Matthew 5.10: 'Blessed are they which are persecuted for right-

eousness' sake: for theirs is the kingdom of heaven.' The narrator
leaves out altogether the biblical idea of 'persecution for righteousness' sake'.[5] Instead he produces a phrase which gives the
beatitude wider application: *Thay ar happen also that con her hert
stere* 'they are blessed also who can steer their hearts' (line 27). By
contrast the narrator of *Cleanness*, before quoting the sixth beatitude (with no reference to the others), seems determined to focus
down its meaning rather than open it up. He announces its subject in unequivocal terms: it *of clannesse uncloses a ful cler speche*
(*Cleanness*, line 26). The *Patience*-narrator chooses not to use the
words 'patience' or 'patient', in his formulation, though it is soon
clear that, following many commentators, he does indeed see
patience as the virtue of the eighth beatitude.[6] By drawing attention to the identity of reward between the first and eighth beatitudes (line 28), he also prepares the reader for his discussion of
the eighth beatitude as linked to the first in lines 35–48.

In *Cleanness* the heavenly reward of the 'cleanness' beatitude,
the sight of God, is constantly alluded to. In *Patience* the heavenly
reward of the 'patience' beatitude, possession of the kingdom of
heaven, is not mentioned again after the paraphrase of the beatitude itself. Indeed, the narrator only mentions God once in his
prologue and epilogue. He is more interested in this world than
the next. When he discusses patience and impatience, he does so
in entirely worldly terms. What he is aware of is that in a situation
which calls for patience, impatience will only make that situation
worse. The threatening eschatological dimension of *Cleanness* is
lacking.

The *Cleanness* narrator no sooner identifies and quotes the
sixth beatitude than he recasts it as a fierce negative. Nothing like
this happens in *Patience*. Instead, after quoting all the beatitudes,
the narrator turns their virtues into ladies, following the well-
established tradition of personifying moral qualities as women:

> These arn the happes alle aght that uus bihyght weren,
> If we thyse ladyes wolde lof in lyknyng of thewes:
> Dame Povert, dame Pitee, dame Penaunce the thrydde,
> Dame Mekenesse, dame Mercy and miry Clannesse,
>
> And thenne dame Pes and Pacyence put in therafter;
> He were happen that hade one, alle were the better. (lines
>   29–34)

[These are all eight of the blessed states that were promised to us, if
we would love these ladies by copying their virtues: Dame Poverty,
Dame Pity, and thirdly Dame Penance, Dame Meekness, Dame
Mercy, and fair Cleanness, and then Dame Peace and Patience put in
at the end; he would be blessed who had one, all would be the better.]

The idea that it is appropriate to love the ladies by copying their
virtues derives from the secular allegory of *The Romance of the
Rose,* in which the lover is advised to win the favour of his mistress by imitating her manners. The same idea is also used in
Cleanness, where, in keeping with the more explicit method of
that poem, *Clopygnel* and his *clene Rose* are mentioned by name
(*Cleanness*, line 1057), the passage of advice to the lover to copy
the ways of his mistress is formally quoted, in paraphrase (*Cleanness*, lines 1059–64), and then the advice is formally applied to the
poem's purpose. In the style of academic argument, *Cleanness*
carefully maintains the distinction between secular idea and
sacred application, and the application is characteristically
remote: the reader is not urged to love a lady, or even to love
Christ, but to imitate Christ's cleanness.[7]

Patience alludes to the *Romance* with a lighter touch, without
explicit quotation or reference, and the transfer works the other
way. Instead of the secular idea being applied to a religious context, the religious is appropriated to the secular, and to the very
worldly world of Jean de Meun's poem. It emerges in this passage
that the narrator's interest in patience comes not so much from
any moral or spiritual conviction as from reflection on his own
personal circumstances, which are what first lead him to associate
patience with poverty:

> Bot syn I am put to a poynt that poverté hatte,
> I schal me porvay pacyence and play me with bothe. (lines
> 35–6)

[But since I am driven to a state which is called poverty, I shall take
patience upon myself and play with both of them.]

He readily equates the poverty of spirit of the first beatitude, usually understood as humility,[8] or as poverty willingly undertaken
for spiritual purposes, with enforced physical poverty. His idea is
that the state of poverty in which he finds himself must lead him
to adopt a patient attitude. His language, in these two lines and in

the subsequent discussion, half-maintains the idea of poverty and patience as ladies to be loved. He does not seek out poverty; rather, she inflicts herself on him. As a result, he says, he has no choice but to woo patience. When he has patience, he is able to love both ladies. The personifications, whimsically managed, bring the narrator's worldly attitude to bear on the sacred text. When he goes on to appeal to the Beatitudes to support his association of poverty with patience he refers to the formal linking in the *tyxte* of these two virtues as first and last in the list, merely noting that they are given the same reward:

> For in the tyxte there thyse two arn in teme layde,
> Hit arn fettled in on forme, the forme and the laste,
> And by quest of her quoyntyse enquylen on mede. (lines 37–9)

[For in the text where these two are spoken of, they are arranged first and last in one formula, and by the judgement of their Lord they receive one reward.]

He does not expand line 39 to discuss the nature and appropriateness of their common reward, the kingdom of heaven, and shows no interest in the possibilities of other connections between them.[9] He is more interested in playing with words and ideas[10] than in probing his text for spiritual insight. Therefore, when he claims that poverty and patience are *of on* ['one'] *kynde* (line 40), his justification for his claim can hardly be other than purely pragmatic. In explaining that poverty can only be suffered in patience he reverts to the worldly-wise style of the opening lines (lines 41–5), and finally applies his worldly wisdom to his own situation (line 46). He comes to the common-sense conclusion that he had better accept poverty and patience gracefully as otherwise he will only make matters worse for himself (lines 47–8).

At the end of the prologue the narrator effects the transition to the story of Jonah by imagining himself in a hypothetical situation in which he, like Jonah, is ordered to go to a distant city against his will (lines 49–52). He concludes that to resist the order would be futile (lines 53–6), and holds up Jonah as a warning example: *Did not Jonas in Judé suche jape sumwhyle?* 'Did not Jonah in Judea do such a foolish thing once?' (line 57). The word *jape* conveys his view of impatience as foolish, foolish because experience teaches that impatient behaviour always turns out badly.

Whereas the narrator of *Cleanness* is constantly assertive, the narrator of *Patience* never presses his case. His rhetoric is reflective and ironic rather than explicit and didactic, his tone conversational rather than authoritative. He directs his teaching not at the reader but either to the world at large or to himself and the reader together, as in lines 29–30. In the passage linking prologue to story he turns on himself the kind of rhetorical question which the *Cleanness*-narrator uses to put the reader on the spot: *What dowes me the dedayn other dispit make?* 'of what use is indignation to me, or defiance?' (line 50), and *What graythed me the grychchyng bot grame more seche?* 'what would grumbling do for me except to invite more trouble?' (line 53). His aim is to disarm and persuade, not to confront.

Jonah (1)

Jonah himself is realised as a 'character' more fully than his biblical counterpart, in some ways more fully than any other of the *Gawain*-poet's character constructions, with words, thoughts, and actions all on show. He becomes an engaging illustration of the frailty of human nature.

The Bible says nothing about Jonah's reception of God's command to him to go to Nineveh to preach against the evil ways of its inhabitants, confining itself to the action he takes: 'But Jonah rose up to flee unto Tarshish from the presence of the Lord' (Jonah 1. 3). The poem however makes much of Jonah's response. He is described as instantly hostile and rebellious: *Al he wrathed in his wyt and wytherly he thoght* 'he became very angry in himself and thought rebelliously' (line 74).[11] His thoughts are primarily for his own safety. He at once jumps to the conclusion that if he does God's bidding and is arrested by the Ninevites he will be in trouble, for God has just told him how villainous they are (lines 75–7). His imagination runs riot as he thinks of what might happen to him. In his mind he is in Nineveh already, enduring one punishment after another, each one worse than the last:

> I com wyth those tythynges, thay ta me bylyve,
> Pynes me in a prysoun, put me in stokkes,
> Wrythe me in a warlok, wrast out myn yyen. (lines 78–80)

[I come with that message, they take me at once, confine me in a prison, put me in stocks, torture me in a foot-shackle, tear out my eyes.]

The accumulation of half-line phrases conveys his rapidly-growing panic.

His fear for himself is mixed with scorn and anger against God (lines 81–4). He thinks first that God must want him dead (line 84). In this way he puts God in the wrong and justifies to himself the avoiding action he proposes to take:

> 'At alle peryles,' quoth the prophete, 'I aproche hit no nerre;
> I wyl me sum other waye that he ne wayte after.
> I schal tee into Tarce and tary there a whyle,
> And lyghtly when I am lest he letes me alone.' (lines 85–8)

['At all risks,' said the prophet, 'I shall approach it no nearer; I will go some other way that he does not watch over. I shall go into Tarshish and tarry there a while, and perhaps when I am gone he will leave me alone.']

His words indicate his determination to stand up for himself against God, his confidence that he will be able to do so, and, in line 88, his sense that God is picking on him unfairly. Already he has demonstrated that, in terms of the narrator's explanation of the eighth beatitude, he is impatient, unable to 'steer his heart'.

As he sets out, still grumbling (line 90) and still determined (line 91), he pictures God's unconcern and his own likely fate in Nineveh still more dramatically, as though trying to convince himself of the rightness of his action:

> 'Oure Syre syttes,' he says, 'on sege so hyghe,
> In his glowande glorye, and gloumbes ful lyttel
> Thagh I be nummen in Nunnive and naked dispoyled,
> On rode rwly torent with rybaudes mony.' (lines 93–6)

['Our father sits,' he says, 'so high on his throne, in his shining glory, and is very little worried though I should be taken in Nineveh and stripped naked, pitifully torn to pieces on a cross by many evil men.']

His view of himself is self-pitying, his image of God childish. Righteous indignation shines through his words. His thought that he will be put to death on a cross by *rybaudes* must suggest the crucifixion of Christ to the reader, and perhaps it brings to mind the standard allegorical interpretation of the Book of Jonah in which Jonah is a type or forerunner of Christ.[12] But the association here must work contrastively, leading the reader to consider the ways in which Jonah in the poem is *not* like Christ, to see him not as type but as antitype.[13] Thus the reader is implicitly invited to reflect that where Christ carried out his father's will to the point of embracing death on the cross, Jonah turns against God as soon as there is any question of danger to himself. Jonah's impatience, demonstrated here by his self-regard, his childishness, his lack of faith, is thrown into relief by the implied comparison with the patience of Christ.[14]

On the ship, Jonah's attitude, like that of the sailors, changes from confidence to fear when the storm blows up. When the sailors question him he admits, in both the Bible and the poem, to worshipping the God of the Hebrews, and he states that the storm is all on his account. But in the poem he acknowledges his error more openly: *For I haf greved my God and gulty am founden* (line 210). For the first time he acknowledges his God as the creator of all things (lines 206–8). The point of this is perhaps not so much to show the reader that Jonah has an admirable side as to emphasise his instability. Throughout the story he lurches from one extreme position to another in response to circumstance. Having been discovered in his attempt to escape from God in secret he now decides that complete candour with the sailors will be best for him. Later, in his preaching to the Ninevites, he carries out God's wishes with extreme zeal, only to react against God with a show of extreme petulance, anger, and despair when God spares the city. The elaborations of the biblical text show him as disproportionately delighted when he discovers his woodbine, disproportionately devastated when he finds that it is gone. Such instability is another mark of his impatience. He reacts to the stimulus of the moment quickly and superficially, without taking the time to consider his response.

In his first prayer[15] from the whale's belly Jonah admits his errors more fully than he does with the sailors, acknowledging his folly and deceit, castigating himself in the strongest terms, and accepting that the creation is God's to do with as he pleases. But he also uses his admissions to work on God, coupling them with pleas on his own behalf in which he appeals to God's mercy and his special status as God's prophet:

> Now, prynce, of thy prophete pité thou have.
> Thagh I be fol and fykel and falce of my hert,
> Dewoyde now thy vengaunce thurgh vertu of rauthe.
>
> Thagh I be gulty of gyle, as gaule of prophetes,
> Thou art God, and alle gowdes ar graythely thyn owen;
> Haf now mercy of thy man and his mysdedes,
> And preve the lyghtly a lorde in londe and in water. (lines
> 282–8)

[Now, prince, take pity on your prophet. Though I am foolish and fickle and false-hearted, forego your vengeance now, through the power of your pity. Though I am guilty of guile, as the scum of prophets, you are God, and all things are truly yours; have mercy now on your man and his misdeeds, and swiftly prove yourself a lord on land and in water.]

The last phrase in particular casts doubt on the genuineness of Jonah's new-found humility. For his own purposes he casts God in the role of a great lord of chivalry, whose duty it is to show magnanimity to those who have offended him. His challenge to God to prove that he really is a lord by forgiving him is presumptuous.

Jonah's second prayer from the whale's belly follows the Bible fairly closely, but it adds lines which make it too, more clearly than in the Bible, a prayer for God to show him mercy:

> Thou schal releve me, renk, whil thy ryght slepes,
> Thurgh myght of thy mercy that mukel is to tryste. (lines
> 323–4)[16]

[You must succour me, sir, while your justice sleeps, through the power of your mercy that one may readily rely on.]

Again the language of Jonah's appeal seems unduly assertive. At the end of the prayer Jonah, as in the Bible, promises to make sacrifice to God when he is saved. But in the poem he takes a further step. Whereas Jonah's last words in the biblical prayer are 'Salvation is of the Lord' (Jonah 2.9), in the poem they convey Jonah's further promise to *halde goud that thou me hetes* 'accept what you command me' (line 336). He has apparently finally acknowledged the need to carry out God's will. It is these words which, in the poem, prompt God's command to the whale to spit Jonah out on dry land (lines 337–8).

The whale

Jonah's progress from the ship to the whale is an index of his dete-
riorating control over his circumstances. The ship's hold in which
he finds himself is an unpleasant subterranean space, and the
whale's stomach a still more unpleasant one. Symbolically, Jonah's
impatience leads him straight to the depths, or straight to hell.
These hell-like places are places of correction, not damnation, in
which Jonah is forced to confront his own weakness and acknowledge God's power. When he emerges from the hold and the whale
he seems on both occasions to be a new man, owning his past
errors and ready to make a fresh start. The narrator himself connects ship and whale when he comments, after Jonah finds a corner of the whale's insides which is free from filth, that he was as
safe there as he was earlier in the ship's hold (lines 291–2). There
is more than a tinge of irony in the statement, as Jonah's security
in the boat's hold soon proves illusory. The place where Jonah
thought he was safe turns out to be not safe at all. In the Prologue's
words, *To sette hym to sewrté, unsounde he hym feches* 'in trying to
achieve safety, he brings disaster upon himself'' (line 58).

The sailor who finds Jonah in the hold is confronted by an
unattractive sight: Jonah sleeps in his secret place (*in derne*, line
182) lying on a plank right at the bottom of the ship, near the rud-
der, slobbering and snoring. He has lost all dignity. One detail in
particular suggests hell: when a sailor kicks him in order to rouse
him, the narrator comments: *Ther Ragnel in his rakentes him rere
of his dremes!* 'so may Ragnel (a devil's name) in his chains rouse
him from his dreams!' (line 188), as though he were being roused
from hell to hear his sentence on the Day of Judgement.

The whale too is to be associated with hell. It is of huge size
(twice Jonah is referred to as a *mote* 'speck' in comparison, lines
268, 299), and its belly is emphasised as a place of darkness,
stench, and filth. For medieval Christian culture at all levels, the
association of whales or sea-monsters with hell was a strong one.[17]
Moreover, the Book of Jonah itself makes the link at the beginning of the psalm which is Jonah's prayer from inside the whale:
'out of the belly of hell cried I' (Jonah 2.2, compare *Patience*, line
306). The narrator refers to the whale as *warlowe* 'monster, devil,
the Devil' (line 258). and makes pointed comparisons: its stomach
stank as the devel (line 274) and *savoured as helle* (line 275).

The biblical commentators' allegorisation of Jonah as a type of Christ derives from Christ's own words in Matthew 12.40: 'For as Jonas was three days and three nights in the whale's belly; so shall the Son of man be three days and three nights in the heart of the earth'. In these words Christ refers to his descent to hell after his death and before his resurrection. But any implicit allegorical reference to Christ in the poem must work contrastively, like the earlier one to Christ's crucifixion. Whereas the story of Christ's descent to hell has him overthrowing hell by force,[18] Jonah as he tumbles down the whale's throat is a figure of weakness. Whereas Christ led the souls of the patriarchs and prophets out of hell in triumph, Jonah remains helpless inside the whale, unable to escape until God intervenes.

The narrator (1)

The characterisation of Jonah makes it evident that the poem's story-telling technique leans towards realism: the sparse biblical detail is filled out in such a way as to suggest real people and events. Along with the realism there is a tendency to rationalise, that is, to provide motives and explanations for events which the Bible leaves unexplained, and in particular to supply detail which de-emphasises the miraculous and brings it more into line with the ordinary world. This realistic, rationalising technique fits with the attitudes of the narrator as revealed in his prologue. It is as though he is not at home in the rarefied spiritual world of the Book of Jonah, which reduces the story to an essential outline and does without contexts and explanations. His narrative methods colour the story so that it expresses his pragmatic view of the world and its need for patience. In this he is the opposite of the *Cleanness*-narrator, who is interested in the transcendental, not the day-to-day.

When Jonah takes ship for Tarshish the poem adds to the biblical verse (Jonah 1.3) in order to provide a detailed account, realistic in terms of a medieval vessel, of the operation of making the ship ready to go to sea and taking it out of harbour:

> Then he tron on tho tres and thay her tramme ruchen,
> Cachen up the crossayl, cables thay fasten,
> Wight at the wyndas weyen her ankres,
> Spynde spak to the sprete the spare bawelyne,

> Gederen to the gyde-ropes – the grete cloth falles.
> Thay layden in on laddeborde and the lofe wynnes;
> The blythe brethe at her bak the bosum he fyndes,
> He swenges me thys swete schip swefte fro the haven. (lines
> 101–8)

[Then he goes aboard (lit. stepped on the boards) and they get the gear ready, hoist the square-sail, fasten cables, swiftly weigh the anchors at the windlass, smartly fasten the bowline, carried in reserve, to the bowsprit, tug at the guy-ropes – the mainsail comes down. They lay in oars on the port side and gain the luff; the merry wind at their back finds the belly of the sail, and swings this sweet ship swiftly from the harbour.]

The sequence of detail conveys the ordered and purposeful nature of the sailors' activity. The wind, semi-personified (*He*) is cheerful and co-operative. The import of the adjective *blythe* transfers from the wind to the *swete schip* and the sailors, suggesting a mood of optimism about the coming voyage in which Jonah himself shares (line 109). Later, when the storm comes and 'the ship was like to be broken' (Jonah 1.4), the poem again adds to the biblical verse. The sail, which had been filled by the *blythe brethe*, now floats uselessly on the sea (line 151). Once more a brief biblical phrase, 'and [the sailors] cast forth the wares that were in the ship into the sea, to lighten it of them' (Jonah.1. 5), is expanded in the service of realism:

> Ther was busy overborde bale to kest,
> Her bagges and her fether-beddes and her bryght wedes,
> Her kysttes and her coferes, her caraldes alle,
> And al to lyghten that lome, yif lethe wolde schape. (lines
> 157–60)

[There was eagerness in casting packages overboard, their bags and their feather-beds and their handsome clothes, all their chests and their boxes and their casks, and all to lighten that vessel, to see if relief would come.]

This time the accumulation of detail conveys the sailors' panic. When later they take to their oars (lines 216–19), their desperate effort to save themselves contrasts with their earlier controlled use of the oars to turn the ship as it leaves harbour. Behind the contrast is the same ironic observation of life that the narrator exhibits in the Prologue. The contrast makes the point that Jonah

and the sailors, and human beings in general, are deluded if they
ever think they are in control of their lives. Any control that they
may think they have is an illusion which can be destroyed in a
moment. This is a lesson which Jonah, and humanity in general,
have to learn. It is enforced, with brutal clarity, in the episode of
the woodbine. 'The Lord hath given, the Lord hath taken away'
(Job 1.21).

Patience makes some rationalising adjustment to the biblical
narrative in its account of the sailors' response to the storm. In
the Bible the sailors first cry to their gods, then throw their goods
overboard. In the poem the order is reversed, perhaps to accord
with the narrator's 'practical' priorities. In the Bible the shipmas-
ter goes down into the ship and discovers Jonah (Jonah 1.6), but
it is not made clear why he does so. In the poem, the sailor's
speech in lines 170–6, urging the casting of lots to identify the
lawles wrech who has offended his god, provides a reason: a sailor
goes below deck to look for men to bring to the casting of lots. To
Jonah's biblical explanation of himself as a Hebrew who worships
the God of creation the poem adds a rationalising detail which
explains how he is able to communicate with the sailors: he uses
signs which they understand (line 213). Once Jonah is gone the sea
becomes calm instantly, as in the Bible, but in the poem this miracle is expanded by the added detail that the ship is described as
still at the mercy of strong currents (lines 233–5), until a propi-
tious current finally brings it to land (line 236). In the Bible it is
not indicated how the sailors return to land to make their sacri-
fices, or even that they return to land at all.

The episode of Jonah in the whale's belly is what the story is
best known for. Whereas spectacular supernatural happenings are
the common currency of *Cleanness*, the whale stands out in the
smaller world of *Patience*, and the narrator twice feels the need to
draw attention to the miracle, almost to apologise for its extreme
unlikeliness. He states that it would be hard to believe it if it were
not for the Bible (line 244), and for God's great power (lines
257–60). These are statements of a kind not found in *Cleanness*.
Much of the considerable expansion of Jonah 1.17 ('Now the
Lord had prepared a great fish to swallow up Jonah. And Jonah
was in the belly of the fish three days and three nights.') is given
over to explanatory and demystifying detail. The whale is not
brought to the ship directly by God, but is *beten fro the abyme*

'driven from the depths (by the storm)', line 248, a detail which is prepared for earlier in the account of the storm when it is stated that *breed fysches / Durst nowhere for rogh arest at the bothem* 'nowhere were terrified fish able to remain quiet at the bottom, on account of the upheaval' (lines 143–4).[19] The whale is described as swimming to the sea bottom after it has swallowed Jonah (lines 253–4), thereby preparing for the biblical emphasis, retained in the poem, on Jonah's prayer as coming from the depths. Later the whale's swimming on through the depths is explained as a response to the irritation which the foreign body in its stomach causes it (lines 299–300). The detail that the whale seizes Jonah while the sailors are still holding his feet provides a graphic 'realistic' touch (line 251). An attempt is made to supply details of the act of swallowing and the whale's insides by mentioning various slimy internal organs.

The narrator's interventions

The prophet Jonah twice rebels against God, and each time is taught a lesson by God. For Jonah's first lesson, in which he tries to escape God's command to go to Nineveh and learns the need for obedience in the belly of the whale, the poem guides the reader's response to the story by means of narratorial comments. For his second lesson, in which God tries to make Jonah understand his forgiveness of the Ninevites by growing a sheltering plant for him and then taking it away again, the narrator leaves the story to its own devices, refraining entirely from comment. This difference in treatment reflects the differing emphasis of the two lessons. The first fits well with the narrator's views as expressed in the prologue, the second goes beyond them. It is as though he gives up on the Book of Jonah when he finds himself siding with Jonah rather than God.

The narrator's longest intervention in the story is his first, when he comments on Jonah's attempt to escape God's command to go to Nineveh by fleeing to Tarshish (lines 109–28). He applies to Jonah the point made in the prologue and epilogue that impatience with suffering only leads to more suffering. As at the end of the prologue, his concern is with the folly rather than the sinfulness of Jonah's action:

> Lo, the wytles wrechche, for he wolde noght suffer,
> Now has he put hym in plyt of peril wel more. (lines 113–14)

[Look, the witless wretch, because he would not suffer, now he has put himself in a state of much greater peril.]

In addition to *wytles wrechche* he calls him *he . . . that dotes for elde* 'he who is foolish in his old age' (line 125), and he castigates Jonah's thought that he could escape God as a *wenyng unwar* 'foolish thought' (line 115). He brings sarcasm to bear on Jonah's misunderstanding of his situation:

> He wende wel that that wyy that all the world plantted
> Hade no maght in that mere no man for to greve. (lines 111–12)

[He knew well that the one who had created all the world had no power in that sea to harm any man.]

To emphasise that Jonah had no excuse for his folly the narrator quotes verses from the Psalms (Psalm 94.8–9) which, he says, make it plain to everyone that one must expect the God who made ears and eyes to hear and see everything. The same biblical verses are paraphrased in *Cleanness* 581–6, where they lead on to the idea of God as seeing into human beings' innermost depths, and using the knowledge he thereby gains to separate the saved from the damned.[20] *Patience*, characteristically, is more restrained in its interpretation of the biblical text. It paraphrases the biblical verses more closely and, with Jonah in mind, confines itself to the idea expressed in them of the foolishness of failing to understand the implications of the fact that God is the creator of all (lines 121–4).

The narrator's imagery is largely made up of commonplace phrases which reflect everyday life. He comments that Jonah *schomely to schort he shote of his ame* 'shot shamefully too short of his mark' (line 128) in trying to escape from God, and that, when he was inside the whale, *colde was his cumfort* (line 264). The ship in the storm has to *suppe . . . of the colde water* (lines 151–2). Jonah passing through the great jaws of the whale is compared to a *mote in at a munster dor* 'a speck of dust in at a cathedral door' (line 268). The whale's stomach where he fetches up is *as brod as a halle* (line 272), it *stank as the devel* (line 274), and *savoured as helle* 'stank as hell' (line 275). When God spares the Ninevites, Jonah

becomes *as wroth as the wynde* (line 410). The account of the
sailors' desperate efforts to bail out their vessel leads the narrator
to generalise in the style of his observations in the prologue and
epilogue: *For be monnes lode never so luther, the lyf is ay swete* 'for
be a man's burden never so heavy, life is always sweet' (line 156).

When Jonah is thrown into the sea and the sailors return safe
to land, the differences between Jonah's state and that of the
sailors, and between his initial aspirations and the outcome of his
flight, are brought out by contrastive couplings:

> Thagh thay be jolef for joye, Jonas yet dredes;
> Thagh he nolde suffer no sore, his seele is on anter. (lines
> 241-2)

[Though they are transported with joy, Jonah is still in fear; though
he did not want to suffer hardship, his welfare is in doubt.]

Jonah's arrival in the whale's belly draws forth similar contrastive
comments (lines 275-6, 296). Such comments, like so much else
in *Patience*, serve irony, not, as with the contrastive comments in
Cleanness, a sense of drama and urgency.

At the end of the lesson of the whale, the narrator's final comment on Jonah comes in the middle of a passage in which he
describes his arrival on dry land:

> Thenne he swepe to the sonde in sluchched clothes;
> Hit may wel be that mester were his mantyle to wasche.
> The bonk that he blosched to and bode hym bisyde
> Wern of the regiounes ryght that he renayed hade. (lines
> 341-4)

[Then he swept to the shore in filthy clothes; it may well be that there
was need for him to wash his mantle. The land that met his gaze,
lying around him, belonged to the very country which he had
renounced.]

In *Cleanness*, which is fundamentally metaphorical, dirty clothes
are a central image for sin, and the symbolism is made explicit
(*Cleanness* 165-76). *Patience* uses this imagery only here, and its
meaning is not made explicit. It is left to the reader to draw the
conclusion that line 342 is to be read in a metaphorical as well as
a literal way (*Patience* is fundamentally literal), with the import
that Jonah needed, not so much to wash himself clean of sin, as to
rid himself of his foolish attitudes: his rebellion has been shown

to be futile, he has been forced to go to Nineveh anyway, and in his effort to avoid doing so he has only suffered the more. The line conveys again the narrator's pragmatic approach to morality, and his ironic approach to Jonah. Its implication, in the context of the extra-biblical observation of lines 343–4, is that Jonah needs to change his attitude to God. *Cleanness*, with its absolutist stance, sees clothes as either clean or dirty, and human beings as either saved or damned. But *Patience* puts the emphasis on the possibility of improvement, of dirty clothes becoming clean and human beings changing for the better.

Jonah (2)

The second movement of the story (which makes up chapters three and four of the Book of Jonah in the Bible) begins with God's second command to Jonah to go to Nineveh. Jonah's words of acknowledgement (not in the Bible), in which he appeals to God for grace, seem to confirm that he has changed his attitude:

> 'Yisse, Lorde,' quoth the lede, 'lene me thy grace
> For to go at thi gre; me gaynes non other.' (lines 347–8)

> ['Yes, Lord,' said the man, 'give me your grace to go at your pleasure; no other course will profit me.']

The last phrase however strikes a discordant note. It indicates that Jonah will do what God tells him not because he wants to but because he now sees that he has to. Events soon demonstrate that his reformation does not go very deep. His own welfare remains his primary concern.

To begin with he is eager to do God's bidding. He travels to Nineveh as fast as he can (lines 351, 355), and preaches the doom of the city. Having finally got to Nineveh, Jonah throws himself into his task with gusto. His preaching, a matter of one short sentence in the Bible ('Yet forty days, and Nineveh shall be overthrown', Jonah 3.4), takes up ten lines in the poem, and two separate passages (lines 357–64, 369–70), and it is made more dramatic.

The Ninevites' repentance takes up five biblical verses and is already dramatic. The poem expands the biblical account and makes it more so. To ensure that the reader understands that the pagans' repentance qualifies as Christian penance the biblical sackcloth and ashes are supplemented by medieval hair shirts, the biblical fasting by tears of contrition. The word *penaunce* itself is used (line 376). In the king's speech more emphasis is given in the poem than the Bible to the idea that even the innocent must undertake penitential fasting:

> Seses childer of her sok, soghe hem so never,
> Ne best bite on no brom, ne no bent nauther. (lines 391–2)

> [Take children from the breast, no matter how much it may distress them, nor shall any beast feed on broom, or grass either.]

The detail in line 391 looks forward to God's pitying reference to innocent children at the breast in line 510. The poem retains the tentative biblical question in which the king expresses his hope that God will respond positively to the city's acts of penance (lines 397–8), a question which recalls the similarly tentative question (only in the poem) of the sailor in the storm (lines 175–6). The king follows it by words in which he expresses his new-found belief in God's mercy (lines 399–404), and the episode ends with a clear narratorial statement to the effect that the people all turned to God in penance and God did indeed forgive them (lines 405–8). The length of the passage itself gives it weight and significance.

The other three *Gawain*-poems are interested in penance too. *Pearl* assigns penance its place in the whole scheme of Christian doctrine, *Cleanness* presents it as more of a theoretical than an actual possibility, and *Gawain* considers it in relation to chivalry. But it comes into its own in *Patience*, where it is fully displayed in the narrative (with its stages of contrition, confession, penance, and absolution), and is seen to work. *Patience* demonstrates that penance is the agency which turns the sinner from pride to humility, and God from justice to mercy. Thus *Cleanness* shows how sin activates God's justice and punishment, and *Patience* how penance activates his mercy and forgiveness. Penance is what Jonah needs if he is to wash his mantle.

But neither the Bible nor the poem shows Jonah ever achieving the humility which a penitential attitude requires. The extent of his self-preoccupation is amply demonstrated by his angry reaction when God forgives the Ninevites. He feels once more that God has not treated him with respect. He has done what God wanted, he thinks, and it is now up to God to play his part appropriately. His prayer of complaint is full of self-pity. He claims, as in the Bible, that it was because he knew God was going to be merciful that he fled to Tarshish instead of going to Nineveh (lines 421–4). In this way he justifies his disobedience. God's courtesy, which the King of Nineveh had praised, and to which Jonah had formerly appealed, he now makes into a weakness:

> Wel knew I thi cortaysye, thy quoynt soffraunce,
> Thy bounté of debonerté, and thy bene grace,
> Thy longe abydyng wyth lur, thy late vengaunce;
> And ay thy mercy is mete, be mysse never so huge. (lines 417–20)

> [I knew well your courtesy, your wise sufferance, the bounty of your kindness, and your good grace, your long endurance of injury, your tardy vengeance; and always your mercy is sufficient, however great the wrong.]

The language of the first two lines belongs entirely to the courtly register. Jonah seems to scorn as 'soft' those very qualities which formerly he had challenged God to demonstrate to him. He evidently sees no inconsistency in blaming God for his mercy to the Ninevites, after he has benefited from God's mercy himself. His complaint culminates in a request to God to end his life. The reason he gives for wanting to die, left implicit in the biblical text but spelt out in the poem, is that God, by sparing the Ninevites, has made him a liar:

> For me were swetter to swelt as swythe, as me thynk,
> Then lede lenger thi lore, that thus me les makes. (lines 427–8)

> [For I would rather die at once, I think, than have anything more to do with your counsel, you who make me untruthful.]

Again he is guilty of inconsistency, for it is not God who had made him a liar; he has made himself into one. In the Bible it is possible to accept the reason he gives at the beginning of his prayer for his not going to Nineveh, that he knew God was going to be merciful, because when his flight to Tarshish is narrated, in Jonah 1.3, the narrative gives no indication of his reasons for fleeing. But in the poem Jonah makes clear at the time his reasons for fleeing, and knowing that God is in the end going to be merciful to the Ninevites is not one of them. In this way the poem makes Jonah's angry words disingenuous as well as self-regarding. His righteous indignation ignores the fact that he is quite happy to stretch the truth when it suits him.

Verbal echoes reinforce the parallel with Jonah's situation at the beginning of the story. Again God angers Jonah, again Jonah gives vent to his feelings, and again he rises, *joyles and janglande* 'grumbling' (line 433, compare *janglande for tene*, line 90) to strike out on his own. One implication of the parallel is that he is about to be taught a second lesson. As in the Bible he leaves the city and builds a *lyttel bothe* for himself out of grasses and leaves from which to watch what will happen, presumably in the hope that God will listen to his prayer and destroy the city after all. In his shelter he falls asleep, as he had earlier fallen asleep in the shelter of the boat's hold. As before the man-made space in which he takes refuge from God is superseded by a space of God's creation. This time it appears to be a version of paradise, not hell. God grows over his head a beautiful bower, a woodbine which is as big as a house. Jonah's anger changes to delight. He glories in what he sees as his new possession, lounging, capering about, laughing like a madman. He loses his dignity as surely as when he was tumbling head over heels down the whale's throat. His delight in the woodbine – *his* woodbine as he thinks of it – is immediate and unquestioning. He plays in it like a child, and like a child he wants to take his new possession home with him.

But his paradise is a fool's paradise. When God destroys the woodbine the next day, his mood swings from elation back to anger and despair. He does not allow God his part in growing the woodbine (*I kevered me a cumfort* 'I acquired a comfort for myself', line 485), but now he attacks him for destroying it, overcome by his sense of the unfairness of it all:

> A, thou maker of man, what maystery the thynkes
> Thus thy freke to forfare forbi alle other?
> With alle meschef that thou may, never thou me spares. (lines 482–4)

[Ah, you maker of man, what kind of achievement does it seem to you thus to ruin your man before all others? You never stop attacking me with all possible mischief.]

He regards himself as the victim of a long-running campaign of persecution, and this is particularly hard for him because he thinks God owes him special consideration as *thy freke* 'your man, your prophet'. He does not consider it strange that God should bend all his powers to the purpose of humiliating him. When God asks Jonah why he has become angry *for so lyttel*, Jonah disputes the word *lyttel* by trying to make God's unfairness (as he sees it) into an issue of principle: *'Hit is not lyttel'*, he says querulously, *'bot lykker to ryght'* [but rather a matter of justice] (line 493). Presumably he means both justice for Nineveh (he thinks it deserves to be destroyed), and justice for himself (he thinks he does not deserve to be made a liar, and to have his woodbine taken away). But his appeal to principle, unconvincing in its own terms, is undermined also by the fact that when it suited him in the past, when he was in the whale's belly, Jonah was very ready for God to suspend his justice.

God

In *Patience* God in his reply to Jonah gives four reasons for his decision to spare Nineveh. The Bible has only the first of these, that in the city there were 'more than sixscore thousand persons that cannot discern between their right hand and their left hand: and also much cattle' (Jonah 4.11). The meaning of this, spelt out in the poem, is that there were many in the city who were innocent of sin (and therefore did not deserve to die).

God's second reason is that as he created and nurtured humanity (lines 503–4), he does not want to destroy it, for this would mean that his long toil would be wasted (line 505). He refers to the Ninevites as his own *hondewerk* whom he would naturally want to help (line 496). This reason is not expressed in the Bible but develops from the implication of Jonah 4.10–11 that if Jonah is sorry to see his woodbine destroyed 'for the which thou hast not laboured, neither made it grow', then he must understand God's reluctance to destroy the Ninevites. The third of God's reasons is that the Ninevites have repented. He refers to their repentance four times (lines 502, 506, 508, 518–19), and in the last of these makes it clear that their repentance is a main reason for his withholding his punishment.

God's fourth and culminating reason (which links with the first) is that it is in his nature to be merciful. The behaviour of the Ninevites had first moved him to anger, but now, as he thinks of man as his own creation, accepts that the Ninevites have repented

their sins, and imagines the innocents amongst them, he is moved
to pity (line 502). Repentant Nineveh has become a *swete place* to
him, and he cannot bear the thought of destroying it: *The sor of*
such a swete place burde synk to myn hert 'the sorrow of such a
sweet place would sink into my heart' (line 507). He thinks of
children at the breast and simple women amongst other innocent
people and animals there. The speech thus refutes Jonah's assertion that what is at stake with Nineveh is the issue of the fairness
of God's justice. Its message, which Jonah and the narrator completely miss, is that God's love for humanity leads him to be merciful to the innocent and the repentant.[21] Jonah's view is that *he*
deserves mercy; the Ninevites, justice. In contrast to the *Clean-*
ness-narrator, who sees the principles of mercy and penance but
not how they work, the *Patience*-narrator and Jonah see penance
and forgiveness demonstrated but do not acknowledge their valid-
ity. Jonah still has to learn that God takes a protective interest in
all his creation, and that his mercy is available to others as well as
to him.

In four climactic extra-biblical lines God draws Jonah's
attention to his lack of patience, and associates his own mercy
with patient endurance:

> Wer I as hastif as thou, heere, were harme lumpen;
> Couthe I not thole bot as thou, ther thryved ful fewe.
> I may not be so malicious and mylde be halden,
> For malyse is nogh to mayntyne boute mercy withinne. (lines
> 520–3)

[Were I as hasty as you, sir, it would be unfortunate; if I could
endure only as you do, few would prosper. I may not be so severe and
(still) be considered gentle, for severity is not to be practised without mercy in one's heart.]

On *his* patience, he says, depends the very survival of humanity.
The speech shows that patience, as manifested in God himself, is
a positive, outgoing virtue, directed to the benefit of others, and
inextricably interwoven with his love for his creation.

God's use of the word *malyse* calls for comment. The usual
senses are 'malice, hostility, evil', which are appropriate to *mali-*
cious earlier in the same speech (line 508), and to God's *malys mer-*
cyles against the sinners of Noah's world in *Cleanness*, line 250.
But when God refers to his *malyse* and his being *malicious* in lines

522–3 the words suggest severity rather than hostility: *malicious* is
opposed to *mylde*, and *malyse* to *mercy*. These two lines of speech
are the last God utters in the *Cleanness-Patience* manuscript
sequence, and they seem to be put there not only to sum up God's
thoughts about patience, but to bring to the surface the dialogic
relationship between the two manifestations of God in *Cleanness*
and *Patience*. God not only alludes to the two sides of his nature
in these two lines, but indicates how the apparent contradiction
between them is to be resolved: justice (*malyse*) must be informed
or tempered by mercy.

As noted above (pp. 5, 6), the idea that God in his own being
reconciles justice and mercy is widely expressed in medieval literature and drama in terms of a debate between the personified four
daughters of God, Justice and Truth on the one hand, Mercy and
Peace on the other. The idea comes from Psalm 85.10: 'Mercy and
truth are met together, righteousness and peace have kissed each
other'; in the developed versions this resolution comes at the end
of the debate. The God of *Cleanness* strikes fear into the hearts
even of his prophets. The God of *Patience* is so little terrifying to
his prophet that Jonah responds to him in anger, not fear. From
the beginning of the story God is closer to Jonah than he ever is
to any human being in *Cleanness*. He first speaks to Jonah *in his
ere* (line 64), and thereafter responds to Jonah's every move. God
even seems to take over something of the narrator's ironic attitude
to Jonah in his final words of remonstrance (especially line 521),
and perhaps also in his earlier questioning of Jonah (especially
line 346).

Thus God's final speech enables the reader to understand the
place of the Jonah-story in the sequence of Old Testament
episodes begun in *Cleanness*. The age of the prophets has moved
on from Daniel to Jonah, and by the end of the Jonah-story it is
evident that God's attitudes to sin and forgiveness have similarly
moved on. His threat to destroy the sinning city of Nineveh
recalls his threats of vengeance in *Cleanness*,[22] but the Ninevites'
thoroughgoing repentance and God's unequivocal acceptance of
it is a new development, although adumbrated in the example of
Nebuchadnezzar in *Cleanness*. His attitude to all his creation is
now more understanding. The poet, in changing biblical detail to
particularise the innocents in Nineveh as women and children as
well as the biblical animals, perhaps intends to recall his account

of the women, children and animals fleeing the rising waters in
Cleanness. In comparing his actions in the two poems, the reader
cannot help but notice that God in *Patience* has become more
human.

God's creation

In the Book of Jonah God makes considerable use of his non-
human creation as his agents. The whale is the chief example of
this, but there are others. *Patience* develops this aspect of the
story in the direction of making these agents into sentient beings.
The most notable example of this, apart from the whale, is the
wind which in Jonah 1.4 God sends to create the sea-storm. The
poem has two winds, which are personified. It refers to them as a
resource available to God, amongst other resources, to carry out
his purposes. It implies that God chooses the winds because, having created them, he knows them and their capabilities well:

> For the welder of wyt that wot alle thynges,
> That ay waykes and waytes, at wylle has he slyghtes.
> He calde on that ilk crafte he carf with his hondes. (lines
> 129–31)

[For the lord of wisdom who knows all things, who always wakes and
watches, has means at his command. He called on those same powers he had made with his hands.]

Line 131 images the physical act of creation and suggests the close
bond between creator and created. God similarly refers to
humanity as his *hondewerk* in line 496. He speaks to the winds and
calls them by their names:

> Ewrus and Aquiloun that on est sittes,
> Blowes bothe at my bode upon blo watteres. (lines 133–4)

[Eurus and Aquilon who sit in the east, both blow at my command
upon the dark waters.]

God's tone is both commanding and personal. The poem emphasises how the winds respond to his mood (*Thay wakened wel the
wrotheloker for wrothely he cleped* 'they wakened the more angrily
in that angrily he called', line 132), and how prompt they are (lines
135–6). They are personified as servants who have a good relationship with their lord and who are ready to do his bidding. It is

as though they seek eagerly to repay the debt they owe to him for having created them. The poet creates a vivid exchange between God and the winds out of a bald biblical statement. By contrast the beginning of the Flood in *Cleanness* is described in entirely impersonal terms, with many intransitive verbs: springs gush and cataracts burst open (*Cleanness*, lines 363–8). The account of the beginning of the destruction of Sodom and Gomorrah is more comparable in that it has God summoning the winds, who come from the four corners of the earth to wrestle together (*Cleanness*, lines 947–50; compare *Patience*, line 141). But God does not speak, the winds are not named, and there is no attempt to convey any closeness of relationship.

God's readiness to call upon his creatures, and their readiness to obey him, is made manifest throughout *Patience*. Though the whale is a proud animal who goes with Jonah wherever it wants (*thurgh ronk of his wylle* 'in the pride of its will', line 298), as soon as God speaks to it it obeys him and goes where *he* wants it to, *at his* [God's] *wylle* (line 339). It finds land and vomits up Jonah *as bede hym oure Lorde* (line 340). In the woodbine episode, God grows the woodbine (line 443–4), sends the dawn (line 445), and sends also the worm which attacks the woodbine (line 467). In a passage of free indirect discourse he calls up one of his winds, again by name (*Zeferus*, line 470), ordering it to blow warm, and he orders the sun to rise and burn like a candle (line 472). Both wind and sun fulfil his commands exactly, destroying the woodbine (lines 476–8).

The willingness of the non-human creation to serve God throws into relief the recalcitrance of the humans. All the human beings in the Jonah story begin in error: the people of Nineveh, who live in wickedness (Jonah 1.2), Jonah himself, who tries to evade God's command (Jonah 1.3), and the sailors, who worship false gods (Jonah 1.5). When God first speaks to Jonah he states his intention of avenging himself on the sin of Nineveh in language which is like the language of *Cleanness*. But when the Ninevites, and the sailors, hear from Jonah about his god, they at once fear him and accept him, and he forgives them. It is only Jonah, the preacher of God's word, who resists God's word. In this the poem sets Jonah apart from all the rest of creation. But Jonah's rebellion still remains within the family, as it were. He never becomes radically disaffected, but rather behaves like a spoilt child, acknowledging his father's authority, including his authority as creator (he calls God *the Fader that hym formed*, line 92, and *maker of man*, line 482) even as he rebels against it. His status as God's prophet, of which he is well aware (he calls himself *thy prophete* line 282, *his prophete* line 327), leads him to expect a privileged relationship with God, and helps explain why he is both hurt at the apparently cavalier treatment which he receives from God and emboldened to make demands on God and challenge him.

Though Jonah first thinks that God has removed himself to a great distance and takes little account of him (lines 93–6), the poem shows God as closely interested in his doings. God does not want to destroy erring humanity, but to get it to see the error of its ways, and he uses Jonah for this purpose. Jonah becomes an agent whose failed (in his eyes) enterprises bring about God's successes, the reformation and conversion of the sailors and the Ninevites. If Jonah behaves like a child with God, then God is like a father to Jonah. He creates miraculous life-experiences for him (the whale, the woodbine) which he intends as learning tools. When God speaks to Jonah, after his abortive attempt to flee to Nineveh, and after his angry reaction to his sparing the Ninevites, he does not merely correct him as a teacher might, but puts questions to him which invite him to reflect on his attitudes (lines 346, 431–2, 490–1, 492).[23] Finally, in the absence of any positive response from Jonah, God gives him explicit instruction in his concluding speech.

Patience shows God becoming aware of his love for his creation, and it is through his patience, through his willingness to tolerate and forgive, that he demonstrates his love. The poem carries the meaning that the whole Christian way of virtue, as summarised in the Beatitudes, is unspectacular and unassertive. Virtue is ordinary and belongs with ordinary people, not the rich and powerful. The Beatitudes convey God's message of reassurance to the poor and lowly of the world. The full quotation of the Beatitudes may suggest the idea, well-established in patristic commentary, that the eighth beatitude has special status, clarifying and summing up the other seven instead of merely being additional to them.[24] Saint Paul writes that charity (or love), the greatest of the spiritual virtues, is not a matter of understanding all mysteries, or having faith sufficient to move mountains, but, essentially, of being patient: 'Charity suffereth long, and is kind; charity envieth not; charity vaunteth not itself, is not puffed up ... [Charity] beareth all things, believeth all things, hopeth all things, endureth all things' (1 Cor. 13.4–7).

The narrator (2)

After he has told his story, the narrator[25] delivers an eight-line conclusion:

> Be noght so gryndel, godman, bot go forth thy wayes,
> Be prevé and be pacient in payne and in joye;
> For he that is to rakel to renden his clothes
> Mot efte sitte with more unsounde to sewe hem togeder.
>
> Forthy when poverté me enpreces and paynes innoghe,
> Ful softly with suffraunce saghttel me bihoves.
> Forthy penaunce and payne topreve hit in syght
> That pacience is a nobel poynt, thagh hit displese ofte. (lines 524–31)

[Be not so angry, good sir, but go on your way, be quiet and be patient in pain and in joy; for he who is too hasty in tearing his clothes must afterwards put up with further annoyance in sewing them together. And so when poverty oppresses me and many sorrows, I must quietly make my peace with patience. And so suffering and sorrow prove it for all to see that patience is a noble virtue, though it often displeases.]

For the first time, the narrator addresses the reader directly (lines 524–5), but he does so unthreateningly. The low-key aphoristic style of the poem's first lines is picked up again, and extended in the mundane generalisation of lines 526–7, which recasts as a proverb the narrator's idea that an attitude of impatience exacts its own retribution.

This conclusion brings the reader down to earth. It does not relate directly to God's speech, but reiterates the narrator's view of patience as above all a matter of acceptance of misfortune, and it relates patience again to his own poverty. Any development in his thinking reflects God's actions in the story, not his words. The narrator's urging the need for patience *in joye* as well as *in payne* (line 525) expands his paraphrase of the eighth beatitude in the prologue, and seems to reflect the significance of the woodbine episode for him. There is a new emphasis, too, on patience as meaning quiet, gentle behaviour (*prevé* line 525, *softly* line 529), which may reflect the narrator's recognition of the lack of restraint which Jonah has demonstrated.

The poem ends with the same one-line generalisation with which it began. The last line is identical to the first, except that the adjective *nobel* is added. This may seem to make no material difference to the meaning of the line, but I believe there is more to it than this. In the first line the manuscript reads not *a poynt* but *apoynt*, without the space. Some readers have argued for retention of manuscript *apoynt*, explaining the form as the past participle of the verb *appoint(en)*, with the meaning 'appointed, enjoined (by God)'. But in all four poems the scribe frequently attaches the indefinite article to the following noun, and most editors print *a poynt*. The one-word reading amounts to 'patience is a necessity', the two-word one to 'patience is a virtue'. It may be, especially in the light of the word-play on *suffer* which follows shortly, that there is word-play also in the first line, in this instance involving form as well as meaning. In other words, the reader of the first line is put in the position of being unable to decide whether *apoynt* or *a poynt* is the reading, and therefore of being unsure what the narrator means. In hindsight, *apoynt* 'enjoined' fits in well with the narrator's view of patience, while *a poynt* 'a virtue' fits in both with the narrator's view and God's. In the last line, the reading and the meaning are unambiguous, and the narrator now clearly sees patience as a virtue. But the second-last line is profoundly ambiguous, in a way which keeps the two views of patience, the narrator's and God's, in front of the reader. If the meaning of *penaunce* is levelled to that of *payne* (*MED* penaunce, sense 5a, 'pain, suffering'), so that the line means 'and so pain and suffering prove convincingly . . .', then the last two lines express the narrator's view that patience is a virtue of necessity, that his tale of his own poverty and Jonah's tribulations has proved the *need* for an attitude of patience if one is to cope with life's ups and downs. But if the meaning of *payne* is levelled to that of *penaunce*, so that it refers to the punishment for sin undertaken by the penitent at the behest of his confessor,[26] then the line means 'and so penance and punishment prove convincingly . . .' This expresses God's view, that a patient attitude is noble because it is allied to a penitential attitude, and a sinner's penance prompts

him to be merciful. But this is a meaning for the reader, not the
narrator, who has not responded to God's speech at all. He does
not see that penance is the key to salvation, and that the attitudes
of the Beatitudes, which patience subsumes, are the key to
penance. The reader is led to suspect that his total lack of comment on Jonah's second lesson indicates that he is not only out of
sympathy with Jonah but himself does not understand God's forgiveness of the Ninevites. If lines 524–7 are to be taken as beginning his conclusion, then his audience, as well as Jonah, are now
the beneficiaries of his attitude of worldly superiority. God's
speech indirectly draws attention to the fact that the narrator's
pragmatism is ultimately based on self-interest as much as Jonah's
rebellion is. Neither Jonah nor he is able to rise to God's message.
Patience is the only one of the four poems not to end with a prayer,
a confirming sign, perhaps, that its narrator is meant to be seen as
not attuned to spiritual matters.

Notes

1   See further my edition of *Patience* (Manchester: Manchester University
    Press, 1969), p. 17.
2   David Williams, 'The point of *Patience*', *Modern Philology*, 68 (1970),
    127–36, finds a calculated discrepancy between narrator and narrative in
    Patience. 'The audience watches Jonah's protracted dialogue with God, with
    the homilist as guide, but they see more than he does.'
3   In line 1, the manuscript has *apoynt*. See below, pp. 154–5.
4   For discussion of these meanings and their significance for *Patience* see Myra
    Stokes, 'Suffering in *Patience*', *Chaucer Review*, 18 (1984), 354–63.
5   Jonah shows he is unwilling to be persecuted for righteousness' sake when he
    refuses God's command to go to Nineveh out of fear for what the Ninevites
    will do to him (see below, pp. 132–3).
6   The verb in the Vulgate version of the beatitude, *patiuntur* 'suffer, endure',
    offers more formal and semantic support for seeing the eighth beatitude as
    enshrining the virtue of patience than the English translations do: 'Beati qui
    persecutionem patiuntur propter iustitiam quoniam ipsorum est regnum
    caelorum.'
7   See above, pp. 62–3.
8   So Augustine, *De Sermone Domini, Patrologia Latina*, 34, 1234.
9   Putter, *Introduction*, pp. 108–13, discusses the *Patience*-poet's ignoring of the
    metaphysical perspective of the beatitudes, a perspective fully supported by
    the commentary tradition.
10 Line 39 provides a good example of word-play. *By quest of her quoyntyse*
    seems likely to mean both 'by (reason of) their nature' (for the sense compare
    the quotation from *Arthur and Merlin* in *MED* under *queyntis(e*, sense 4a)

and 'by the judgement of their Lord', with reference to Christ as the author of the Beatitudes (the primary meaning of *quoyntyse* is 'wisdom', and Wisdom was a name given to Christ in medieval theological writing; see my edition of *Patience*, p. 51). The fact that the narrator continues to flirt with the idea of poverty and patience as his mistresses (poverty is still referred to as 'she' and 'her' in lines 41–2) suggests a third possible meaning for *quoyntyse* here: 'beauty, elegance, refinement' (*MED queyntis(e*, sense 3a).

11   It is significant to the poem's construction of Jonah as the opposite of patient that the first word conveying his response to God's first command should be *wrathed*, and that the words *wroth* (*wrath*) and *anger* are several times used subsequently in the context of Jonah's behaviour. In the scheme of the seven deadly sins and their seven opposite virtues, anger (wrath) and patience are the regular pairing.

12   See also below, p. 137.

13   So Spearing, *Gawain-Poet*, p. 87.

14   Christ himself, especially in his willing acceptance of his crucifixion, was the great example of patience for the medieval Christian. See for instance Chaucer's *Parson's Tale*: 'Heer agayns suffred Crist ful paciently, and taughte us pacience, whan he baar upon his blissed shulder the croys upon which he sholde suffren despitous deeth' (*Canterbury Tales* X. 667).

15   This prayer has no basis in the Bible. It seems to be supplied primarily in order to make sense of the past tense verbs in Jonah's long prayer in lines 305–36, which *is* based in the Bible (Jonah 2.2–9; in the Vulgate, 2.3–10) and keeps the biblical past tenses. So, when Jonah says in the first line of his long prayer: *Lorde, to the haf I cleped in cares ful stronge* 'Lord, I have called to you in great trouble' (line 305), he may be taken to be referring to his prayer in lines 282–8. The supplied prayer also adjusts the import of the biblical prayer to bring it more into line with the poem's interests.

16   These lines apparently correspond to Jonah 2.6: 'yet hast thou brought up my life from corruption, O Lord my God'. The poem follows the past tenses of the biblical prayer until Jonah 2.4 (*Patience* line 316), but then it switches to the present tense from line 317 to line 324; so Jonah 2.5 'The waters compassed me about,' becomes *Patience* line 317: *I am wrapped in water* . . . In line 323 the biblical present tense is turned into a future. Thus lines 317–24 express, more clearly than the Bible, Jonah's acknowledgement of his present difficulty and his future hope.

17   It is standard in the Bestiary, which tells the story of sailors who mistake the whale for an island, land on it, and make a fire. The whale submerges, taking their ship with it, and they are drowned. The whale also lures fish into its mouth with its sweet breath. In the appended moralisation the whale is the deceitful Devil who lures the unwary down to hell by his trickery. See e.g. the extract from the only surviving Middle English Bestiary in Bennett and Smithers, *Early Middle English Verse and Prose* pp. 171–3. In medieval visual art it was not uncommon to represent hell as the jaws of a whale-like monster, and the monstrous hell-mouth was the most famous prop of the English mystery plays.

18   See, e.g., the mystery plays on the episode of the Harrowing of Hell.

19   The idea that whales were driven by storms from the depths of the sea to the surface is from medieval natural history; see p. 172 of the edition of extracts from the English Bestiary referred to in note 17, above.

20   See above, pp. 101–2.

21   The maiden expounds this doctrine in *Pearl*. See above, pp. 48–51.

22   God's phrase *vilanye and venym* (line 71), for instance, echoes *The venym and the vylanye*, applied to the sin of Sodom and Gomorrah in *Cleanness* 574.

23   In this the poet follows the biblical model; cf. God's questions to Jonah in the woodbine episode: 'Doest thou well to be angry?' (Jonah 4.4), and 'Doest thou well to be angry for the gourd?' (Jonah 4.9).

24   Vantuono in his edition refers to Jay Schleusener, '*Patience* lines 35–40', *Modern Philology*, 67 (1969–70), 64–6, who cites Augustine, *De Sermone Domini, Patrologia Latina*, 34.1234: 'Septem sunt ergo quae perficiunt: nam octava clarificat, et quod perfectum est demonstrat.' [Therefore there are seven (beatitudes) which make perfect: for the eighth clarifies, and demonstrates what is perfect.]

25   Opinions differ as to where the narrator's voice takes over from God's, whether at line 524 or line 528. I prefer the former view; others, e.g. Putter, *Introduction*, pp. 145–6, prefer the latter. In my opinion the homely generalisation of lines 526–7 accords better with the tone of the narrator's generalisations in the prologue than with the kind of speech given elsewhere in the poem to God, in particular the dignified generalisation of line 523. Putter argues that God generally speaks colloquially to Jonah, and that the one who is urged to be *noght so gryndel* must be Jonah: 'The narrator of *Patience* is not one to address his audience directly . . . [nor] in the singular of *god-man*' (p. 145). However the narrator elsewhere does speak directly to his audience of listeners (lines 59–60). He does not do so in the singular in *Patience*, but the singular is usual in *Cleanness* in passages of exhortation directed at the audience, e.g. *Cleanness* lines 1133–6: *Bot war the wel, if thou be waschen wyth water of schryfte* . . . As a term of address, *godman* 'good man, good sir' is I think in keeping with the generally easy language of the narrator, but a little out of keeping with the brusquer language God uses with Jonah elsewhere, including terms of address, as in *renk* (line 431), *thou renk* (line 490), *wyye* (line 492), *mon* (line 495), *heere* (line 520), all meaning 'man, sir'.

26   For this specific sense see *MED* under *pein(e*, sense 2a: 'suffering endured in penance or mortification', and the supporting quotation from *The Parson's Tale*, X.109: 'Penitence destreyneth a man to accepte benygnely every peyne that hym is enjoyned'. *MED* also notes, under *pein(e*, sense 2b, that Latin *penitentia* is translated as *peyne takinge* in the earlier version of the Wyclif Bible, *penaunce* in the later.

4

Sir Gawain and the Green Knight: the beautiful lie

The story

Sir Gawain and the Green Knight tells a good story. On New Year's Day a fearsome green-skinned knight rides into King Arthur's court, where all are feasting, and issues a challenge: will one of the assembled knights strike a blow at him with his axe, and agree to receive a return blow in a year's time? The knights are struck dumb, and it looks as though Arthur himself will have to meet the challenge. At the last moment Gawain offers himself, and strikes off the Green Knight's head. But the Green Knight picks up his head and rides out of the hall, reminding Gawain of his promise.

When the time comes, Gawain leaves the court to seek out the challenger. He interrupts his journey to accept the Christmas hospitality offered by a castle which he finds on his route. There he is entertained by the lord of the castle, the lord's beautiful wife, and a mysterious old woman. The lord suggests that they make a pact: he will go hunting, and give Gawain his days' winnings, and Gawain will stay in the castle and give him whatever he wins there in return. Gawain agrees; the pact, renewed each evening, runs for three days. While the lord is out hunting, his wife visits Gawain in his bedroom each morning, and tries to seduce him. He parries her advances, but allows her to kiss him, and on the third day he accepts also her offer of her magic girdle, which, as she explains, has the property of protecting the wearer from harm. When they meet each evening, the lord delivers the animals he has killed to Gawain, and Gawain gives him the kisses he has received. On the third evening he does not however hand over the girdle.

On New Year's Day Gawain, with the help of a guide supplied by the castle, rides out to meet the Green Knight. He finds him in a desolate place, and offers his neck to the axe. The Green Knight prepares to strike, but witholds his blow at the last moment. This process is repeated a second time. The third time he allows the axe-blade to descend, but it merely grazes Gawain's neck. Delighted at his unexpected escape, Gawain prepares to defend himself. The Green Knight however offers him words, not battle. He explains that he and the lord of the castle are one and the same; that the two feinted blows were for his faithfulness to the exchange of winnings agreement on the first two days, and that the slight wound he received with the third blow was because he failed *a lyttel* on the third day, when he did not hand over the girdle.

The Green Knight makes light of Gawain's failure, calling him the best knight in the world. But Gawain is utterly mortified. He refuses the Green Knight's invitation to return with him and be reconciled with his wife and the old woman of the castle, whom he now reveals to be the enchantress Morgan le Fay. It was Morgan, he explains, who sent him to Arthur in the first place, with the intention of testing the honour of the court. Gawain goes back to Arthur, wearing the girdle as a badge of his shame. He is inconsolable, but the king and court all welcome him back and laugh at his tale of woe. They decide to institute the wearing of green baldrics as a sign of the esteem in which they hold him, and the green baldric becomes a mark of honour for all who wear it.

The interest of the story is enhanced by careful management, so that the reader's attention is constantly engaged. The poet exploits his chosen metre (he constructs stanzas consisting of a variable number of alliterating long lines, ending with five shorter rhyming lines, the 'bob and wheel') to shape the flow of his narrative. The bob and wheel is also used to control the narrative by summarising what has gone before, and introducing the matter of the next stanza. Commonly he builds up the sense of his stanza towards a culminating statement at the end. A striking example is the stanza of description of the challenger. The most significant thing about him, his colour, is introduced only in the fourth last line *(For wonder of his hwe men hade* 'men wondered at his colour', line 147), and it is only in the last line, and the last word of the last line, that his colour is finally revealed (*And overal enker grene* 'and bright green all over', line 149). Another example is the first stanza of bedroom conversation between Gawain and the lady.

Twenty-eight lines of elegant amatory banter culminate in the last four lines of the stanza with what seems to be the lady's direct offer of her body (line 1237–40). In these two examples (and there are others) the stanza form is used to help create mini-climaxes. The narrative constantly leads the reader forward. It is governed by the overarching and forward-looking romance motif of the quest. It is set in the context of the legendary history of Britain, which links it to the forward movement of human history, and of the advancing year, which connects it with the forward movement of time. Above all, it generates suspense. King Arthur will not eat until he has heard about or seen an adventure. What will happen to allow him to begin his meal? Will Gawain keep his promises to the Green Knight and to his host? Will the Lady succeed in seducing Gawain? Will her girdle protect its wearer as she claims it will? What will happen to Gawain if the girdle is discovered in his possession? The reader is constantly intrigued and puzzled, led to read on by the desire to find out what will happen next and the desire for explanation. Who is the huge challenger, with his green skin and green horse? Why is he there and where does he come from? Later there are questions about the castle. What is it doing in so remote a place? Who are its lord and lady, and who is the strikingly ugly older lady to whom all seem to defer?

Such a story-telling technique, which holds the reader's interest by looking to the future and leaving much unexplained, or only half-explained, is unusual in medieval romances, at least in this developed form. It is more usual for romance writers of all kinds to fill in the details of who people are, what is happening, and why it is happening. Putter has contrasted the sixteenth-century retelling of the story of *Sir Gawain and the Green Knight* in the ballad-romance known as *The Grene Knight*, pointing out that in the latter the narrative tends to explain as it goes. Thus, when Gawain arrives at the castle, it explains at once that his host and the Green Knight are the same person.[1] Malory, in *Le Morte Darthur*, though well able to create suspense when he wants to, also usually explains people and events as he goes, or in advance. Chaucer at the beginning of The Knight's Tale explains fully who Theseus is, how he comes to be married to Ypolita, who Emily, Palamon, and Arcite are, why Theseus wars against Thebes, and how Palamon and Arcite come to find themselves in prison.

Notably, *Gawain* does not 'introduce' or single out Gawain in any way at the beginning. He is brought into the story unobtrusively as one name in a list of of names of courtiers seated at Arthur's high table (lines 109–13). Without the help of the modern title (the poem is untitled in the manuscript) the reader only gathers that Gawain is to be the hero of the adventure when he offers to take over the challenge from Arthur (lines 339–61). The narrative throughout gives little help to the reader in enabling him to see where it is going. Indeed it seems at times that, just as the Green Knight/Bercilak and the Lady deliberately mislead Gawain, so the story is told in such a way as to deliberately mislead the reader.[2]

Like *Pearl* and *Patience* the poem is dialogic, putting different points of view alongside each other without comment. It is up to the reader to come to his own conclusions, and to decide, if he wishes, that the author tells the story in such a way as to indicate that he favours one point of view over another. In its largest constituents and smallest details, the narrative throughout works by implication, offering not meaning but possible meaning. It prompts questions, but does not answer them. The reader is not told what attitude to take to Gawain, Arthur, the Green Knight/Bercilak, Morgan, and chivalry itself, as they are represented in the poem. Such an inexplicit narrative method is more than a means of stimulating and holding the reader's attention. It helps construct the world of chivalry as one where the surface is not necessarily a good guide to what lies beneath.

The narrator

As in *Cleanness* and *Patience*, the narrator brings himself into the narrative from time to time. But he does not act as a signpost for the reader, guiding him as to what to think, as he does in *Cleanness* and *Patience*. He is part of the poem's refusal to commit itself to clear meaning. His voice is primarily that of a storyteller, serving the story and not any message it might contain.

Towards the end of his opening account of the founding of Britain he establishes his presence by means of phrases which use the first-person pronoun: *Then in any other that I wot* 'than in any other that I know of' (line 24); *as I haf herde telle* (line 26); *I attle*

to schawe 'I intend to show' (line 27). Then he invites his audience
to listen to his story, hoping to impress them, it seems, by establishing its oral and written credentials. He maintains that it has
been told him by another, as he himself is telling it, in live performance. The polite, easy tone he establishes here, and maintains
throughout, indicates the relaxed relationship he wants with his
audience:

> If ye wyl lysten this laye bot on littel quile,
> I schal telle his astit, as I in toun herde,
>> with tonge,
>> As hit is stad and stoken
>> In stori stif and stronge,
>> With lel letteres loken,
>> In londe so has ben longe. (lines 30–6)

[If you will listen to this lay for just a little while, I shall tell it at
once, as I heard it in town (*or* court?), recited aloud, as it is set down
and fixed in bold and strong story, linked (*or* fastened?) with true letters, as it has long been in this land.]

These lines seem designed to enhance the status of the story by
making a point of its antiquity. The narrator calls it a *laye*, which
in a general sense may mean no more than a poem or story, though
the word also has the specific sense of a short poem about love and
adventure which was usually recited. *In toun* may indicate that the
poet heard it in a town or village, or else in the hall of a great
house. He promises to recite his lay to his audience just as he has
heard it himself, invoking the widespread medieval practice of
oral storytelling and the circulation of tales by oral transmission
from one performer to another, and claiming oral authenticity for
his performance. At the same time the phrase *stad and stoken*
seems more appropriate to the written record. On the face of it the
word *letteres* refers to the written letters of the alphabet, suggesting that the source of the poem was written down. If *loken* is
understood in the sense of 'linked', the whole phrase may be
taken to refer to the alliterative style of poetic composition. When
later the narrator describes Gawain setting out from Arthur's
court he refers to the source for his description as *the bok*, but in
the phrase *The bok as I herde say* 'as I heard the book say' (line
690). At the end of the poem he refers to the *Brutus bokes*, i.e. the

chronicles of Britain, as bearing witness to the fact that the events he has retold happened in Arthur's day (lines 2522–3).[3]

So the ultimate source of the story is said to be a written one, but the narrator thinks of the written source as the script for an oral performance. He hears books rather than reads them. He alludes to himself several times as a listener and makes it clear that he puts his poem together from what he has heard, not what he has read. If his immediate input is oral, so is his output. The poem has several references to an audience of listeners, but readers are never mentioned. Typically the narrator announces to his audience, envisaged as a group, what they are about to hear, as in lines 30–1, quoted above. In lines 1996–7 he appears to envisage his audience so concretely as to take into account the possibility of their becoming restless as they listen to his long recital. Clearly the narrator presents himself as part of the oral culture of story-telling, a minstrel who tells stories and hears stories from others. However, it would be rash to conclude from this that *Gawain* is intended only for oral performance. The verbal precision of the poem, including its references to the story and the audience, is of a kind that readers, rather than listeners, are best placed to appreciate. The narrator seems to want to claim for his story both the freshness of oral storytelling and the authority of the written word. The antecedents of his story as he explains them, his narrative style, his language, and the world of chivalry his narrative constructs, are alike ambiguous.

The narrator's interventions take many different forms and have a range of different imports. Sometimes they heighten the narrative in the most obvious way, as in comments of the kind *Hit were to tore for to telle of the tenthe dole* 'it would be too difficult to tell the tenth part of it', that is, of what Gawain endured during his journey to the green chapel (line 719; lines 1008–9, 2483 are similar). Some comments suggest the immediate story-telling situation, as that already noted at the end of the third fitt:

> Let hym lyye there stille,
> He has nere that he soght;
> And ye wyl a whyle be stille,
> I schal telle yow how thay wroght. (lines 1994–7)

[Let him lie there quietly, he has what he sought close at hand. If *you* will be quiet for a while, I shall tell you what they did.]

The story and the audience are cleverly linked through the idea of being quiet, at the same time as the audience's appetite is whetted for what comes next. In his longest intervention the narrator signals the importance of his explanation of the pentangle by indicating that he is prepared to break the basic rule of storytelling, 'Keep the story moving!', in order to give space to it:

> And quy the pentangel apendes to that prynce noble
> I am intent yow to telle, thof tary hyt me schulde. (lines 623–4)

> [And why the pentangle belongs to that noble prince I am intent on telling you, though it should delay me.]

He keeps the long expository passage alive by phrases which draw attention to his own involvement in it: *as I here* (line 630), *that I finde* (line 651), *I noquere fynde* (line 660).

Some comments engage the reader/audience by drawing attention to the seriousness of what is going on. Thus at the end of the first fitt and the beginning of the second the narrator seems to point a moralistic finger. He apostrophises Gawain to warn him in so many words not to shrink from the adventure he has undertaken because of the danger (lines 487–90). He then implies that Arthur is to blame for what has happened, and prefaces his description of the passing seasons with gloomy moralising which appears to be linked to disapproval of Gawain's enjoyment of the festivities (lines 495–9). In the account of the third day's wooing a summary comment at the end of the stanza both identifies an important moment in the story and alerts the reader to the moral dimension of the action (*Gret perile bitwene hem stod,/Nif Maré of hir knyght con mynne* 'great peril stood between them, unless Mary remembered her knight', lines 1768–9). Such 'serious' comments are counterbalanced by others which lighten the tone, as when the narrator sums up his descriptions of the younger and the older woman, again in the last two lines of the stanza (*More lykkerwys on to lyk/Was that scho hade on lode* ' Tastier to taste was the one she had in tow', lines 968–9).

Several interventions point to ambiguities in the story, for example the comment which draws attention to the ambiguous appearance of the Green Knight (see below, p. 173). Other comments are themselves ambiguous. A comment on Arthur (lines 86–9) seems to have an element of negative value judgement, but how much is uncertain.[4] In describing the courtiers' failure to respond to the Green Knight's demand to speak with their leader, the narrator records that they sat still in utter silence, and remarks: *I deme hit not al for doute,/Bot sum for cortaysye* 'I think not all (sat still and silent) out of fear, but some out of courtesy' (lines 246–7). This is difficult to interpret. Is the narrator seeking to mitigate the court's failure of nerve, perhaps with Arthur and Gawain particularly in mind, or is the comment to be read ironically, in which case it magnifies the failure by a mocking judgement of it? A summary comment on the lord of the castle at the end of the second fitt is also enigmatic, directing attention to the uncertainties surrounding him: *The olde lorde of that leude/ Cowthe wel halde layk alofte* 'The old lord of that household was well able to keep a game going' (lines 1124–5). Does the word *olde* imply 'experienced, wily'? Bercilak has earlier been described as *of hyghe eldee* 'of mature years' (line 844), but he does not behave as an old man would. The *layk* seems to be firstly the Christmas games that have occupied the evenings of Gawain and his hosts, and secondly the exchange of winnings game, the terms (*covenauntes*, line 1123) of which have just been agreed between Gawain and Bercilak. But line 1125 seems to have a resonance which goes beyond the immediate context. Where does the *layk* begin and end?

Thus the narrator's comments do not contribute to meaning in any consistent way. Indeed, as part of the inexplicit narrative method of the story, they problematise rather than clarify meaning. A superficially innocent comment can have a probing, questioning effect. At the same time the comments have an important rhetorical function. Spearing sees them as part of a generally deictic or demonstrative narrative style.[5] Like the fiction of orality, they make the story seem more immediate, personal, and dramatic.

History (1)

The 'history' which begins the poem would have been familiar to the readers of romances and chronicles having to do with Britain and Arthur. The first lines locate Arthur as one of a line of kings going back to the fall of Troy and the founding of Britain by Brutus, great-grandson of Aeneas. One might expect the connection with the heroes and heroic deeds of the ancient world to be used for the purpose of enhancing the status of Britain, Arthur, his knights, and their exploits.

But this history as told in *Gawain* conveys confusing messages. The fall of Troy is a famous epic event associated with great heroes, but one of the greatest of them is referred to here in the context of treachery:

> The tulk that the trammes of tresoun ther wroght
> Was tried for his tricherie, the trewest on erthe.
> Hit was Ennias the athel and his highe kynde,
> That sithen depreced provinces, and patrounes bicome
> Welneghe of al the wele in the west iles. (lines 3–7)

[The man who hatched treacherous plots there was tried for his treachery, the most certain on earth. It was the noble Aeneas and his high-born kindred, who afterwards conquered provinces and became lords of almost all the wealth in the western lands.]

Is the traitor unnamed (if so, it seems that the Trojan Antenor, who in some accounts was made primarily responsible for betraying Troy to the Greeks, is meant), or is it Aeneas himself, who in important medieval traditions was also held to be a traitor? The lines can be read either way, depending on whether line 5 is linked to the previous lines or not. To identify Aeneas as the traitor has implications for the story of Gawain, suggesting that the Arthurian world of knightly honour owes its existence ultimately to one guilty of dishonourable action.

The implication that the pedigree of Arthurian chivalry is not entirely straightforward is strengthened when the history of Britain is described as one of alternating *blysse and blunder* (lines 18–19), a mixture of the good and the bad. There is a reference to fighting men who made mischief in troubled times (lines 21–3). The narrator states that he has heard it said that Arthur was the noblest of all the kings of Britain (lines 25–6), but when he comes to the story he is about to tell he says nothing about the worth of Arthur, Gawain, or the Round Table. Instead he concentrates on its 'tale of wonder' aspect, calling it *an aunter in erde* 'a great adventure' (line 27), *a selly in sight* 'a supreme marvel' (line 28), and *an outtrage awenture of Arthures wonderes* 'a most strange adventure amongst the wonders of Arthur' (line 29).[6] The founding of Britain tradition, as used here, establishes an ambiguous historical context for the story to come, with possible implications for real-life courtly society, insofar as it was seen as modelled on the Arthurian court of chronicles and romances.[7]

Arthur and the court

The reader's first impression of Arthur's court is of a place entirely given over to high-spirited revelry. There is a full account of its fifteen-day-long Christmas and New Year festivities. Tournaments and jousting, singing and dancing, feasting, games, and gift-giving are mentioned in swift succession. The splendour of the court is brought out in the description of the high dais on which Guinevere sits, with its fine canopy and tapestries (lines 76–9), and of the New Year's day feast, accompanied by music, with its great variety of elaborate dishes served on silver (lines 116–29).

The narrative emphasises the youth, reputation, and attractiveness of the courtiers. The knights are described as the most renowned on earth (line 51), and the ladies as *the lovelokkest ladies that ever lif haden* (line 52). Arthur himself is introduced in superlative terms as young, handsome, and high-spirited (lines 53–7), and Guinevere is described as of supreme beauty (lines 81–4).

But these glowing words appear to be qualified a little when the narrator pointedly draws attention to Arthur's restlessness:

> Bot Arthure wolde not ete til al were served,
> He was so joly of his joyfnes, and sumquat childgered;
> His lif liked hym lyght, he lovied the lasse
> Auther to lenge lye or to longe sitte,
> So bisied him his yonge blod and his brayn wylde. (lines 85–9)

[But Arthur would not eat till all were served, he was so light-hearted in his youthfulness, and somewhat boyish; his life pleased him (when it was) light, the less he liked either to lie for long or sit for long, his young blood and restless brain stirred him so much.]

There seems to be a hint of narratorial criticism in the adjective *childgered*,[8] and the phrase *brayn wylde* seems to carry a suggestion of youthful irresponsibility ill befitting a king. Linked to this criticism is a reference to another reason for his refusal to eat, namely that it was his custom not to eat on any great feast day

until he had heard a tale of chivalric adventure or seen a joust
between two knights (lines 90–9). It is as though the narrator sees
him as at fault in inviting an adventure which will, as it turns out,
disrupt the festivities and severely test the chivalry of the court.
Arthur is evidently not looking for this to happen at all. What he
wants is excitement within the bounds of courtly routine (such as
a joust might provide), which will contribute to the festive spirit.
But he gets more than he bargained for. At the beginning of the
second fitt, the narrator appears to confirm his critical view of
Arthur:

> This hanselle has Arthur of aventurus on fyrst
> In yonge yer, for he yerned yelpyng to here. (lines 491–2)

> [Arthur has (received) this gift of marvels at the beginning of the
> young year, because he yearned to hear brave talk.]

The conjunction *for* leaves no room for doubt that the meaning is
that Arthur has brought the situation upon himself, and the
implication is that he has paid the price of his rashness.

The emphasis on Arthur's youthfulness and the youthfulness
of the court (*in her first age*, line 54) is striking. There are various
possible significances. In terms of traditional romance motifs
Gawain's quest, because of his youth, becomes a *rite de passage*
(although not the usual kind), in which his chivalric qualities are
put to the test. In terms of the whole Arthurian story as it developed through the middle ages, the poem is set in the time of the
court's innocence, when its chivalric values are not under strain
(as they are later, especially with the adultery of Lancelot and
Guinevere), and may therefore be displayed all the more clearly.
From the point of view of realism Gawain's seriousness, and the
powers of physical endurance which he demonstrates, as well as
Arthur's restlessness, are young men's attributes. Symbolically,
the youth of the court signals that chivalry, in its values and its
manifestations, its interest in combat and love and show (amongst
other things), is essentially a young person's ethos, with both the
virtues and defects of youth.

When the Green Knight appears Arthur, like the rest of the
court, is placed on the defensive, not knowing what to make of the
intruder or the situation. The courtiers stare at him and edge
close to him, fearful and at the same time curious (lines 237–40).
Their fear makes them fall silent (lines 241–3). After Arthur has

elicited from the Green Knight his challenge to the knights to *strike a strok for an other* (line 287), the narrative again expresses the courtiers' response, or lack of it, in terms of their silence and stillness (lines 301–2). Their continuing silence gives the Green Knight his chance to taunt them with an accusation of cowardice, and this puts Arthur himself in the position of having to defend the honour of the court.

As the situation develops, and first Arthur and then Gawain take up the challenge, the knights play no significant part, merely going along with events. When the king gets angry, so do they (lines 319–20). When Gawain puts it to them that he should be allowed to take over the challenge, they agree (lines 360–5). After the Green Knight is 'safely' decapitated they kick at his head as it rolls on the floor (line 428). As the Green Knight rides out with his headless trunk and talking head, the narrator refers again to their fear (lines 442–3), and after he has gone they react with excited talk (lines 465–6).

But Arthur himself is, the narrator states, unafraid (*rad was he never*, line 251), and he offers the Green Knight a courteous welcome (lines 252–5). He then has to listen to the Green Knight's challenge, observe his knights' failure to take it up, and listen again to the Green Knight's taunts. The taunting finally overcomes his courtesy. He speaks angrily, scorning the challenge as foolish bombast, and doing his best to defend his knights. He demands and gets the Green Knights's axe and brandishes it in practice swings (*stures hit aboute*, line 331). His activity recalls the earlier description of him as unwilling to be still, and contrasts with the Green Knight's coolness as he stands waiting for the blow (lines 332–8).

After the Green Knight has gone the courtiers talk openly about what has happened (lines 465–6). It is significant that Arthur's priority is to restore order. Arthur and Gawain fall to joking about the intruder (lines 463–4), presumably in an attempt to reassure the courtiers and no doubt themselves. Arthur offers soothing words not directly to the court, whom he politely pretends have no need of them, but to Guinevere, whom he addresses *wyth cortays speche* (line 469). However, he speaks loudly (line 468), for all to hear. He makes no mention of the event's serious consequences for Gawain, nor does he rally the court in Gawain's support, or call on his knights to meet to work out what to do. He admits the strangeness of the event, but appropriates it to the routine of Christmas entertainments, implying that it is no more than an 'interlude' (line 472), a technical term meaning a play or other kind of dramatic entertainment performed at a feast.

In this way Arthur diminishes the event's significance, reasserts his authority, and brings the court's attention back to the feast, which continues as before. The narrator points out that like everyone else he is amazed at what has happened, but, unlike them, he does not let his amazement show (line 468). He recovers his social poise. Underlying his sense of priorities is evidently a belief in the overriding importance of maintaining the highest standards of chivalric behaviour. He is aware that the shock of events has caused his own standards to slip, those of his courtiers to slip further. All have been discomfited, but this is not what concerns him most. His main problem is that they have all let their discomfiture show. What he now does is to try to restore not normality, for that is impossible after what has happened, but the appearance of normality. He hides his own discomfiture behind his courtly speech and behaviour, and succeeds in calming the court.

Ten months later, Gawain is about to set out for the Green Chapel, and Arthur holds a feast in his honour. The courtiers are distressed on his behalf, but on this occasion they keep their feelings to themselves and do not lose their composure. The narrative dwells on the contrast between their inner and outer states:

> Knyghtes ful cortays and comlych ladies
> Al for luf of that lede in longynge thay were,
> Bot never-the-lece ne the later thay nevened bot merthe;
> Mony joyles for that jentyle japes ther maden. (lines 539–42)

[Courteous knights and comely ladies were all distressed for the sake of that man, but nevertheless they talked of pleasant things only; many who were joyless on account of that noble knight made jokes there.]

Then, after the meal, the best of Arthur's knights come to give their parting advice to Gawain. They too have *care at her hert* (line 557), but again they keep it to themselves as *derne doel* 'secret sorrow' (line 558).

But the next day, as they watch Gawain riding off, they weep openly (line 684). They also talk amongst themselves, and indulge in guarded criticism of the king: what a waste of a fine knight, they say – he should have been made a duke, not sent to his death through *angardes pryde* 'overweening pride' (line 681). This *angardes pryde* must be the king's, though the precise application of the phrase is unclear. It may refer to the king's tempting fate by refusing to eat until he had seen or heard of a marvel, or to his insistence on meeting the Green Knight's challenge instead of refusing to engage with what he himself calls *foly* (line 324). They end with less guarded criticism:

> Who knew ever any kyng such counsel to take
> As knyghtes in cavelacioiuns on Crystenmas gomnes? (lines 682–3)

> [Who knew any king ever to take such counsel as knights give in arguments over Christmas games?]

Diminishing the event and their own part in it, and blaming the king for taking their own advice, is unreasonable. In criticising Arthur they give vent to their grief, frustration, and perhaps feelings of guilt at what they see as the loss of Gawain.

The whole episode demonstrates the public nature of chivalry. On the public occasion of the farewell feast, the knights submit to the discipline of the chivalric code, maintaining a calm and cheerful demeanour which, as the narrator makes clear, does not correspond at all to their true feelings. The next day, when they come together informally to see Gawain off, what they say and do confirms that their behaviour at the feast was a performance. When the best knights gather round the king to give their parting advice to Gawain (lines 550–7), their action not only shows their concern for Gawain but also implies their belief in the brotherhood of the Round Table and their king as its head. But the next day this apparently high-minded behaviour is shown up as hollow. They are seen to be not above petty private disloyalty to the ruler whom they had honoured in public.

Apart from Arthur, Gawain, and Guinevere, the knights and ladies of the court are never differentiated from each other in any significant way. They function as a single unit. There are two lists of Arthurian names (lines 109–113, 551–5), but the people so named, heroes though they may be in other romances, never do anything individually in *Gawain*. Their larger significance may be that, as a group, the knights establish a kind of average or norm of knightly conduct. They demonstrate, as Arthur does, that chivalry is a public matter, and that the poise and politeness characteristic of chivalric behaviour may be very much at odds with private thoughts and feelings. They also demonstrate, as does Arthur to a lesser extent, that the chivalric façade of poise and politeness may crack under the pressure of emotions such as fear or anger, and that chivalry by itself does not make ordinary human beings into extraordinary ones.

The Green Knight

The Green Knight is a spectacular and complex version of the challenger figure of romance literature. The narrative makes the most of his supernatural characteristics – his green skin, hair, and beard, red eyes, and green horse – and, after the axe-blow, it dwells on the weirdness of the decapitated trunk and speaking head. Some details connect him with the world of nature beyond the castle – his greenness, his great beard compared to a bush (line 182), and the holly branch which he carries. The holly is described as *grattest in grene when greves ar bare* 'greenest when the woods are bare' (line 207). This detail, in drawing attention to the fact that holly is evergreen, invites the reader to see it as a symbol of natural life. The Green Knight tells Arthur's court that he lives in a place called the green chapel, which Gawain eventually discovers to be a rugged natural feature in a wild landscape, where he finds the Green Knight perfectly at home. It seems that the Green Knight is a supernatural creature who is in touch with 'natural' forces.

There are however many details which present the Green Knight as a member of refined knightly society. He has, for instance, a fashionably slender waist (line 144), and rich and fashionable dress (lines 151–67). The ambiguity of the challenger's appearance is highlighted by the difficulty which the narrator has in working out his own view of him. His difficulty is encapsulated in the phrase which he first uses of him, *an aghlich mayster* (line 136). *Aghlych* 'fearsome', cognate with Old English *egeslic* 'terrible' (used of Grendel's head and the dragon in *Beowulf*) suggests a Grendel-like monster, while the French word *mayster* (glossed in this instance 'lord, knight' by Tolkien-Gordon-Davis) suggests a man of high culture. The narrator's difficulty is manifest again when he tries to categorise the visitor's great size:

> Half etayn in erde I hope that her were;
> Bot mon most I algate mynn hym to bene. (lines 140–1)

[I believe that he may have been half giant indeed; but at any rate I consider him to be the biggest of men.]

Etayn (used again in line 723), Old English *eoten*, unequivocally means a giant or monster in the supernatural sense. The narrator cannot make up his mind whether the Green Knight's size is supernatural or not.

The Green Knight's appearance conveys ambiguity of purpose as well as of nature. The axe which he carries in one hand appears to contradict the import of the holly branch in the other, which he explains as a sign that he comes in peace (lines 265–6). His axe is, like himself, a mixture of the outlandish and the civilised. It is huge and fearsome (lines 208–9), with an axe-head almost four feet in length (line 210), but it also has a shaft carved with elegant designs (line 216), and an elaborate tasselled *lace* or cord wound round the shaft (lines 217–20).

However puzzling the Green Knight is, it is clear that he belongs to the same aristocratic culture as Arthur and Gawain. He is not beyond the pale, like Grendel or, say, the giant of St Michael's Mount whom Arthur overcomes in Geoffrey of Monmouth's *History of the Kings of Britain* and in stories descended from that work.[9] The similarity of his dress to Gawain's, described as Gawain is about to leave for the green chapel (lines 566–622), makes the point well. Both wear quantities of gold, silk, and precious stones. There are parallels of detail too. The *capados* that Gawain wears at the beginning of his arming, trimmed on the inside with *bryght blaunner* 'white fur' (lines 572–3), recalls the Green Knight's cloak (*mantile*), which is also trimmed with *blaunner ful bryght* (lines 153–5). The decoration of Gawain's *urysoun,* with bejewelled silken embroidery depicting birds and true-love-knots (lines 608–14), is reminiscent of the bejewelled silken embroidery on the Green Knight's clothing, depicting birds and butterflies (lines 161–6). Both men have gold spurs. The Green Knight's horse is described in two passages (lines 168–78, 187–95). It too is green-skinned and huge, and it has rich trappings of the highest standard, similar to the trappings of Gawain's horse: both have *brydel, payttrure, cropore, skyrtes,* and *arsounes.* If Gawain's horse, Gryngolet, is splendid in gold on red, then the Green Knight's horse is splendid in gold on green.

When he rides into the court the terrified courtiers see him as unreal, as *fantoum and fayryye* 'illusion and magic' (line 240)[10]. But Arthur addresses him politely as *'Sir cortays knyght'* (line 276), and Gawain later asks him to tell him from which court he comes (line 400). He uses the word *knyght* of himself (line 454), and his speech reveals, despite his brusque and even contemptuous tone, full understanding of the ways of chivalry. He knows the symbolism of the holly branch, and knows that the courtiers will know. He explains that he is drawn to the court as a place where knights are brave (lines 260–1), and also courteous (line 263). He is a knight with supernatural characteristics which heighten the puzzlement and terror he inspires, not a monster dressed as a knight.

Jeffrey J. Cohen, the 'monster theorist', goes further. He sees the poem as exploring 'the lack of a firm boundary between manhood and monstrousness . . . The giant is not a force to be overcome and banished . . . but rather an interior Other, foundational rather than antithetical to chivalric identity'.[11] This view resonates with Gawain's discovery that he and Morgan are closely related (see below, p. 214). The Green Knight may be thought of as, in one way at least, a model for the court as well as a challenge to it. In failing to come to terms with the natural world to which the Green Knight is visibly allied, Arthur's knights (and especially Gawain) are in danger of becoming over-refined. Chivalric culture (so the poem implies) makes a mistake in excluding nature and the forces of nature from its equations.

Games (1)

From the moment he begins to speak the Green Knight shows himself to be less than open with the court. When he issues his challenge he says that he comes in peace and that what he wants is not a fight but a game. Twice he uses the word *gomen* 'game', first when he intimates to Arthur that he wants something from him:

> Bot if thou be so bold as alle burnes tellen,
> Thou wyl grant me godly the gomen that I ask
>   bi ryght. (lines 272–4)

[But if you are as bold as all men say, you will allow me with goodwill the game that I ask for, as a matter of right.]

His *bi ryght*, which indicates his attitude that, by the rules of
chivalric behaviour, he has the right to have his request for a game
accepted, is the first hint of an interest in the legalities of chivalry.
When Arthur, despite the challenger's disclaimer, offers him battle, he dismisses the offer, claiming that Arthur's knights are no
match for him (lines 279–82). He says again that all he asks for is
a *Crystemas gomen* (line 283).

But if by this he means something light-hearted appropriate
to the festive season, then he is being misleading. It becomes
apparent that the game which he has in mind is not the kind that
Arthur's knights and ladies have been playing, but something
more serious. He offers to give his axe to anyone prepared to strike
him with it, and states that he will take the blow unarmed and
unprotected. However, whoever takes up the challenge must agree
to take a return blow from him (lines 285–90). He then reiterates
and adds to these terms:

> If any freke be so felle to fonde that I telle,
> Lepe lyghtly me to, and lach this weppen;
> I quit-clayme hit for ever, kepe hit as his auen.
> And I schal stonde hym a strok, stif on this flet,
> Elles thou wyl dight me the dom to dele hym an other,
> > Barlay.
> > And yet gif hym respite
> > A twelmonyth and a day. (lines 291–8)

[If any man is so bold as to put to the test what I propose, let him
run quickly to me and seize this weapon; I give it up for ever, let him
keep it as his own. And I shall stand a stroke from him, firm on the
floor, provided that you will give me the right to deal him another,
claim my turn. And yet (I) give him respite for a year and a day.]

The language here keeps the idea of a game in the word *barlay*,
from children's games,[12] but there is also more use of legal language (*I quit-clayme hit for ever, A twelmonyth and a day*). Before
he allows Gawain to strike the blow the Green Knight insists on
hearing from him that he knows and accepts the terms of what he
now presents as a legal contract: *Refourme we oure forwardes er we
fyrre passe* 'Let us restate our agreement before we go further'
(line 378). When Gawain tells him his name and agrees to take the

return blow (lines 381–5), the Green Knight notes that he has cor-
rectly rehearsed the contract (*covenaunt*, line 393) and adds a further term: Gawain must promise to seek him out and stand the
return blow on the Green Knight's own ground (lines 394–7).
When Gawain agrees to do this, he mentions the need for Gawain
to keep to the agreement once more (line 409). As he rides out, he
bluntly and at length reminds Gawain yet again of his solemn
undertaking *herande thise knyghtes* 'with these knights as witnesses' (line 450), and spells out the disastrous consequences for
his honour if he does not keep his promise (line 456). By his
emphasis on their agreement as a binding contractual arrangement he does not allow Gawain to avoid taking his side of the bargain seriously. He has turned what he had offered as a Christmas
game into a matter of life and death for Gawain.

The Green Knight is also, if not misleading, at least evasive
as to who he is. He asks Gawain for his name *as I tryst may* 'so that
I may be sure of you' (line 380). Gawain promptly gives it. But
when Gawain asks him about the court he comes from and what
his name is (lines 400–1), he delays his reply. At the last moment,
as he rides out holding his head in his hand, he states that *The
knyght of the grene chapel men knowen me mony* 'many men know
me as the knight of the green chapel' (line 454). This gives little
away, and he gives no more information about himself. He does
not tell Gawain what the green chapel is or where it is, only that
he will have to find it by asking.

The whole long speech in which Gawain offers to take over
the challenge is a *tour de force* of verbal courtesy,[13] a performance
in which he demonstrates, and seems indeed to revel in, his
alertness to every nuance of verbal good manners which the situation might possibly be thought to call for. He implies in what he
says to Arthur that he is not eager for the adventure and the
chance to distinguish himself, but rather believes that to allow
Arthur to continue will not save the court from shame, as it is not
Arthur's part to accept the challenge. Like Arthur, he is evidently
motivated to act because he feels that the honour of the court
is at stake. But his manner of acting, and speaking, is very different from Arthur's. Whereas Arthur becomes agitated, Gawain
remains poised in the extreme.

As Gawain speaks, he effectively turns the problem of the
Green Knight and how to respond to him into a problem of cour-

tesy. How can he put himself in the king's place without giving offence to others or otherwise breaching the rules of courteous behaviour? His first difficulty, to which he devotes his first sentence, is how to get up from the table *wythoute vylanye* 'without (showing) discourtesy' (line 345). With elaborate politeness he asks the king to command him to join him (lines 343–4), at the same time taking care to defer to Guinevere, who is sitting next to him (line 346). In his second sentence he gives his reason for his intervention (it is not fitting for the king to take up the challenge) in such a way as to incorporate both a compliment to the king and high praise for the assembled knights (lines 348–53).

His third sentence is devoted to a statement of his own unworthiness. His language is still the language of extreme politeness: if the other knights are the best in the world, then he is the worst. Whereas before he had implied that the other knights were qualified to take up the challenge by their excellence, he now finds a way of offering his lack of worth as a good qualification:

> I am the wakkest, I wot, and of wyt feblest,
> And lest lur of my lyf, quo laytes the sothe. (lines 354–5)

> [I am the weakest, I know, and feeblest of wit, and my life would be the smallest loss, to tell the truth.]

But he now risks falling into a trap. If he is so unworthy, will this not reflect on his family, and especially the king, his uncle? He avoids the danger:

> Bot for as much as ye ar myn em, I am only to prayse;
> No bounté bot your blod I in my bodé knowe. (lines 356–7)

> [I am only to be esteemed inasmuch as you are my uncle; I know no virtue in my body except for your blood.]

In this way he turns what might have been taken as a slight into a compliment while continuing to announce his own unworthiness.

In his fourth and last sentence Gawain reiterates the point with which he began, that the challenge rightly belongs with him and not the king. Again he finds reasons which do not impugn the fitness of others. He states that the challenge should be his because it is beneath the king's dignity (line 358), and because he has asked first (line 359). The implication of this last point is that many other knights would have wanted to offer themselves, but he

has managed to get in before them. Throughout his speech he is
at pains to avoid giving the impression that he is thrusting himself forward. He ends on a note of further non-assertiveness by
putting his offer in the hands of the court, leaving them to decide
whether or not he has spoken well (lines 360–1). In making his
offer of a game the Green Knight is already playing a game with
the court, in that to begin with he conceals from them what his
proposed game is, and then holds out for as long as possible before
giving them any clue to his identity. In taking up the Green
Knight's offer, Gawain plays another game, in which his main
concern is to acquit himself honourably – the game of courtesy,
which is also a game of concealment. It is impossible to penetrate
his courteous phrases to discover what is his true attitude to the
behaviour of the Green Knight and the court. Even his striking
off of the Green Knight's head is accompanied by an ironic courtesy (lines 415–16). It is evident that he takes the ideal of courtesy
more seriously than the rest of the court. But there is a downside
to this. Despite apparently having the advantage in the situation,
he is never able to obtain any psychological leverage against the
Green Knight. He follows the Green Knight's lead, and accedes
to all his requests. His courtesy appears to hold him back. Gawain
might have taken up the challenge when it was first issued, but did
not. He puts himself forward only when matters have got to the
stage where the Green Knight has readied himself and Arthur is
preparing to strike his blow. From what he says when he begins to
speak, the reader may put this down to his concern not to give the
impression that he is pre-empting the leader's role. But in that the
silence lasts so long that the Green Knight is given the opportunity to accuse the court of cowardice and Arthur is embarrassed,
the narrative perhaps hints that it may be unwise for a knight to
be as particular about matters of courtesy as Gawain is.

The pentangle

The account of Gawain's arming is divided equally between
description of his appearance and exposition of the meaning of
his pentangle emblem. The description of his appearance is
straightforward. In two stanzas (lines 566–618) Gawain's armour
and the accoutrements of his horse are detailed piece by piece.
Everything is of the very best, and there is particular emphasis on

the fine *appearance* of the armour, its richness and brightness.
There is a strong element of ritual; each piece of armour is
brought to Gawain in turn, and then in his full armour he goes to
hear mass (ceremoniously *Offred and honoured at the heghe auter*,
line 593), after which he takes formal leave of the court. Such ceremony and such finery suggest that Gawain and the king want to
make his standing as a knight apparent to all. The climactic
moment comes when, after he has made his farewells and his
richly-dressed horse has been brought to him, Gawain puts on his
helmet. The helmet is described in more detail than the other
pieces of armour, especially the *urysoun* or horson, a band of silk
which attached the neck-armour to the helmet (lines 606–18). It
is elaborately embroidered, with motifs which include the courtly
love motifs of turtledoves and true-love-knots, the work of many
ladies at court (lines 608–14). The emphasis on the *urysoun*, its
love motifs, and the women who embroidered it, has forward-
looking significance. It is on his neck that Gawain will receive his
wound from the Green Knight, as a consequence of his love-
games with the lady of the castle.

Gawain's shield is brought to him as the last piece of his
armour:

> Then they schewed hym the schelde, that was of schyr goules,
> Wyth the pentangel depaynt of pure golde hwes.
> He braydes hit by the bauderyk, aboute the hals kestes;
> That bisemed the segge semlyly fayre. (lines 619–22)

[Then they showed him the shield, that was of bright gules (red),
with the pentangle (five-pointed star) painted on it in pure gold
colours. He takes it by the baldric, slings it round his neck; it suited
the man most becomingly.]

The lines confirm that gold and red are Gawain's heraldic colours
(*goules* is a heraldic term), and establish further the richness and
attractiveness of his appearance. At the same time the pentangle
device is slipped into the narrative. It is a surprising emblem for
a knight to have on his shield (and on his surcoat, line 637) as his
blazon. In other romances the pentangle is not so used by Gawain
or any other knight, and in history there is no record of it as a
heraldic device.

The narrator devotes almost two stanzas (lines 625–65) to
expounding the appropriateness of the pentangle as a symbol of

Gawain's chivalry. He begins by calling it a sign of *trawthe* established by Solomon (lines 625–6). In the Christian middle ages
Solomon had a mixed reputation. On the one hand he was revered
as the builder of the Temple at Jerusalem and as a fount of divine
wisdom, on whom God himself bestowed directly the gifts of
wisdom and intelligence.[14] He was thus regarded as one of the
great spiritual authorities of the Old Testament (and is appealed
to as such by the maiden in *Pearl*, line 689). But he was also
regarded more problematically, as an example of a great man led
astray by women. The fact that Gawain later includes Solomon in
his list of such (line 2417) makes it all the more possible to see an
irony in his being associated now with Gawain and his pentangle,
in that Gawain too is eventually led astray by a woman.

There was another way in which the middle ages regarded
Solomon as problematic: as a founder of occult and magic arts.
Many medieval learned works on magic claimed Solomonic origin.
The most significant of these, known as the Solomonic *Ars Notoria*[15] ('The Notory Art', or 'Art of Signs') was condemned by most
church authorities as a work of ritual magic. Five-sided figures
such as pentangles were sometimes identified or confused with the
five-pointed star of the learned Pythagorean tradition, which was
a symbol of physical and spiritual wholeness. But they were better
known in the middle ages as Solomonic magic signs than as anything else.[16] Thorndike refers to a sweeping condemnation of
Solomonic rings, seals, and signs in the *De Legibus* of William of
Auvergne, a thirteenth-century Bishop of Paris, who states that
'there is no divinity in the angles of Solomon's pentagon'.[17] Hardman notes that Ranulph Higden, in his *Speculum Curatorum*
(1340) states, more mildly than William, 'that no faith is to be put
in Solomon's ring, pentacle, or seal' (249), and she concludes that,
on the evidence, there is 'a reasonable case for assuming that the
pentangle sign could be understood by the poet's contemporaries
to have apotropaic power' (250).[18] *OED* notes (under Pentacle) that
the Pentacles of Solomon to which Henry More refers in 1664 in
the context of conjuring spirits must have the same origin as
Gawain's pentangle. According to Powell, 'The pentangle . . . is
ambivalent as a Christian symbol: it finds a context in black, as well
as white, magic.'[19] This context leads the reader to see Gawain's
pentangle as indicating his interest in magic, and to see his *trawthe*
as ambiguously related to Christian truth.

The narrator complicates the matter further when he gives the pentangle another name, *the endeles knot* (line 630, and again *the knot*, line 662), which is, as he explains, what the ordinary people call it all over England. It is not difficult to see the star figure, with its criss-crossing and interlocking lines, as a stylised version of a knot.[20] There is no firm evidence however that the word *knot* ever meant such a figure in the middle ages. It appears that the poem has gone out of its way to claim popular currency for the symbol, perhaps to make the point that Gawain may have come to know of it otherwise than through learned writings.

When the narrator goes on to give a detailed account of the significance of the pentangle for Gawain, he describes the five points as bound together in an endless figure. Contextually, there-fore, *trawthe* would seem to mean 'truth' in some such sense as 'wholeness, integrity'. The pentangle is specifically linked to Gawain's armour: *Forthy hit acordes to this knyght and to his cler armes* 'and so it befits this knight and his bright armour' (line 631). The implication is that the pentangle conveys the same mes-sage of high standards as his armour does. The reason that the pentangle is said to suit Gawain is that he is *faythful in fyve and sere fyve sythes* 'faithful in five ways and five times in each way' (line 632). So his *trawthe* is evidently to be understood as the sum total of all the ways in which he is faithful. It looks as though the explanation is going to concentrate on Gawain's moral and per-haps spiritual worth.

But in what follows it is necessary to look particularly closely at the wording. Gawain is not said to be a good knight but 'known' as a good knight (*Gawan was for gode knawen*, line 633), that is, that he had the reputation of being one. He is 'adorned' with virtues (*wyth vertues ennourned*, line 634), and a little later his virtues are said to be 'fastened' on him (*happed on*, line 655; *fetled on*, line 656). It is as though the narrator sees his virtue, like his armour, as something external to him,[21] rather than as part of his inner nature. As the passage proceeds, social virtues, rather than moral or spiritual, are indicated. Gawain is compared to refined gold which is *Voyded of uche vylany* 'purged of every impurity' (line 634). Does *vylany* in this context mean 'villainy, evil, sin', or 'ill-breeding, discourtesy', or both? Both meanings are found elsewhere in the *Gawain*-poet's usage, but the second meaning is

the primary one in Middle English. Even the bob line *in mote* 'in
the castle' (line 635) is ambiguous. The phrase may be more or
less meaningless, as it often is in other texts, or it may imply that
the virtues Gawain is adorned with are those particularly suited to
life in a castle, that is, social virtues. The wheel lines, as often,
seem to sum up the meaning of the stanza:

> Forthy the pentangel nwe
> He ber in schelde and cote,
> As tulk of tale most trwe,
> And gentylest knyght of lote. (lines 636–9)

[And so he wore the new [newly painted/worked?] pentangle on his
shield and surcoat, as a man most true to his word (*or* correct in his
speech), and a knight most noble of bearing (*or* speech).]

Gawain's *trawthe*, the reason that the pentangle is an appropriate
symbol for him, seems to be thought of here in terms primarily of
social worth. He is not said to be *most trwe* but *of tale most trwe*.
This may mean no more than that he uses refined language. It
may mean also that he keeps his word, which brings in the moral
dimension. But keeping one's word is often a matter of social as
much as moral probity. There is nothing here to indicate that
Gawain's morality is more than a social morality.

The narrator explains in detail the five times five ways in
which Gawain is faithful, to which he had alluded in line 632. He
is described as *founden fautles* in his five senses (line 640), and as
never having failed in his five fingers (line 641). These first two
sets of five presumably point to Gawain's physical prowess. The
five fingers, in particular, suggest the strength of grip needed to
hold a weapon. The next two sets of five are the five wounds of
Christ, in which Gawain is said to put all his trust, and the five
joys of the Virgin. His interest in the five wounds and the five
joys, the objects of popular devotion, suggest the simplicity of
Gawain's Christian faith. Moreover, they are introduced in such a
way as to continue the theme of his physical prowess, begun by
the first two sets of five As his body gives him physical strength,
so his faith gives him the moral strength necessary to success as a
warrior. In other words, his faith serves his military and chivalric
prowess, not vice versa. The narrator observes that, when hard-
pressed in battle, Gawain drew all his strength from thinking
about the five joys, and that, for this reason (*At this cause*, line

648) he had an image of the Virgin painted on the inside of his shield, *That quen he blusched therto his belde never payred* 'so that when he looked at it his courage never failed' (line 650). But the detail has a touch of ambiguity. Knights in romances might look to an image of Mary to give them strength and courage, but most looked to their mistresses.[22]

The fifth sct of five is a list of moral qualities: *fraunchyse, felawschyp, clannes, cortaysye*,[23] *pité* ('pity/piety'). There is no mention of *lewté* 'loyalty, faithfulness', the virtue which the Green Knight later accuses Gawain of failing in (line 2366), and which Gawain admits to forsaking (line 2381). However, *lewté* may be taken as very similar to *trawthe*, the sum total of the pentangle's meaning.[24] Though there is overlap with religious virtues, these are primarily courtly-chivalric ones, with a strong social aspect.[25] The narrator relates the five sets of five back to the pentangle figure, with the implication that not only do the five sets link up with each other, but that together they make a coherent scheme of virtue. The endlessness of the figure, further implying the interdependence of the five sets of five virtues, is reiterated at length (lines 656–61). The idea seems to be that the figure needs all of its points and all of its lines. Take anything away, and it is a pentangle no longer. Applied to Gawain, the idea is that he must maintain every aspect of his *trawthe*. To fail in any one aspect is to lose everything.

The poem has taken advantage of a significant epic/romance moment (the moment when the hero is about to begin his undertaking) to offer a formal description of Gawain which takes in his values as well as his appearance. The excellence of his armour is complemented by the idealism of his outlook, as conveyed by the commentary on the pentangle. The commentary gives clear notice that Gawain regards the demands of the code of chivalry as absolute. But it is by no means clear that his pentangle emblem is to be understood as a symbol of unqualified perfection, let alone one which unites chivalric and Christian virtue, as it is often taken to be.[26] There are many indications that his Christian belief takes second place to his chivalry. His religious or moral virtue sits uneasily with social virtue, and his religious faith sits uneasily with his belief in magic. The narrative goes on to demonstrate that the various elements of his belief system, as symbolised by the pentangle, are ultimately incompatible.

But at his farewell meal Gawain is as poised and courteous as when he offered to take over the Green Knight's challenge from Arthur. On his eight-week journey through the wilderness he is tested by difficult terrain, solitude, fierce adversaries, and bad winter weather, and he passes these tests without compromising his pentangle standards. On Christmas Eve he remembers his duty to attend a religious service on the anniversary of Christ's birth, and he prays that he may find lodging where it would be possible for him to do this. It is only when his prayer is answered by the miraculous appearance of a great castle in the middle of the wilderness that the first small signs of problems ahead begin to appear.

Nature and time

Medieval romance is usually not much interested in what goes on beyond its castles and towns, where courtly civilisation can flourish. The romance countryside tends to be seen as an alien unknown quantity. It may take the shape of a wild place or forest with few inhabitants apart from hermits and animals. Supernatural creatures and outlaws lurk there. It is for knights to pass through and encounters to take place in. Descriptions of landscapes in the romances are usually sketchy. There are only a few chivalric activities, chiefly the sport of hunting, which take place in the country.

In *Gawain* however the world beyond the castle is described in detail, particularised as carefully as any item of courtly finery. It is more than a mere backdrop to Gawain's journeys and Bercilak's hunting. An example is the description of the forest where Gawain finds Bercilak's castle:

> Highe hilles on uche a halve, and holtwodes under
> Of hore okes ful hoge a hundreth togeder.
> The hasel and the hawthorne were harled al samen,
> With roghe raged mosse rayled aywhere,
> With mony bryddes unblythe upon bare twyges,
> That pitosly ther piped for pyne of the colde. (lines 742–7)

[(There were) high hills on every side, and woods below of huge grey oaks, a hundred at a time. The hazel and the hawthorn were all tangled together, covered all over with rough shaggy moss, with many unhappy birds on bare twigs, piping there piteously for pain of the cold.]

Such descriptions are the product of observation, or observation and imagination combined, not of reading other romances. The identification of real places which Gawain passes through – North Wales, Anglesey, Wirral – encourages the reader to relate the imaginary site of Bercilak's castle and the green chapel to actual landscapes of the north of England.

For Gawain the natural world is an enemy. The landscapes he rides through are always wild and threatening to him. The green chapel is a strange rocky cave or crevice in a wild valley, so forbidding to him that he thinks it must belong to the devil (lines 2180–96). For Bercilak, who hunts in the same landscape that Gawain journeys through, nature is a friend. He is after all the Green Knight in another shape. Though he and those in his castle always treat Gawain as an honoured guest, they are not as refined in their behaviour as Arthur's court, especially Gawain. Bercilak's men acknowledge this when they talk of learning the finer points of courtesy from him (lines 915–27). Bercilak is as energetic in his speech and actions as the Green Knight is. He rises at or before the crack of dawn, hunts all day, and then revels the night away with his household and Gawain. While hunting he observes the rules, but at the same time he hunts with a dedication and exuberance (lines 1174–5) which threaten to burst the bounds of courtly decorum. The lady too seems to have her elemental side. She has the same high level of energy that her husband has. Over the three days of the exchange of winnings game Gawain sleeps late, but the lady is up early (line 1474). Then, after spending most of the morning in the bedroom with him, she plays social games with him and others for most of the afternoon, and in the evening does so again until late at night. In the bedroom she matches Gawain in courteous speech, but she sees courtesy as a means to an end, not, like Gawain, as an end in itself. It is evident that she is prepared to use any means to achieve her end, including predatory exploitation of her sexual attractiveness.

A very different view of nature is given by the passage on the passing of the seasons at the beginning of the second fitt, which is a rhetorical flourish made up of traditional seasons imagery. The need to get the story from the New Year's Day on which

Gawain beheads the Green Knight to the following All Saints'
Day, when he sets out to find the green chapel, is met by one line:
Forthi this Yol overyede, and the yere after 'and so this Yule passed
by, and the year after' (line 500). But the poem chooses to amplify
this statement by providing a version of the familiar *topos* of the
seasons,[27] in which characteristic features or activities of the different seasons are described. The result is a vivid, idealised
impression of the changing face of the English countryside in the
course of a year. The regularity of the progession of the seasons
is brought out (line 501), and the seasons are named: *Wynter* (line
504) is succeeded by *somer* (lines 510, 516), then *hervest* 'autumn'
(line 521), then *wynter* again (lines 522, 530, 533). If the passage
is there for more than its own sake, then it must be to comment in
one way or another on the story and its concerns.

The purpose of the comment is indicated most clearly at the
beginning and end of the passage. The idea of the passing year is
linked to Gawain's merrymaking:

> Gawan was glad to begynne those gomnes in halle,
> Bot thagh the ende be hevy, haf ye no wonder;
> For thagh men ben mery in mynde quen thay han mayn
> drynk,
> A yere yernes ful yerne, and yeldes never lyke;
> The forme to the fynisment foldes ful selden. (lines 495–9)

[Gawain was glad to begin those games in the hall, but do not be surprised though the end should be heavy, for though men are merry in
mind when they have strong drink, a year passes very quickly, and
never gives back the same; the beginning is very seldom like the
end.]

Here heavy *sententiae* point to the reckoning that awaits Gawain.
In their emphasis on the changes wrought by the passing of time
they echo the sentiments and language of the Book of Proverbs
and the Psalms.[28] At the other end of the seasons passage the biblical language and imagery return. The details of leaves falling
from the tree (line 526) and the green grass withering (line 527)
are emblematic of decay and are commonly used in literature, as
they are in the Bible, to express the idea of the transitory nature
of life. One line sums up the whole passage: *And thus yirnes the
yere in yisterdayes mony* 'and thus the year passes in many yester-
days' (line 529). This points to the slow, steady slipping away of

time, and recalls biblical texts on transitoriness again.[29] The same idea is conveyed in the body of the seasons passage by the manner in which nature is described as always in motion, one season merging into another as the year proceeds towards winter, the dead season.

Possibly one purpose of the passage is to draw attention to the fact that chivalry has no answer to the passing of time. In Arthurian tradition even Merlin dies, for all his magic, and in *Gawain* his disciple, Morgan, is old and decayed. The message of this image of Morgan is appropriate to time conceived of as linear, moving forward in a straight line from the beginning to the end of the world, and bringing death to all the animate creation. But the seasons passage also invokes the idea of time as cyclic. The natural year comes to an end in the winter season, but then, without pause, the whole cycle of renewal, growth, and decay begins again. Mixed in with the names of the seasons are the names of religious festivals, also used as markers of the advancing year: *Yol* (line 500), *Crystenmasse, Lentoun* (line 502), *Meghelmas* (line 532). Like the natural year the religious year is cyclic and ongoing, year after year, century after century. Christians saw both the seasons, and the church with its festivals, as ordained by God, and enduring till the end of the world.

There is a difference between the way time is indicated in the seasons passsage and in the story. In the former the time-words, whether religious or secular, all indicate seasons, imprecise periods ot time, and as such they help convey a sense of time as it manifests itself in the natural world, as a ceaseless flow. In the story most of the references indicate a particular day in the calendar. The day of the Green Knight's challenge is New Year's Day (lines 60–1). The feast in Gawain's honour, before he sets out for the green chapel, is held on All Saint's Day (line 536). Gawain reaches the castle on Christmas Eve (lines 751–2). He joins in the merrymaking on Christmas Day (lines 995–6) and the following two days, ending with St John's Day (lines 1020–2). The hunting and the wooing take place on the three days before New Year's Day, and then Gawain's second encounter with the Green Knight takes place on the second New Year's Day (line 1998). Calendar time becomes part of the legalistic arrangement in the agreement Gawain enters into with the Green Knight, who insists three times (lines 288, 383, 453) that Gawain must be ready to receive the return blow in exactly a year's time. Gawain too is acutely conscious of the importance of his being at the green chapel on New Year's Day (lines 1054–5, 1670–1).

The main actions of the story are thus precisely plotted in terms of the calendar. Human time takes over from natural time. A famous passage in Malory may help the reader to see meaning in this. The idea that the regulated life of chivalry is at odds with the rhythms of nature is given memorable expression at the beginning of the last book of *Le Morte Darthur*. Malory remarks that it is in May, the time of year when the world comes to life again and ordinary people escape from their winter fires and are happy, that the Round Table chooses to begin its long descent to destruction.[30]

Thus the account of the passing of the seasons does more than heighten the ominousness of Gawain's situation. It evokes the *ubi sunt* motif of the transience of all earthly life. When Gawain first sees the lady, in the chapel, an old and ugly woman is leading her by the hand (lines 947–8). This, together with the fact that the description of the young woman is intertwined with that of the old (lines 950–6), leads the reader to look for other possible connections between them. One implication may be that the lady shares Morgan's combination of courtly attributes and dangerous female power. But another is that Morgan, who in the traditions was herself beautiful when young, may be seen as a picture of what the young woman will become.[31] The passage, read in this way, is an example of the traditional *topos* of feminine beauty quickly fading. It thereby gives a memorable image of the tyranny of time over the glamour of courtly life.

The seasons passage may lead the reader to see a similar *ubi sunt* significance in the descriptions of the wilderness beyond the castles. The most striking aspect of these descriptions, in the medieval romance context, is that the wilderness is made to seem so solidly *there*. The fact that it exists, and will continue to exist, regardless of what men do in it or to it, is borne in upon the reader. Long after the knights' lives and chivalry itself are no more, the forest and the crags will remain, the deer will still run and the sun will still rise, as God ordains (line 1999). But the knights themselves are not alert to *ubi sunt* significances. When they do not ignore nature and time, they try to make them serve their programmes of courtly pleasure. Nature is a source of sport, prominent calendar days are occasions for entertainment, seasons are hunting and festive seasons. The natural world might have prompted the knights to reflect on the ultimate significance of their individual lives and the chivalry of which they are so proud, as the narrator's thoughts at the beginning and end of the seasons passage encourage the reader to do. But they are too preoccupied, and not given to reflection.

Religion

The speech of Arthur, Gawain, the Green Knight/Bercilak, and the Lady has numerous brief references to God, Christ, Mary, the saints, heaven and so on in conventional exclamations and formulae, making it clear that all share the same basic Christian beliefs. They make conventional religious gestures also, such as the sign of the cross. Religion and ceremony may come together, as when Arthur blesses Gawain when he takes over the Green Knight's challenge, and Gawain goes to mass dressed in his armour before he leaves Arthur's court.

The Christian faith is part of the fabric of the knights' lives, but it seems to be no more than that. In the courts of Arthur and Bercilak at Christmas and New Year, Christian observance is attended to but subordinated to the daily round of pleasure. In Arthur's court the chapel service on New Year's day, referred to in a phrase which is tucked into its sentence parenthetically (line 63), is mentioned only as preliminary to the high-spirited kissing games[32] and the feasting which follow (lines 62–71). In Bercilak's castle on Christmas Eve chaplains make their way to the chapels (line 930) and ring the bells *ryght as thay schulden* 'as was proper for them to do' (line 931). Everyone goes to the chapel for the Christmas Eve service, but there is no sign that they do so other than as a matter of custom. There is no mention of any details of the service, only that Bercilak and Gawain *seten soberly samen the servise-quyle* 'sat quietly together while the service lasted' (line 940). The Advent fast is respected insofar as Gawain is given only fish dishes to eat on Christmas Eve, but the dishes are so elaborate that the courtiers joke about it (lines 895–8), and it is plain that they are keeping the letter of the law rather than the spirit.

Morning mass is evidently performed on a daily basis in the castle, and the inhabitants attend. In proposing the exchange of winnings game the lord suggests to Gawain that he should take his ease in bed *quyle the messe-quyle* 'until the time for mass' (line 1097). On the subsequent three days the lord hears mass before he goes hunting, and on the first two days Gawain goes to mass when he gets up. In all these instances hearing mass is mentioned together with taking breakfast. It is one of the routines for beginning the day.

The indications in the account of Gawain's shield that his Christian faith is simplistic and watered down by superstition are borne out by his actions. The narrator describes him riding through the wilderness on Christmas Eve, anxious that he will miss the Christmas services. He prays to Christ and Mary for help, says his *pater and ave and crede*, cries out for his sins, and crosses himself many times, ending his prayer with the phrase *Cros Kryst me spede!* 'May Christ's cross help me!' (line 762). His recital of the three elementary prayers (the first prayers to be learned by children), his crossing himself, and his use of the phrase *Cros Kryst me spede* as he does so, mimic the practice of children at school reading from the Primer.[33] At the same time the word-order of the first phrase (*Cros Kryst* instead of the usual *Kryst Cros*) suggests an English version of the 'Letter to Charlemagne', a Latin charm (in its simplest form *Crux Christi + sit mecum* 'may Christ's cross be with me') widely used for protective purposes.[34]

In thanking Jesus and Saint Julian for their courtesy to him in answering his prayer for lodging, he asks them for one more boon, that they should bring it about that he is granted *good* lodging in the castle which has appeared (lines 773–6). His purpose in seeking lodging already seems a little less religious than it was. He takes his changed emphasis further after he has scrutinised the castle, when he decides that it would be a good and pleasant place to spend the Christmas holiday (lines 803–6). When he finally attends the Christmas Eve service in the castle there is no indication of any interest on his part in the service. He seems to be conscious mainly of the beauty of his host's wife (lines 943–6). There is nothing to indicate that Gawain does not want to be a good Christian knight, but there is much to indicate that he does not understand what this might entail. He has little deeper interest in spiritual things, and fits his faith into his programme of chivalry without difficulty.[35] If, despite this, he seems at times more serious about his faith than his fellow knights, he is also more serious than they are about everything else.

Games (2)

Like Camelot, the castle at Christmas is dedicated to the pursuit of pleasure. As head of the household, Bercilak makes sure that Gawain is kept entertained day and night, from Christmas Eve until Saint John's Day (27 December). This emphasis on merry-making may be explained in terms of the designs which Bercilak has on him. He wants to lull him into a sense of security, so that he will not be suspicious when he proposes his exchange of winnings game. He therefore wants to make the proposal and its delivery as different as possible from the challenge in Arthur's court. So he sees to it that the community of the castle appears to be an 'ordinary' community like Arthur's, engaged in 'ordinary' Christmas and New Year revelling. The Green Knight had challenged Arthur's court to play a game with him which turned out to be no game at all. Bercilak offers *his* proposal as an entirely unthreatening game, one more for Gawain to enjoy during his stay in the castle. Whereas the Green Knight was at his most terrifying in reminding Gawain to keep his promise, Bercilak is at his most genial when he does the same, sealing their bargain by calling for drinks.

Bercilak's strategy works. Gawain evidently does not make connections or see anything untoward in the behaviour of those in the castle. He has no suspicion that the friendliness he finds at every turn might hide an ulterior purpose. When he first meets Bercilak he thinks him well fitted to lead his household (lines 848–9). He does not connect (though the reader might) Bercilak's huge size, great beard, *Felle face as the fyre* 'a face fierce as fire' (lines 844–7), and boisterous manner with the Green Knight. There has been indication already that Gawain keeps to the surface of things. In addition, the comfort of the castle may have led him to lower his guard, and the warm welcome he has received may have induced him to make a special effort of courtesy, which leaves him no room to be suspicious. When those in the castle first learn that he is the famous Gawain they look forward to lessons from him in *sleghtes of thewes* 'the arts of good manners' (line 916), *the teccheles termes of talkyng noble* 'the polished phrases of noble conversation' (line 917), and *luf-talkyng* 'courteous conversation' (line 927). They call him *that fyne fader of nurture* 'that excellent master of good breeding' (line 919). In this way they put him on his mettle, in effect challenging him to justify their praise. Later, in the bedroom, the lady issues similar challenges. It would be understandable if Gawain did his best to live up to the flattering role assigned to him.

For the first three days of his stay Gawain puts himself at his host's disposal. As with the Green Knight in Arthur's court, he does not assert himself in any way. He allows his armour and clothes to be taken away from him, including his shield (line 828), and with them his pentangle emblem. He accepts his hosts' offering of new 'soft' clothes. When those who attend him in his chamber on his arrival ask him during his meal who he is and where he comes from he gives the information requested without putting any such questions to them in return. On Christmas Eve he goes to the chapel as he had always intended, but once there he is commandeered by his host (lines 936–9), and eventually by the ladies: *Thay tan hym bytwene hem, wyth talkyng hym leden / To chambre* . . . (lines 977–8). In the chamber the lord leads the way in high-spirited Christmas games, and Gawain falls in with him (line 989).

Gawain has no difficulty in maintaining this pattern until the evening of the third day of Christmas, St. John's Day. The poem explains that St John's Day is the last day of the festivities, and that the guests are due to leave the next day. At the end of St John's Day Gawain demonstrates his courtesy again when he thanks his host for his hospitality. He ends by putting himself totally at his host's command, in particularly fulsome language (lines 1039–41). But when his host responds to this by asking him to stay on, Gawain is caught, for the first but not the last time in the castle, between duty and courtesy, or between one promise and another. In this first test he sees his way clear:

> To hym answres Gawayn
> Bi non way that he myght. (lines 1044–5)

[Gawain answers him that he might by no means (stay longer).]

The free indirect discourse of line 1045 is uncharacteristically emphatic, and Gawain's subsequent explanation, which includes several exclamatory statements, betrays some agitation (lines 1050–67). He is still courteous, but there are signs that he is under strain. Then, when his host tells him that the green chapel is very close and that he will be able to go there from the castle on New Year's Day itself, he finds that he can keep both his promises after all. He thinks that his difficulties are over, and laughs in relief (line 1079). He at once agrees to stay and places himself in his host's hands (lines 1081–2). It is soon after this, with Gawain still eager to return to the role of perfect guest, that his host makes his exchange of winnings proposition, reminding Gawain of his ful-some promise to do his bidding (lines 1089–90). In the circum-stances Gawain can hardly refuse, and so agrees to the proposition before he has heard what it is.

The host and Gawain renew their exchange of winnings bar-gain twice, so that it runs for three days in all. For three days Gawain stays in bed late, as he had agreed to do. What he had nei-ther agreed to nor expected was that the lady would visit him in his bedroom each morning. He finds again that his promise to place himself in his host's hands has led him into a difficult situ-ation. For three days the lady tries to get him to make love to her, and for three days he fends her off. In the account of the third day, the narrator articulates Gawain's dilemma and his reasons for refusing:

> He cared for his cortaysye, lest crathayn he were,
> And more for his meschef, yif he schulde make synne
> And be traytor to that tolke that that telde aght. (lines 1773–5)

[He was anxious about his courtesy, lest he should be a boor, and more about his wrongdoing, if he should commit sin and be traitor to the man who owned the house.]

This statement spells out the conflict between Gawain's desire to maintain his courtesy and his still greater desire to avoid wrongdo-ing. It also indicates that he sees 'making sin', that is making love to the lady, in terms of chivalric rather than Christian morality. The moral/religious sin of adultery is in the particular circum-stances also a sin against chivalry, and Gawain does not want to betray his host. This is presented as his overriding concern, but the reader is left uncertain as to whether the betrayal he is so anxious to avoid takes the form of failure to respect his host's marriage, or failure to respect the exchange of winnings agreement, or both. In any event he finds that his pentangle virtues of *cortaysye, clannes,* and *trawthe* are in conflict with each other. Because of his devotion to *cortaysye* especially, this is a particular problem for him.

The lady turns on its head the idea of the lover using the language of *cortaysye* to offer his service to his mistress. She makes offers of love to him, and Gawain uses the language of *cortaysye* to turn the offers aside. As in his dealings with the Green Knight and the host, Gawain finds himself placed at a disadvantage by his determination to maintain his *cortaysye*. The lady is able to dictate both the matter and the manner of their exchanges, and Gawain can only deploy self-protective stratagems. His skill in the art of conversation allows him to keep the lady at bay, but never to wrest control from her. He is in retreat from the moment when, in bed and half asleep on the first morning, he hears the door stealthily open (lines 1182–3). The narrative emphasises the cautiousness of his reaction:

> A corner of the cortyn he caght up a lyttel,
> And waytes warly thiderwarde quat hit be myght. (lines
>   1185–6)

[He caught up a corner of the bedcurtain a little, and looks warily towards it (the door) to see what it might be.]

He is embarrassed when he sees the lady, and is driven to playing for time by pretending to be asleep while he assesses the situation and works out what to do next. The narrative takes the reader through the actions involved in his pretence:

> Then he wakenede and wroth and to-hir-warde torned,
> And unlouked his yye-lyddes and let as hym wondered,
> And sayned hym, as bi his sawe the saver to worthe,
>   With hande. (lines 1200–3)

[Then he awoke and stretched himself and turned towards her, and opened his eyelids and pretended to be surprised, and crossed himself with his hand, as though to make himself the safer by his prayer.]

He uses his play-acting to cover his confusion and preserve his composure. From time to time the narrator draws attention to a disparity between Gawain's manner and what he really thinks and feels, as in the account of his response to the lady's forwardness on the second evening of the exchange of winnings:

> . . . al forwondered was the wyye, and wroth with hymselven;
> Bot he nolde not for his nurture nurne hir ayaynes,
> Bot dalt with hir al in daynté . . (lines 1660–63)

[He (lit. the man) was all astonished, and angry within himself; but he would not repulse her on account of his good breeding, but dealt with her in all courtesy.]

When the lady first speaks to him in the bedroom, Gawain responds to her as he had to her husband, by following her lead. She adopts a light teasing tone, appropriate to courtly conversation between the sexes,[36] which Gawain catches precisely. The matching nature of his response is brought out by the matching pattern of the two five-line passages which convey their exchange, one conveying her mock threat to take him prisoner in his bed, and the other his mock alarm. They both use the same salutation in first lines which are of similar structure: *'God moroun, Sir Gawayn,' sayde that gay lady* (line 1208), and *'Goud moroun, gay,' quoth Gawayn the blythe* (line 1213). The last lines of the two passages also echo each other in that each line comments in similar language on the joking nature of the conversation: *Al laghande the lady lauced tho bourdes* 'All laughing the lady uttered those pleasantries' (line 1212), and *And thus he bourded ayayn with mony a blythe laghter* 'And so he joked in return with many a cheerful laugh' (line 1217). In the three lines in between, the lady in her passage claims to have taken Gawain prisoner, and Gawain in his picks up and continues her military metaphor by offering his surrender and asking for mercy. He falls at once into the reciprocal and defensive role which he maintains throughout the three days of their exchanges, in which they spar with each other in an elegant display of *the teccheles termes of talkyng noble* 'the polished phrases of noble conversation' (line 917).

When Gawain tries to move the situation forward as he wishes by asking the lady to release him, she refuses. Instead she intensifies her attack, and Gawain is forced back on the defensive. His tactic is to try to hold to the line that their encounter is social, not sexual. His responses to the lady's suggestive remarks take the sexual import out of them. At the same time he is careful to maintain a respectful attitude, thereby maintaining his courtesy. He reiterates his desire to serve her (in a social sense), and he combines self-deprecation with statements of her great worth. Their

first day's sparring leads to the first crisis, when the lady seems
suddenly to offer him her body:

> Ye ar welcum to my cors,
> Yowre awen won to wale;
> Me behoves of fyne force
> Your servaunt be, and schale. (lines 1237–40)

[You are welcome to my body, to choose your own pleasure; I must
of absolute necessity be your servant, and I shall be.]

This is clever, as the phrase of the first line has another, innocent,
meaning in Middle English: 'you are welcome to me' in the sense
of 'I welcome you'. Which meaning does the lady intend? No
doubt she is aware of the ambiguity, and uses it to set a trap for
Gawain. If he takes it that she is literally offering her body and
accepts the offer, she can respond with a shocked refusal and
explain that she only meant to welcome him to her home, thereby
leaving his courtesy in tatters. Gawain opts however for the innocent meaning. This allows him to take it that in line 1238 she is
inviting him to choose any pleasure which, as his hostess, she can
facilitate, not specifically the pleasure of making love to her. He
replies by paying her a compliment; his greatest pleasure would
be to please her, but he makes it clear that he does not mean sex-
ually:

> Bi God, I were glad and yow god thoght
> At sawe other at servyce that I sette myght
> To the plesaunce of your prys – hit were a pure joye. (lines
> 1245–7)

[By God, I would be glad if you thought it good that I might devote
myself, with words or with service, to pleasing you – it would be a
pure joy to me.]

His words seem to mean that he would count himself fortunate if
she deigned to accept even ordinary knightly service from one so
unworthy as he, and by implication they put the idea that he
might aspire to be her lover entirely out of court.

On the second day the lady asks Gawain why it is that, for all
his youth and reputation as a chivalrous knight, she has heard no
words of love from him. She asks him to 'teach' her about love
(line 1527, 1533), and states her readiness to 'learn' (line 1532).
Gawain finds a defence by taking her words 'teach' and 'learn' lit-

erally, as though he thinks that all she wants him to do is to give her an academic exposition of the arts of love. He is then able to pay her another compliment, and to retreat further, by suggesting that she is far better qualified in such matters than he is:

> Bot to take the torvayle to myself to trwluf expoun,
> And towche the temes of tyxt and tales of armes
> To yow that, I wot wel, weldes more slyght
> Of that art, bi the half, or a hundreth of seche
> As I am other ever schal, in erde ther I leve –
> Hit were a folé felefolde, my fre, by my trawthe. (lines 1540–5)

[But to take the task upon myself to expound true love, and discourse on the main themes and stories of chivalry to you who, I well know, have more skill in that art by far than a hundred such as I am or ever shall be, for as long as I live in the world – it would be a manifold folly, my noble lady, upon my word.]

As often in their encounter, the elaborateness of Gawain's language is itself a defence, buying time and blunting the edge of the lady's attack.

Kissing is a key issue over which they join battle. The lady argues on the first and second days that courtesy requires a knight to claim a kiss from any lady he converses with in private (lines 1297–1301, 1489–91). On the first day Gawain does not take up her argument but states his readiness, not to claim a kiss, but to receive one from her as a matter of duty, a compromise which he hopes will save his courtesy (lines 1302–4). At the start of the second day the lady returns to the same issue. She introduces it obliquely, accusing him of forgetting the lesson of the previous day. This gives Gawain the opportunity to stall by pretending not to know what she is talking about, which he does with his usual self-deprecation (lines 1487–8). When she presses him further he retreats into hypothesis, arguing that he would be in the wrong to offer a kiss if he were then refused. When the lady replies to this that he would be strong enough to overcome any resistance, he takes advantage of the opportunity she has now given him to seize the high moral ground:

> 'Ye, be God,' quoth Gawayn, 'good is your speche,
> Bot threte is unthryvande in thede ther I lende,
> And uche gift that is geven not with goud wylle.' (lines 1498–1500)

['Yes, by God,' said Gawain, 'your speech is good, but force is igno-
ble in the land where I live, and every gift that is not given with
goodwill.']

As usual he begins with a courteous phrase indicating that he values what she has just said, even though he is about to disagree
with it. Having thwarted once more the lady's attempts to get him
to kiss her, Gawain repeats his first day's offer of allowing her to
kiss him (lines 1501–2). He succeeds in his 'thus far and no further' defence over the three days. The lady kisses him six times in
all, and he does no more than passively allow himself to be kissed.

   Does the narrative give any indication of the lady's true feelings for Gawain? She appears at first to have fallen in love with
him, but a comment summing up the first day's wooing opens up
the possibility of pretence to the reader: *And ay the lady let lyk a
hym loved mych* 'and always the lady behaved as though she loved
him greatly' (line 1281). Another comment sums up the second
day's wooing:

> Thus hym frayned that fre and fondet hym ofte,
> For to haf wonnen hym to woghe . . . (lines 1549–50)

[So that noble lady tested him and tempted him often, in order to
have brought him to harm.]

These lines leave the reader in no doubt that the lady's loving
manner is a means to an end, and, in general terms, what that end
is. Later, when on the third day she finally leaves him, after he has
accepted the girdle, the narrator states that she does so because
she can get no more out of him (line 1871). Their encounter
points again to what the poem sees as the fundamental issue of
chivalric courtesy: that the elegant surface may not correspond to
what lies underneath. Both Gawain and the lady use courtesy not
only as a weapon (for both attack and defence), but as a means of
hiding their true intentions.

The girdle

The third day begins in the same way as the other two, with the lady
coming into Gawain's bedroom to wake him. The narrative refers
to the lady's determination to carry out her purpose (line 1734), and
for the first time in the bedroom scenes there is a description of her

appearance. She is dressed seductively (lines 1740–41). There are indications of heightened tension in Gawain. For the first time his sleep is described as troubled by thoughts of his encounter at the green chapel, now imminent (lines 1750–4). Also for the first time there is an explicit indication of the strong sexual attraction he feels for the lady. The narrative has made it obvious that he found her very attractive from the moment he first saw her, when he thought her *wener then Wenore* 'more beautiful than Guinevere' (line 945). Now her beauty fills him with desire for her:

> He sey hir so glorious and gayly atyred,
> So fautles of hir fetures and of so fyne hewes,
> Wight wallande joye warmed his hert. (lines 1760–2)

[He saw her so glorious and beautifully dressed, so faultless in her features and of such fine colouring, strong swelling joy warmed his heart.]

The narrator intervenes to warn of the danger he is in (lines 1768–9, quoted above, p. 164). But still he succeeds in keeping her at bay (lines 1777–8).

Just when it seems that the wooing has reached its usual impasse, there is a new development. Seeming to accept that Gawain will not be her lover, the lady offers him an honourable way out. She gives him the opportunity to declare that he loves another (lines 1779–87). Gawain does not make such a declaration, but takes his chance to put an end once and for all to the lady's aspirations:

> In fayth I welde right non
> Ne non wil welde the quile. (lines 1790–1)

[Truly I have none (i.e. no mistress) at all, nor will I have anyone at present.]

It appears that Gawain has won the long struggle, for the lady now gracefully accepts that Gawain will never be her lover (lines 1792–5). But she is not finished with him yet. She asks for a parting gift from him. He excuses himself again, telling her for the first time, in explaining that he has brought with him nothing suitable to give her, that he is on a mission (lines 1808–9). She presses gifts on him herself, first a gold ring and then her girdle, but he courteously refuses them, and in refusing the girdle he again gives his mission as his reason (lines 1836–8).

His attitude changes however when she explains that the girdle has the property of protecting the wearer from death. On this third day, the day before his departure for the green chapel, Gawain's responses to the lady seem to be determined by awareness of his forthcoming encounter with the Green Knight in a way they have not been before. Does the lady, who as Bercilak's wife must know what he has to face, sense his increased anxiety, and conclude that, as she cannot get him to make love to her, she will abandon the attempt and steer him towards taking the girdle? If she cannot trap him in one way, she will trap him in another. The narrative reveals Gawain's thought-processes, and in doing so clarifies the nature of the attraction the girdle has for him:

> Then kest the knyght, and hit come to his hert
> Hit were a juel for the jopardé that hym jugged were,
> When he acheved to the chapel his chek for to fech;
> Myght he haf slypped to be unslayn, the sleght were noble.
> (lines 1855–8)

[Then the knight pondered, and it came to his heart that it would be a jewel for the peril that had been decreed for him, when he came to the chapel to meet his fate; if he might escape alive, that would be an excellent trick.]

This is the decisive moment in the story, when Gawain's instinct of self-preservation takes over from that of sexual desire, nature finally defeats chivalry, and religion gives way to magic. Gawain finds that, having held out against all the lady's attempts to seduce him (and perhaps exhausted by his efforts), he cannot resist the promise of a magical escape from death, a *sleght* which will make everything right for him.[37] Sexual desire and fear of death, the elemental life-forces which his conniving hosts have activated in him, and which his chivalry has successfully resisted until now, weaken his resistance and finally break through. The wording of the quoted passage indicates that the idea of saving himself with the girdle is not strictly his but comes to him from somewhere outside himself and plants itself in his heart. Thus at the very moment he decides to take the girdle, he begins to deny to himself that he is to blame for his action. At the same time as he defends himself against himself, he defends himself against the possibility of adverse judgement from the lady. He does not reveal his thoughts to her but, as when she first entered his bedroom, he indulges in play-acting:

> Thenne he thulged with hir threpe and tholed hir to speke,
> And ho bere on hym the belt and bede hit hym swythe,
> And he granted, and ho hym gafe with a goud wylle. (lines 1859–61)

[Then he bore with her importunity and allowed her to speak, and she pressed the belt on him and offered it to him eagerly, and he consented, and she gave it to him with goodwill.]

In this way he pretends to her that his change of heart is not sudden, and that it is not necesssarily to do with her revelation of the girdle's powers. He makes his taking of the girdle into an act of courtesy towards her, a concession to her importunity.

From now on Gawain cannot honour his bargain with his host. If he needs to have the girdle with him at the green chapel then he cannot return it to Bercilak as the exchange of winnings agreement requires. The lady presses her advantage when she specifically urges him, for her sake, to *lelly layne fro hir lorde* 'loyally conceal (the girdle) from her lord' (line 1863). The phrase *lelly layne* points to the contradiction now inherent in Gawain's position. He cannot keep faith with both the lady and the lord. He pins himself down when he agrees, emphatically, to her request:

> The leude hym acordes
> That never wyye schulde hit wyt, iwysse, bot thay twayne,
> for noghte.
> He thonkked hir ofte ful swythe,
> Ful thro with hert and thoght. (lines 1863–7)

[The man agrees that no one should ever know of it, indeed, except the two of them, for any reason at all. He gave her heartfelt thanks again and again, with all his heart and mind, most earnestly.]

His transfer of loyalty from Bercilak to his wife has echoes of Criseyde's 'slyding of corage' as she leaves one lover for another in Chaucer's poem. To the lady at least he will be true. He is not to know that she has at last succeeded in her aim of bringing him *to woghe*. He does not know that, in taking what seems to be the gift of life, he is putting his life in peril.

Though Gawain maintains his persona of the exemplary knight, there are signs of the increased strain he is now under. In particular, his speech and actions become more demonstrative. The emphasis of his language as he makes his promise to the lady and thanks her is the first such sign. After the lady has left he rises, dresses, and carefully puts the girdle away in a safe place (lines 1873–5). Then, instead of simply hearing mass as he does on the previous two days when he gets up, he goes to make his confession:

> Sythen chevely to the chapel choses he the waye,
> Prevely aproched to a prest, and prayed hym there
> That he wolde lyfte his lyf and lern hym better
> How his sawle schulde be saved when he schuld seye hethen.
> There he schrof hym schyrly and schewed his mysdedes
> Of the more and the mynne, and merci beseches,
> And of absolucioun he on the segge calles;
> And he asoyled hym surely and sette hym so clene
> As domesday schulde haf ben dight on the morn. (lines 1876–84)

[Then quickly he makes his way to the chapel, approached a priest privately, and prayed him there that he would lift up his life and teach him the better how his soul should be saved when he should go hence (i.e. die). There he confessed himself fully and showed his misdeeds, the greater and the lesser, and begs for mercy, and calls on the man for absolution; and he absolved him fully and made him as clean as if doomsday had been appointed for the next day.]

Again the emphasis of the language is striking. It seems that Gawain makes a full confession, and it is stated that he receives full absolution. The fact that he goes directly from hiding the girdle to making his confession may raise in the reader's mind the question: does he confess to taking the girdle, all the time with the intention of keeping it? And this question may raise the further question: if so, is his confession valid? But because the narrative gives no detail of what he actually says to the priest these questions cannot be answered, and in any event they are effectively beside the point. What is to the point is that the passage indicates what his subsequent behaviour demonstrates, that he appears to see no incompatibility between his receiving absolution and keeping the girdle. The narrative simply follows through the stages of the confession process, and this suggests Gawain's characteristic concern with outer form. From the way his confession is presented, for him making a good confession is like performing well in other areas of life, a matter of following the rules. But the language indicates that, whatever he confesses, he confesses it in an unrestrained manner.

After making his confession he falls into his customary afternoon partying with the ladies. The courtiers, and the narrator, note that he is unprecedentedly cheerful (lines 1885–92). In the scene of the hunters' return, the narrative focus for the first time is not on Bercilak but on Gawain. Again there is emphasis on his cheerfulness. For the first time on these occasions his fine clothing is described, and its colour specified: he wears a long cloak of blue (line 1928), a colour which is particularly associated with the Virgin Mary and with the virtue of faithfulness. He breaks the established pattern for the exchange of winnings by not waiting for his host to make the first move. He steps forward to meet him in the middle of the hall (line 1932), is the first with his greeting (line 1933), and announces his intention of carrying out his part of their bargain forthwith (lines 1934–5). Whereas on the first and second evenings Gawain had given him the kisses *comlyly* 'graciously' (line 1389) and *hendely* 'courteously' (line 1639), he now does so uninhibitedly (*As saverly and sadly as he hem sette couthe* 'as feelingly and firmly as he might plant them', line 1937).

At the end of the evening, when Gawain comes to take his final leave of the household, he is profuse with his thanks. He thanks the lord both for looking after him (lines 1962–3), and for assigning a guide to him (lines 1975–6). To the ladies he offers *fele thryvande thonkkes* 'many heartfelt thanks' (line 1980). He does not forget the rest of the company, and thanks them all individually (lines 1984–6). The next morning, as he leaves the castle, he thanks his hosts again, four times, in their absence (lines 2019–20, 2045–6, 2052–9, 2067–8). His speech in lines 2052–9, uttered as he stands in the castle courtyard with Gryngolet and his guide, is particularly effusive.

On the way to the green chapel, the guide tells him of the fearsome knight who lives there, and advises him to abandon his quest quietly. He promises that he will not say anything if he does so: *I schal lelly yow layne, and lauce never tale / That ever ye fondet to fle for freke that I wyst* 'I shall faithfully keep your secret, and never breathe a word that you were ever minded to flee because of any man that I knew of' (lines 2124–5). Gawain is displeased but

still, characteristically, speaks courteously to him. But he says that
he cannot take his advice:

> 'Grant merci,' quoth Gawayn, and gruchyng he sayde:
> 'Wel worth the, wyye, that woldes my gode,
> And that lelly me layne I leve wel thou woldes.
> Bot helde thou hit never so holde, and I here passed,
> Founded for ferde for to fle, in fourme that thou telles,
> I were a knyght kowarde, I myght not be excused.
> Bot I wyl to the chapel, for chaunce that may falle,
> And talk wyth that ilk tulk the tale that me lyste,
> Worthe hit wele other wo, as the wyrde lykes
>   Hit hafe. (lines 2126–35)

['Thank you,' said Gawain, and he spoke with displeasure: 'Good
fortune befall you, sir, who have my good at heart, and I well believe
that you would loyally keep my secret. But however faithfully you
kept it, if I went away from here, minded out of fear to flee, in the
way that you describe, I would be a cowardly knight, I might not be
excused. But I will go to the chapel, whatever may happen, and
speak whatever words I wish to that same man, whether good or ill
will come of it, as fate is pleased to have it.']

This is an uncharacteristic assertion of the high knightly standards
he sets himself. The only time he had spoken in this way before
was when he feared he was caught between his promise to the
Green Knight and his promise to do his host's bidding (above, pp.
192–3), and felt his honour to be threatened. Now he feels his honour to be threatened again by his wearing of the girdle. Gawain
picks up the phrase that the guide uses when he promises not to say
anything if Gawain accepts his advice to ride away from his meeting with the Green Knight: *lelly yow layne*. The same phrase, *lelly
layne*, had been used by the lady when she asked Gawain to conceal the girdle from her husband. Gawain's use of the phrase now
points to the complex ironies in his situation. Even as he speaks his
noble words to the guide he is wearing the girdle, which he should
have handed over to Bercilak by the terms of the exchange of winnings agreement. If before he had felt in danger of being caught
between his promises to the Green Knight and to Bercilak, now
the phrase *lelly layne* must remind him that he is well and truly
caught between his promises to Bercilak and to the lady

A lengthy passage describes Gawain's putting on his armour
before he sets out for the green chapel. He now seems more inter-

ested in the 'soft' items of dress than in the armour itself. The
narrative singles out his surcoat and the lady's girdle for special
mention. They take up a whole stanza, and are differentiated from
the rest of his dress in that they are described as the *wlonkest wedes*
'richest garments'. Gawain puts them on himself without allowing the chamberlain to help him (line 2025), an indication of the
importance he attaches to them. Back in the second fitt there is a
full account of Gawain's shield and the pentangle painted on it,
including the significance of the pentangle, but no description at
all of the surcoat; merely an indication that Gawain had the pentangle *in scheld and cote* (lines 637–8). Now, though some individual pieces of his armour are mentioned (lines 2017–18), there is
no mention of his shield. On the other hand his surcoat *is*
described fully:

> Hys cote wyth the conysaunce of the clere werkes
> Ennurned upon velvet, vertuus stones
> Aboute beten and bounden, enbrauded semes,
> Ande fayre furred withinne wyth fayre pelures. (lines 2026–9)

[His surcoat with the device of bright embroidery worked on velvet,
(with) gems of special power inlaid and set round it, embroidered
seams, and beautifully furred on the inside with fine fur-skins.]

The pentangle is not now called a pentangle. Instead the narrator
uses a vague descriptive phrase. The reader may have to think
twice before concluding that *the conysaunce of the clere werkes*
must indeed be the pentangle. It registers no longer as a figure of
trawthe but as a figure of embroidery, and as only one of the surcoat's decorative features. Equally prominent in the description
are the precious stones which are set round it. These are said to be
vertuus 'of special power', with reference to the belief that some
jewels had magical powers of various kinds, especially protective
powers.[38] The gems fit in with and draw attention to the magic
aspect of the pentangle. The implication is that Gawain is now
mainly interested in the pentangle for its decorative aspect and
magic properties. Its significance for him as a symbol of *trawthe*
has faded.

The girdle is more prominent in the account of Gawain's
dressing than the surcoat. Three times as many lines are devoted
to it. Gawain's putting it on is presented as the climactic moment
of his preparations. Gawain does not expect to see his host again,

and the lady has told him that he must have the girdle closely fastened round him for its magic to work (lines 1851–2); nevertheless
his readiness to display it so openly is unexpected, given that he
had hidden it away as soon as he received it. There is nothing sur-
reptitious about the way he handles it as he puts it on, and nothing discreet about the way he wears it. It makes Gawain look more
courtly and less military than he did in the second fitt. It is introduced in two lines which send out mixed messages as to his reason for wearing it:

> Yet laft he not the lace, the ladies gifte;
> That forgat not Gawayn, for gode of hymselven. (lines
> 2030–1)

> [Yet he did not leave off the girdle, the lady's gift; Gawain did not
> forget that, for his own good.]

The idea of the girdle as the lady's gift is continued in lines
2033–4, in which it is called a *drurye* 'love-token', and Gawain is
described as putting it on in the way a knight might put on a love-
token, winding it *swetely* twice about his waist. It must cover the
belt to which his sword is attached (line 2032), and show against
that ryol red clothe that ryche was to schewe 'the splendid red cloth
of rich appearance' (line 2036), presumably the surcoat. However,
the statement that Gawain wore the girdle for his own good can
only mean for protection against the Green Knight, and there follows in lines 2037–42 a lengthy and precise narratorial statement
to the effect that Gawain wears the girdle not for its beauty but for
its protective powers. So why the emphasis on the fine appearance
of Gawain and the surcoat and girdle together (lines 2035–6)?

The explanation of Gawain's changed behaviour may lie with
his psychology. From the moment of his taking the girdle,
Gawain is aware that all is not well with him, and begins a process
of denial. He tries to conceal his anxiety by over-assertive behaviour. He covers his unease at his yielding to the lady by being
exceptionally cheerful with her in the afternoon entertainments.
His enthusiastic return of the kisses compensates for his awareness that he should have handed over the girdle too. His over-
elaborate thanks to Bercilak and his household compensates for
his recognition that to take the girdle away with him is poor return
for the hospitality he has enjoyed. He counteracts his sense that
he has been unfaithful to both his host and his patron saint by

wearing blue, the colour of faithfulness and of the Virgin. His
protest to the guide responds to his sense that he has been cowardly. His uninhibited confession may be an attempt to assert the
strength of his faith against his sense that he has betrayed it by
putting his trust in a magic talisman.[39] He continues with strong
assertions of his faith in God both when he is with his guide (lines
2138–9), and again after the guide has left him:

> To Goddes wylle I am ful bayn,
> And to hym I haf me tone. (lines 2158–9)

[I am fully obedient to God's will, and I have committed myself to
him.]

This last utterance especially seems to be for the purpose of convincing himself, for there is no one but himself to hear it.

His most spectacular act of denial is to flaunt the girdle on his
person for all to see, as a parting gift from the lady which is his by
right. The parallelism between the arming scenes in the second
and fourth fitts encourages the reader to see that in dressing for
his encounter in the green chapel he is no longer the pentangle
knight. There is no mention of his shield, a functional piece of
equipment which gave him physical protection and also gave clear
indication, through the symbolism of the pentangle painted on its
surface, of his whole military and courtly programme. In its place
(it seems) he has a woman's (as he thinks) decorative garment,
which gives him (as he thinks) magical protection. In contrast to
the shield, a symbol of masculinity, the girdle is a symbol of fem-
ininity. His acceptance of it marks the culmination of the soften-
ing process that Gawain has been subjected to during his stay in
the castle. Again in contrast to the shield and the pentangle, its
meaning is uncertain, and it focuses Gawain's uncertainty of
mind.[40] The fact that the narrator insists that Gawain took the girdle not for its beauty but for the protection it offered makes it
clear that this is its chief meaning for him, and the emphasis of
the comment implies that this meaning would have remained with
him and supported him through his ordeal. But he evidently cannot dissociate his acceptance of the girdle as a magic talisman
from his desire for the lady, and it seems he allows himself to
think that the lady also intends the girdle to be a love-token
indicative of her desire for him. The girdle is a reminder to him
of the lady herself, beautiful and with a strong sexual charge (she

unties the girdle from round her waist to give it to Gawain). In wearing it so ostentatiously he denies that he has done any wrong in taking it, either because he has broken faith with Bercilak (by not handing it over), or because he has betrayed his religion (by turning to magic to protect him), or because he has failed to live up to the standards of sexual morality (by accepting the love of another man's wife).

The catastrophe

Whether fortified by his possession of the green girdle or not, Gawain is resolute under the Green Knight's axe. He has a moment of elation when he realises that he is still alive after the Green Knight has struck his two feinted blows and the third 'real' one. Freed from both his ordeal and his promise, and with the events of the castle far from his mind, he assumes one of the classic poses of the hero knight, alert and ready to act, sword in hand. But his triumph is short-lived. The Green Knight immediately re-establishes his dominance of the situation. His action of standing back and leaning on his axe (lines 2331–2) makes Gawain's stance seem a little absurd.

His first words (*Bolde burne, on this bent be not so gryndel* 'bold knight, do not be so fierce on this (battle-)field', line 2338) are soothing. But when he begins his explanations of what has happened, he manages them as he had managed his challenge in Arthur's court, in such as way as to cause the greatest confusion. He does not state directly that he and the lord of the castle are one and the same, but leaves it to Gawain (and the reader) to work it out: *. . with ryght I the profered, / For the forwarde that we fest in the fyrst nyght* 'I offered (this first feinted blow) to you with justice, on account of the agreement that we made on the first night' (lines 2346–7). He explains the first two harmless blows as the result of Gawain's immaculate behaviour on the first two days of the exchange of winnings game, and the third blow, which nicked Gawain's neck, as the result of his failure to hand over the girdle on the third day. He reveals that he put his wife up to the whole business. He praises Gawain and makes light of his fault in keeping the girdle, but his praise carries a sting in the tail – that he knows his reason for keeping it:

> Bot her yow lakked a lyttel, sir, and lewté yow wonted;
> Bot that was for no wylyde werke, ne wowyng nauther,
> Bot for ye lufed your lyf – the lasse I yow blame. (lines
> 2366–8)

[But that was not for any underhand behaviour, or love-making either, but because you loved your life – the less I blame you.]

Gawain does not accept this invitation to go lightly on himself. His persona of a knight of the highest standards, under strain since he took the girdle, is finally shattered, and in the most humiliating way. He is overcome by shame and mortification. His first move however is not to blame himself but to attack the two vices which he thinks have undone him:

> Corsed worth cowarddyse and covetyse bothe!
> In yow is vylany and vyse that vertue disstryes. (lines 2374–5)

[A curse on both cowardice and covetousness! In you is villainy and vice that destroy virtue.]

Next he takes off the girdle, flings it at the Green Knight, and curses it too:

> Lo! ther the falssyng, foule mot hit falle!
> For care of thy knokke cowardyse me taght
> To acorde me with covetyse, my kynde to forsake
> That is larges and lewté that longes to knyghtes.
> Now am I fawty and falce, and ferde haf ben ever
> Of trecherye and untrawthe – bothe bityde sorwe
>   and care! (lines 2378–84)

[Look! So much for the false thing, bad luck to it! For fear of your blow cowardice taught me to ally myself with covetousness, (and) to forsake my true nature, which is the generosity and loyalty which belong to knights. Now I am faulty and false, and I have always been afraid of treachery and dishonour – may sorrow and care befall both of them!]

It is evident that the control that formerly characterised his speech is gone. Angry exclamations replace his polished phrases and elaborately crafted sentences. Twice he refers to *cowarddyse* and *covetyse* as bringing about his downfall, and he does so again when he returns to the court and explains to Arthur what has happened to him (line 2508). He picks on *cowarddyse* first no doubt because the Green Knight has just identified his desire to live as the reason for his failure to return the girdle. His use of the word *covetyse* perhaps suggests that he is taking a religious view of his failure, as the word is much used in Middle English for the deadly sin *avaricia*, and for Augustinian *cupiditas*, the root of all sin. But other words he uses – *cowarddyse, larges, lewté, falce, trecherye, untrawthe* – suggest chivalric rather than Christian values, and make it likely that he gives *covetyse* also chivalric import. Just as *cowarddyse* offends against the knightly virtue of courage, so *covetyse* offends against the knightly virtue of *larges*. By *cowarddyse* in this context Gawain must mean his fear of losing his life, and by *covetyse* his desiring and taking the girdle for the purpose of saving his life. He appears to see his retention of the girdle not only as a breach of faith (*lewté*) with Bercilak, but also as breaching his duty to give (*larges*), that is, in context, his duty to give the girdle back. These breaches have, he thinks, led him to lose his identity as a knight (*my kynde to forsake*). Gawain's linking of one vice to another suggests that he is constructing a kind of anti-pentangle in his mind. The Green Knight commends Gawain for his *grete trauthe* (line 2470), but Gawain sees himself revealed as a follower of anti-*trawthe*.

Just as Gawain's virtues were described in the pentangle passage as though they were external to him, so now Gawain appears to think of his vices as external entities, lying in wait for him as it were. He confesses to the Green Knight that he has behaved badly:

> I biknowe yow, knyght, here stylle,
> Al fawty is my fare;
> Letes me overtake your wylle,
> And efte I schal be ware. (lines 2385–8)

> [I humbly confess here to you, knight, my conduct is all at fault; let me know your pleasure, and henceforth I shall be on my guard.]

Confession is a ritual of the church, but this confession is of course to a fellow-knight, not a priest, nor do Gawain's words suggest the frame of mind of a Christian penitent. What he offers is a mock-confession, though the reader may conclude that he takes it more seriously than the 'true' confession he makes in the castle. He admits that his behaviour is at fault, but not that *he* is. The last line may mean either 'I shall be careful not to fail again', or 'I shall be careful not to get caught again'. He has not so far squarely laid the blame for what has happened at the door of his own weakness, and indeed he never does so. Instead he has blamed first *cowarddyse* and *covetyse*, then the girdle, and now he proceeds to blame the two women in the castle and the treachery of women in general. His wish to be remembered to the two women, which he asks the Green Knight to convey, is expressed ironically:

> And comaundes me to that cortays, your comlych fere,
> Bothe that on and that other, myn honoured ladyes,
> That thus hor knyght wyth hor kest han koyntly bigyled.
> (lines 2411–13)

> [And commend me to that courteous lady, your beautiful wife, both the one and the other, my honoured ladies, who have thus skilfully beguiled their knight with their trick.]

His use of the possessive adjective *hor* is significant. It implies his understanding that they had abused his courteous offer to be their servant by treating him as their possession and plaything, to do with as they pleased. His attitude suggests he may be aware of a ridiculous aspect to his encounters with the lady in the bedroom. Both the code of courtesy and Gawain himself, immobilised by his principles as he struggles against the lady's onslaught, are made to seem absurd. Indeed, in the literature of the war between the sexes, these scenes are among the great passages of high comedy.

In his attack on women in general Gawain refers to the many illustrious men of old – he names Adam, Solomon, Samson, and David – who came to grief through women's wiles, and draws the conclusion that in the light of such precedent it is no wonder that he should fall also: *Me think me burde be excused* 'I think I ought to be excused' (line 2428). He intimates that he sees himself not as a sinner but as a fool (line 2414), not only in the sense that he was foolish in putting himself in the hands of the two women, but also in the sense, implicit in his ironic compliment to them, that they have made a fool of him.

Gawain's list of examples is a commonplace of antifeminist pulpit rhetoric. The fact that not only has his flowery language all gone but he has now adopted a discourse formerly entirely alien to him indicates the extent to which his whole outlook has changed. The difference is confirmed by the manner in which, having rejected the Green Knight's invitation to go back to the castle, he accepts his offer of the girdle. Emphasising that it is *grene as my goune* (line 2396), the Green Knight offers it to him as an appropriate souvenir of their encounter at the green chapel (line 2399), fit for him to wear in the company of noble princes (line 2398). But Gawain replies that he will wear it to counteract rather than enhance his pride in being a knight:

> 'Bot your gordel,' quoth Gawayn, 'God yow foryelde!
> That wyl I welde wyth guod wylle, not for the wynne golde,
> Ne the saynt, ne the sylk, ne the syde pendaundes,
> For wele ne for worchyp, ne for the wlonk werkkes.
> Bot in syngne of my surfet I schal se hit ofte
> When I ride in renoun, remorde to myselven
> The faut and the fayntyse of the flesche crabbed,
> How tender hit is to entyse teches of fylthe.
> And thus quen pryde schal me pryk for prowes of armes,
> The loke to this luf-lace schal lethe my hert.' (lines 2429–38)

['But your girdle,' said Gawain, 'God reward you! I will have that with good will, not for the precious gold, nor the sash, nor the silk, nor the long pendants, (neither) for the pleasure nor the honour (of having it), nor for the beautiful workmanship. But as a sign of my fault I shall look at it often when I ride in renown, remember with remorse the fault and the frailty of the perverse flesh, how prone it is to attract spots of filth. And so when pride in my prowess in arms shall spur me on, looking at this love-lace shall humble my heart.]

When the lady had offered him the girdle, Gawain had taken it because he accepted what she had said about its protective properties. Now he is faced with an offer of the girdle again, this time from the lady's husband. Again he takes it, though this time not in the spirit in which it is offered. But does the girdle catch him out again? Would he not have been better to leave the girdle with the Green Knight, as before with the lady?

Gawain's enumeration and rejection of the girdle's beauties is a symbolic renunciation of the whole world of courtesy which was his special milieu. Knightly devotion to women and all that that implied had been the foundation of his chivalric creed and, encouraged by Bercilak, he had lived according to that creed in the castle, spending most of his time with women. But the girdle no longer has the meanings for Gawain that it had when he put it on, a thing of beauty, a love-token, and a protective talisman.

When he had first worn the girdle he did so, in part, as a sign of his capitulation to the lady and her way of doing things, an acceptance of her feminine values against those of his knightly code. Now he turns against her and sees his capitulation as the source of all his problems. He calls the girdle a *luf-lace* but will wear it, he says, not as a love-token but penitentially, a symbol not of the glory of the flesh but its weakness. As he talks of renown and fighting prowess, he implies that he sees an assertively masculine role for himself in the future. When he eventually returns to Arthur's court, he no longer wears the girdle round his waist, but military style, as a baldric (line 2486).

The word *lace* has been used before several times for the girdle, and now one of the meanings of *lace*, 'snare', often 'the snare of love' (*MED* under *las*, sense 4), latent in the earlier uses, is activated. This meaning connects with what Gawain has just said about his being ensnared by the wiles of women. Like the lady herself, and the whole world of Bercilak's castle, the girdle misleads Gawain. It must come as another shock to him, dissipating in a moment his perception of the girdle as a sign of the lady's support and interest, when the Green Knight tells him bluntly that the girdle is his, not his wife's (line 2358)[41]. For the reader, the movement from shield to girdle images Gawain's experience, as he finds that his solid rock of chivalry turns into shifting sands.

Gawain's language in this speech has a religious intensity. In the environment of the castle he had shown off his handsome body in handsome clothes. Now he sees the body as *crabbed flesch* and bodily pleasures as *teches of fylthe*, a phrase which recalls the strong language of *Cleanness*. Does this language indicate that Gawain has gone over to an attitude of religious asceticism? Or is the intensity of the language to be read as expressing his anguish over his now-exposed failure in chivalry? Does he now see the girdle as an object which has brought him to his Christian senses, or as one which will remind him forever that he is no longer able to hold his head up amongst his fellow-knights? In other words, does he see the pride he refers to in line 2437 as Christian sin or chivalric virtue, and the humble heart of line 2438 as strength or weakness? The answer comes when he returns to Camelot.

Morgan

Before he leaves the green chapel Gawain asks the Green Knight
to tell him his real name. He has yet another shock when he learns
from the Green Knight's reply that his whole adventure is down
to the machinations of Morgan.[42] The Green Knight reminds him
that Arthur's court knows Morgan well (lines 2450–1), and
reminds him too of another connection, that she is related to him
and to Arthur: *Ho is even thyn aunt, Arthures half-suster* (line
2464). He appeals to this family relationship as he tries to persuade Gawain to return to Hautdesert: *Therfore I ethe* ['urge'] *the,
hathel* ['sir'], *to com to thyn aunt* (line 2467). At the start of his
adventure Gawain is proud to be able to claim that he has Arthur's
blood flowing through his veins. Now he is reminded that he also
has Morgan's. He discovers, no doubt to his further chagrin, that
his adversaries are of the same ilk as he is, and that he has been
tricked by his old aunt. He must also be reminded, by Bercilak's
account of family history, of the moral ambiguities which surrounded his own origins and those of Arthur and Morgan.[43] This
is further news that Gawain, already reeling from what the Green
Knight has told him, does not want to hear.

Arthurian stories attest to a long-running feud between Morgan and the court, particularly between Morgan and Guinevere.
But the Green Knight does not explain why Morgan decides to
act when she does. There is no indication that she is is responding
to any particular injury done to her by the court, or that she has a
particular grievance against the court. Her action is presented
simply as something she takes it into her head to do on the spur of
the moment, as though to amuse herself. The Green Knight says
to Gawain that she is well able to bring down the proud (lines
2454–5), and her target, apart from Guinevere, is the honour of
the court, not the court itself. Her intention is evidently to show
the court up, not destroy it.

Neither Morgan, nor the Green Knight/Bercilak, nor the
Lady show any animosity towards Gawain. When the narrator
describes the Green Knight, after delivering his third blow, con-
templating the figure of Gawain, he uniquely takes the reader
inside the Green Knight's mind, revealing that his view of
Gawain accords with his soon-to-follow words of praise: *in hert
hit hym lykes* 'he is pleased in his heart' (line 2335). When the nar-

rator explains that the lady tempted Gawain in order to bring him to harm, he adds the words *what-so scho thoght elles* 'whatever she thought besides' (line 1550). Unlike the comment on the Green Knight's thoughts this phrase is enigmatic, but it suggests that the lady's private opinion of Gawain too is positive and at odds with the role assigned to her to trap him. When the Green Knight invites Gawain back to the castle he promises to reconcile him with his wife, *That was your enmy kene* (line 2406). His past tense verb implies that she is his enemy no longer, and further that she was his enemy only in role. He seems to be saying, in effect: 'Now that our game is over, and you have done so well in it, why don't you come back home with me? We want to show you how much we all like you. No hard feelings, I hope.'

It is no surprise that Gawain refuses the Green Knight's invitation. From his point of view, he is the victim of a heartless deceit[44], tricked into a situation where he has had to endure for a year what he believed to be the fate of certain death hanging over him, and it can be no comfort to him when the Green Knight reveals that his painful experience was no more than a by-product of Morgan's feud. Bercilak had put the exchange of winnings to him as a way of passing the time, and Gawain had gone along with the game in order to indulge him. But when all is explained he learns that the exchange of winnings was the real test. The lady had misled him by presenting her visits to his bedroom as an opportunist attempt on her part to take advantage of her husband's absence (lines 1533–4). Gawain had assumed she was deceiving her husband, and had indeed reminded her that she was married in one of his attempts to put her off (line 1276). Now he finds that she has been acting on her husband's instructions. That Morgan and her agents have nothing against Gawain must make their conduct all the more unacceptable in his eyes.

The end of the story brings out the pointlessness of Morgan's action in sending the Green Knight to Arthur's court, for she does not achieve her aims. The court is reinforced in its pride, in all but his own eyes Gawain passes his tests with honours, and Guinevere remains alive. Ironically, the only one who Morgan damages is her nephew, Gawain, towards whom she is not hostile.

Illusion

When the Green Knight first revealed himself to Gawain as the host of the castle in another shape, he finally established his credentials as a member of knightly society. Now he appears to say that he owes his name and position as Sir Bercilak de Hautdesert to Morgan (lines 2445–6),[45] and he becomes an even more ambiguous figure. Not only is he a shape-shifter, but there is the question of which of his two shapes is the primary one, and, following on from this, the question of whether he has any real being at all, or is simply conjured up by Morgan in a shape appropriate to her purpose of the moment. He states that Morgan made him terrifying by her magic, that is gave him the shape of the Green Knight, specifically for the purposes of testing the renown of Arthur's court and frightening Guinevere to death.

Is Arthur's court right then to see the Green Knight as a phantom? And is the world of Bercilak's castle to be understood as no more than phantasm? The Green Knight tells Gawain that it was he who had sent his wife to tempt him (lines 2361–2), but it appears from his explanations that none of those in the castle, including Bercilak and his wife, have the power to act independently of Morgan. She thus bears the responsibility for all that happens. If the poem leads the reader to think along these lines, then it raises the further possibility that the Green Knight/Bercilak, Bercilak's wife, and the castle are to be understood as having no ongoing reality but are also created by Morgan's magic for a particular purpose. The fact that the castle and its inhabitants are not in the story except when Gawain is there supports this idea. There is no 'independent' verification of the castle's existence, or of the green chapel's. In Arthur's court the Green Knight tells Gawain that many men know him as the knight of the green chapel (line 454), but all those Gawain asks on his journey say they know nothing of a green knight or a green chapel (lines 703–8). Only the guide, who belongs to the castle and is therefore not an independent witness, tells Gawain of a huge man who has lived in the *chapel grene* a long time and who kills all passers-by (lines 2098–117). Now, when Bercilak finally explains who he is, Gawain's reaction indicates that he has never heard of him or Hautdesert. From the moment Gawain sees the castle to the moment he starts on his return journey to Arthur's court he seems to be in a self-contained enclave insulated from everything around it. The only item belonging to the castle which returns with Gawain to the 'real' world is the girdle.[46]

Descriptive details support this reading of the castle as Morgan's creation. Though its individual architectural features, as first seen by Gawain, correspond to those of actual fourteenth-century castles which the poet might have known, the whole effect of the detailed description is one of unreality. It is a picture-book castle. Three times its excellence as it appears to Gawain is stated (lines 767, 793, 803), and the description is full of superlatives. The details that it shimmers and shines (line 772) and has a fantastic roofline (lines 795–801) gives it a dream-vision quality, as does the comparison with a paper cut-out (line 802). It appears very suddenly; no sooner has Gawain finished his prayer than it is there. Again, when the Green Knight finally parts from Gawain, not to return to the castle but *Whiderwarde-so-ever he wolde* 'to wherever he wished, to wherever it might be' (line 2478), the effect is as though he and the castle, having served their purpose, vanish into air.

Inside the castle everything looks as superlative as the building itself – again to an unreal degree. The narrative pays attention to the richness of materials. Gawain when he arrives is given *Ryche robes* (line 862), including a *meré mantyle* of richly embroidered brown silk (lines 878–9). The blue mantle which he wears when he welcomes Bercilak home on the third day, and which he has also presumably been given, is similarly rich (lines 1928–31). Bercilak's wife in the chapel wears kerchiefs decorated with lustrous pearls (line 954). On the third morning in the bedroom she wears a beautiful long furred robe (lines 1736–7) and an elaborate head-band with clusters of precious stones set round it (lines 1738–9). The gold ring that she offers Gawain, with its glittering stone, is described as very costly (line 1820). Though she dismisses it as *unworthi* (line 1835), her girdle is described as made of silk, embroidered round the edges (lines 1832–3), and with gold pendants (lines 2038–9). The older lady in the chapel is also richly dressed. The rich materials and workmanship of Gawain's clothes are matched by those of the furnishings in his bedroom, which are described in detail (lines 853–9). The table which is set up in the bedroom for Gawain to eat from is laid with a clean white table-cloth, an over-cloth, a salt-cellar, and silver spoons (lines 885–6).

Though it is the extensive descriptive passages which are mainly responsible for communicating the effect of richness, words indicative of brightness, beauty, fine workmanship and so on occur more or less incidentally from time to time in passages of narrative. The closed pew which the lady enters in the chapel is *cumly* (line 954), the bed Gawain lies in when the lady first visits him is *gay* (line 1179), and its coverlet is *ful clere* 'most bright, most beautiful' (line 1181). To some extent the free use of intensifying adjectives and adverbs is a general feature of alliterative style, but the cumulative effect of the reiterated emphasis on the beauty and richness of materials and workmanship creates the impression that the castle is a place of the highest courtly standards.

The manner in which Gawain is treated conveys the same message. It may be significant in this regard that there is no surprise in the castle on Gawain's arrival. Everyone is prepared to receive him. When Gawain calls from outside the gate, the gatekeeper comes immediately, and without hesitation invites him to stay as long as he likes (lines 813–14). The reader may wonder whether the gatekeeper usually issues such invitations to stray knights without first finding out more about them, or whether, perhaps, his readiness to do so comes from the fact that he has been told to expect Gawain and to make him welcome. The servants give him faultless service. The castle seems to have an endless supply of men and resources, and it runs like clockwork. On the surface the public behaviour of everybody towards Gawain is immaculate.

Four stanzas are devoted to the account of Gawain's reception. The narrative presents him as the sole focus of attention. There is a single-minded desire to honour him and accommodate his every need. When Gawain rides over the drawbridge and into the courtyard men are ready to hold his saddle while he dismounts, to take his horse to the stable, and to relieve him of his helmet, sword, and shield. Knights and squires come to meet him, and to escort him into the hall. In the hall he meets the lord of the castle, and, after they have greeted each other, the lord accompanies him to a private room and assigns a servant to him. From there he is taken by others to his splendid and immaculately prepared bedchamber. There men assist him to take off his armour and clothes, and bring him a choice of the finest courtiers' garments to put on. A richly-covered chair is prepared for him in front of the fireplace, where a charcoal fire is already burning, and a sumptuous mantle and hood are placed over his shoulders. The meals he is given are the best of their kind, whether the 'fasting meal' which Gawain takes on Christmas Eve, with its many kinds of fish, its well-seasoned soups, and cunning sauces (lines 888–93), or the meals on Christmas Day, described as consisting of exquisite dishes served in the best manner (lines 999–1000), and, like Arthur's feast, accompanied by the music of horns and pipes (lines 1016–17). As a guest, Gawain's every material need is attended to from beginning to end. His armour, returned to him on his last morning, has been kept *holdely* 'carefully' (line 2016), and cleaned for him so that it is as good as new (lines 2017–19). Gryngolet has been stabled *saverly and in a siker wyse* 'comfortably and securely' (line 2048), and is in prime condition (line 2049).

There is one activity where Gawain is not the centre of attention. Three times Bercilak goes hunting, and each hunt is a model of its kind. Each day follows the same pattern: Bercilak rises early, goes to mass, eats breakfast, sets out with his hunters and his hounds, hunts and kills his quarry, skins it and/or cuts it up, and then in the evening returns home to deliver it to Gawain. The animals all behave in archetypal fashion, testing the hunters in their characteristic ways. The first day's hunt is a deer-drive, in which the female deer, in large numbers, flee in fear. The boar on the second day is a single massive specimen, a dangerous quarry which turns to confront its adversaries, and the fox on the third day tries every trick to elude them.

The hunters' methods and skills are also exemplary, according to medieval hunting practice. The deer hunters are assisted by beaters and others, and two kinds of hounds, small *rachches* who hunt by scent and larger *grehoundes*. The deer are shot at with bow and arrow and pulled down by the large hounds. The very detailed account of the cutting up of one of the carcases, almost two stanzas long, takes the reader step by step through the procedure and shows the meticulous attention paid to the details of the operation. The boar likewise is hunted with appropriate hounds, *rachches* to track the animal, and larger *blodhoundes* to attack it at close quarters. In contrast to the deer drive, the boar hunt is full of excitement and danger, until after a long chase the lord of the

castle himself confronts and kills the animal in the middle of a
stream, showing great courage and skill in doing so (lines
1589–96).[47] The boar carcase is then cut up, with the narrative
once more paying meticulous attention to the detail of the procedure. The fox is hunted and its carcase dealt with with less
ceremony, but this is appropriate to the low status of the fox as
a quarry, and the fox hunt has no less of an archetypal quality
about it than the other two: the fox displays its full bag of tricks
as it tries to elude its pursuers. Bercilak appears to be the complete hunter as well as the perfect host. Only a magic castle,
one might suppose, could deliver such an exemplary version of
chivalric life.

The supernatural

Gawain exemplifies the fact that romances characteristically do
not set up well-defined boundary lines or oppositions between
natural and supernatural, but use the supernatural to extend reality in the direction of the marvellous, in order to heighten the
interest of the story and, usually, the courage of the hero. These
functions of the supernatural are clearly illustrated in the account
of Gawain's journey from Arthur's court, in the course of which
he has to face many dangers:

> Sumwhyle wyth wormes he werres, and with wolves als,
> Sumwhyle wyth wodwos that woned in the knarres,
> Bothe wyth bulles and beres, and bores otherquyle,
> And etaynes that hym anelede of the heghe felle. (lines 720–3)

> [At times he fights with dragons, and with wolves also, sometimes
> with trolls who lived in the crags, with both bulls and bears, and
> boars at other times, and giants who pursued him from the high fell.]

In these lines supernatural creatures vie with non-supernatural
ones, implying that there is no significant difference between
them. The 'natural' landscape is given supernatural additions
which heighten the reader's sense of the perilous nature of
Gawain's enterprise.

   Gawain also exemplifies the fact that the supernatural in the
romances is usually more than simply part of the landscape. In
Arthurian tradition Merlin the magician is almost as significant
and famous a figure as Arthur himself, and Morgan le Fay is not

far behind. In *Gawain*, Morgan and her magic arts propel the hero-knight's whole adventure. Gawain's own interest in magic, indicated by the pentangle, is confirmed when he accepts the girdle and clarified when the Green Knight reminds him that he is Morgan's nephew. Thus although initially Gawain seems to stand largely apart from the supernatural world of the Green Knight, he is in the end shown to be deeply involved in it.

In many romances the interplay of chivalry, religion and the supernatural is taken for granted, but this is not so in *Gawain*. The focus in this work is precisely on the way in which, as the poet sees it, chivalry's preference for magic over religion, or for a magic and/or a superstitious kind of religion,[48] undermines its worth as an ideal to live by. Following Augustine, the medieval church was predominantly hostile to practitioners of magic, often regarding them as demonic, even when they were not obviously so.[49] Didactic writers especially spoke out strongly against them, though intellectuals might debate particular issues. For the author of *Pearl, Cleanness,* and *Patience*, as for most religious writers of his time, religion must be clearly distinguished from magic and superstition.

The return

By the time Gawain returns to Camelot the shock of the Green Knight's revelations is over, and he speaks more deliberately about what he feels and thinks. In both *Pearl* and *Gawain* the protagonist, in responding to the crisis-event which concludes his 'quest', goes through the two stages of immediate reaction and considered judgement (for *Pearl*, see above, pp. 73–4). Gawain's words reveal that though time may have healed his neck-wound until only a nick in the skin is visible, it has only intensified his sense of shame. He is described as riding into the court wearing the girdle as a symbol of his fault (line 2488). There is no mention of the pentangle. The narrative presents the story he tells the court as another confession (*Biknowes* 'confesses', line 2495). He saves the girdle to the last and dwells on the nick in his neck, going red in the face with shame when he shows it to the court, groaning as he speaks. His confession becomes still more anguished when he addresses himself specifically to the king:

> 'Lo! Lorde,' quoth the leude, and the lace hondeled,
> 'This is the bende of this blame I bere on my nek;
> This is the lathe and the losse that I laght have
> Of couardise and covetyse that I haf caght thare.
> This is the token of untrawthe that I am tan inne,
> And I mot nedes hit were wyle I may last.
> For mon may hyden his harme bot unhap ne may hit,
> For ther hit ones is tachched twynne wil hit never.'
>   (lines 2505–12)

['Look! Lord,' said the knight, and handled the lace, 'this is the sign of this reproof which I bear in my neck; this is the injury and the loss that I have sustained from the cowardice and covetousness which I caught there. This is the symbol of the dishonour which I am taken in, and I must needs wear it as long as I live. For a man may hide his guilt but may not undo it, for once it is attached it will never be parted.']

But this confession is unlike his two earlier confessions in that he does not ask his confessor to help him. He is full of humiliation, but not humility. *Bend* is the technical term in heraldry for a diagonal band in the field of a coat of arms. His own *bend*, the girdle, goes over his right shoulder and is tied under his left arm (line 2487). The fact that he sees the girdle as a heraldic sign, replacing the pentangle, confirms his continuing loyalty to the knightly ideal (minus courtesy). When he confessed to the Green Knight, he had envisaged a future for himself in which he tried to be more careful in his conduct. Later he had imagined himself performing feats of arms. But now he indicates, especially in the last two lines (the last words he speaks in the poem), that he is overcome by the realisation that once a knight is dishonoured there is no way back. He sees himself condemned to a life of perpetual shame. And, whereas before his confrontation with the Green Knight he was at pains to conceal his breach of trust, he now insists on parading it. As is the way of idealists he has moved from one extreme position to another.

With his sense that he is irredeemably lost, Gawain might be better talking to a priest, not to Arthur. Arthur cannot help him, and in any event, though he tries to comfort him, he does not take his tale of woe seriously. At the end of the story the court is as it was at the beginning, a cheerful company of knights and ladies. They show no understanding of his hurt. They laugh at his self-recrimination and decide to institute the wearing of green baldrics in his honour, though he has told them that he is going to continue to wear the girdle as a badge of shame.

The Green Knight's response to Gawain's mock-confession earlier, though like the court's it also failed to comprehend his anxieties, at least attended to his sense of having done wrong. The Green Knight acknowledges that Gawain has been at fault (*ye lakked a lyttel*), but sees the fault as entirely understandable (*ye lufed your lyf – the lasse I yow blame*), and concludes that Gawain is not a failure but, on the contrary, a knight without peer. This may seem to the reader to be a reasonable judgement, but Gawain cannot accept it. The root of his difficulty is, as always, the seriousness with which he takes his chivalric duty. Whatever others may tell him, he stands condemned in his own eyes.

History (2)

The end of the poem returns to the idea of adventure and story, and to the ambiguous historical context of the beginning. There is the same concern as at the beginning with establishing the story's faultless literary credentials; so it is claimed that the story of how the green baldric came to be honoured is found in *the best boke of romaunce* (whatever that book may be), and that Gawain's adventure is authenticated by the chronicles (lines 2521–3). Arthur, Brutus, and the siege of Troy are mentioned again, and the story of Gawain is said to be only one episode in a long sequence of similarly adventurous episodes (lines 2527–8). The fact that the last long line is almost identical to the first plays its part in returning the reader to the beginning of the poem. The implication of this going back to the beginning may be that, like the year in the seasons passage at the start of Fitt 2, Gawain's adventure both comes to an end and goes round again, and there is nothing new under the sun: a knight's individual story, however exceptional it may seem at the time, is neither exceptional nor significant in the long perspective of British history, in which (so the reference to Brutus may remind the reader) the individual event is only one small element in a meaningless pattern of *blysse and blunder*. So the historical ending is as ambiguous as the historical beginning: on the surface, the tone of the passage is entirely positive, but there is an undercurrent of negative implication which has a diminishing effect.

In its last two lines, the poem makes an explicit Christian reference which may be designed to lift the reader out of the story's secular cycle. The poet uses a conventional formula of ending which is found in one variation or another in other medieval romances, chronicles, and religious pieces:

> Now that bere the croun of thorne,
> He bryng uus to his blysse. (liines 2529–30)

[Now may he who wore the crown of thorns bring us to his bliss.]

The formula signals the end of the poem, but these lines may carry more meaning than that. The reference to Christ, conventional as it is,[50] may lead the reader to compare Arthur to a spiritual king who is not bound to 'fallen' history, whose crown of thorns is a symbol not of earthly honour but lack of such honour, and in whose heavenly realm *blysse* exists without *blunder*. Read in this way the formula reinforces the possibility that, like the other three poems in the manuscript, *Gawain* encourages the reader to bring heavenly perspectives to bear on earthly ones.

Conclusion

In one of its aspects *Gawain* is a record of, and tribute to, the beauties and pleasures of chivalric life. The lavishly detailed descriptions of idealised examples of the material culture and characteristic activities of high chivalry testify to the poet's positive interest. They communicate the knights' pride and confidence in their position in the world, and the energy which this pride and confidence generates. Without any hint of ironic undercutting, these descriptions present the chivalric world as compellingly attractive. Indeed, the admiration of the poet shines forth. He has evident admiration, too, for the aspirational nature of chivalric values, the ideals symbolised by the 'five fives' of Gawain's pentangle. But, from the religious perspective of his other three poems, he also sees chivalry as not taking religion seriously enough. He does not accept the view, implicit in the crusading ideal, that chivalry and religion are as one, that there is 'no need to try to prise apart the goals of worldly honour and of service acceptable to God',[51] a view which no doubt appealed to many in his courtly audience. Prising them apart is precisely what he does. *Cleanness* holds that an attractive surface is theologically a minus quantity unless it reflects what lies beneath. In *Gawain*, chivalry is presented throughout as offering an attractive front to the world with nothing solid underpinning it. In life as well as in literature, chivalry emphasises the importance of polite and honourable behaviour and speech, lavish display, and other external manifestations. Because it attaches so high a value to appearance,[52] it easily leads to an acceptance of life as a matter of performance and to deceitful practices.[53] The poem demonstrates this through its story, thereby showing chivalry to be flawed as a moral and spiritual system and, if taken seriously enough, unworkable in practical terms as well. But the poem also demonstrates that doubts about it as a creed to live by need not invalidate or even temper admiration for its beauties. If ultimately the poem shares the religious and moral outlook of its companion poems, and of later medieval alliterative poems generally, nevertheless the attractions of chivalry are not displayed so fully merely to be castigated and condemned. There is nothing crude or sour about the poet's morality. He may expose chivalry as a beautiful lie, but he admires its beauty and its ideal of honour even as his story shows how potentially dangerous they are.

The confessions in the last part of the poem point to a fundamental difference between the secular chivalric and the Christian ethical systems. Chivalry asks its practitioners for a quasi-religious level of devotion to it, a demand not usually met, but which the fictional Gawain does meet. It was an ideal which had potent appeal for the high culture of the later middle ages. But it can hardly take the place of religion in people's lives, for it has no theology, no metaphysics, and no concept of salvation. It deals in honour and dishonour, not sin, and these are a matter of men's perception, not God's. Accordingly, if a knight's unchivalric act does not come to light, his honour is safe. But the problem with this, which Gawain fastens on at the end of the story, is that once the unchivalric act becomes public knowledge the knight loses his reputation and, in theory at least, is dishonoured forever.[54] In the Christian faith, sin is ultimately a matter between the sinner and God, and God, through Christ and his church, offers mercy. *Pearl* and, especially, *Patience* teach that God's mercy will be activated if the sinner makes proper confession. But chivalry does not make such allowance for human weakness, and has no equivalent to the

Christian sacrament of penance. The knight may live by the sword and die by the sword, but, according to the chivalric ideal, he also lives and dies by his public reputation. This concern for reputation underlies chivalry's obsession with surfaces at the expense of attention to the sub-surface realities.

The 'shame culture' of chivalry helps to explain both Gawain's behaviour with the girdle and his reaction to the Green Knight's revelations. He puts his reputation for *trawthe* ahead of *trawthe* itself. Virtue and vice are given meaning for him by being visible to others. He keeps the girdle in the knowledge that he is breaking his promise to Bercilak, but he thinks that neither Bercilak nor anyone else will ever find out, and tries to behave as though nothing has happened. He may be uneasy about his failure, but he is not appalled by it until the Green Knight reveals that he knows what he has done. Only then is he overcome by shame. When he returns to Arthur's court he is described as wearing the girdle not simply as a sign of his failure, but as a sign of his being *caught out* in his failure (*In tokenyng he was tane in tech of a faute* 'as a sign that he had been caught [lit. 'taken'] in the disgrace of a fault', line 2488). When he himself speaks, he expresses the same idea and uses the same verb (line 2509, quoted above).[55]

The English *locus classicus* of the operation of the chivalric 'shame culture' is Lancelot's adultery with Guinevere in Malory, which is of little moment to Arthur and his court until Aggravayne and Mordred make a public issue of it. In some ways what happens to Gawain is a microcosmic version of what happens to Malory's Round Table. The process acted out within a society in the one instance is much the same as that acted out within an individual in the other. In Malory the adultery is like a time-bomb ticking away beneath the public surface of the Round Table, which, despite tensions of various kinds, maintains its surface integrity as it goes about its business. It has an idea of what is going on, but prefers to turn a blind eye. The bomb explodes when the adultery is proclaimed, and, as Arthur and the knights see at once, the Round Table is dishonoured and will not be able to survive its collective disgrace. From that moment its public surface collapses and it falls to warring with itself. Gawain plants his time-bomb on himself when he takes the girdle. He tries to maintain his chivalric persona and carry on as though nothing had happened, but the bomb explodes with the Green Knight's revelations.

Do Gawain's problems lie with chivalry, or with his attitude to chivalry? What the poem seems to see as fundamentally wrong with chivalry is that its interest in more superficial values such as courtesy, good reputation, and impressive display undermines its interest in the more solid values it espouses, especially loyalty, reliability, and courage. The story demonstrates this at length, principally through the way in which Gawain's activities in the bedroom impinge on the beheading game through his taking and wearing the magic girdle, which puts a question mark over his bravery and other virtues when he comes to face the Green Knight. But it is Gawain's attitude to chivalry, and specifically to his lapse of chivalry, which condemns him, in that he pretends for as long as he can that there has been no lapse, and then, when he is no longer able to pretend, he refuses to take full responsibility for it. By blaming *cowarddyse and covetyse*, the girdle, the young and the old lady, women in general, and finally the weakness of the flesh, he tries to keep intact his inner core, his sense of himself, or so it seems. But does he have an inner self? There is no mention of more inward moral, emotional, and spiritual qualities in the explanation of the pentangle, and little evidence in the story that inner qualities matter much to him. There is no sign of any emotional bond with his king, or with his fellow-knights. The Green Knight warms to him (line 2335), his wife and Morgan want to see him, and the knights of Camelot weep for him and are glad for him; but can one imagine Gawain responding to them in the same way? He is physically drawn to the lady, but there is no statement or sign that this physical attraction is accompanied by feeling for her. There is mention of a love-token, and love-talk, but for Gawain the word *luf* never seems unambiguously to have an emotional sense, and it is usually clear that it does not. The narrator sees his chivalric virtues as extrinsic to him, and Gawain sees his vices in the same way. His courage is more physical than moral. His formulaic religious language is perhaps a sign not only of the immaturity of his faith, but that there is little to his faith apart from language. If he possesses any cognitive or 'higher' faculties, then they seem much under-used.

Unlike the other knights and ladies Gawain does not display any zest for the Christmas festivities at Camelot and Hautdesert, except on his last day at Hautdesert, when, as discussed above

(p. 203), his behaviour is exceptional. He seems to have a fear of death but not a love of life, usually acting out of a sense of obligation rather than from more positive motives. All at Camelot are cut off by their chivalry from the energies of the natural world to some extent (as those in Bercilak's castle are not), but none so completely as Gawain. It is true that when Gawain succeeds in remaining utterly unflinching while he waits for the Green Knight's second blow a simile links him for the first time to something in nature: he remains *stylle as the ston other a stubbe auther / That ratheled is in roché grounde with rotes a hundreth* 'still as stone, or else a tree-stump that is entwined in rocky ground with a hundred roots'. It is an impressive simile, but one cannot take it to imply that Gawain, in his moment of crisis, turns for strength not to the code but to the life-force within him, for both the stone and the tree-stump are dead.

In trying to become the perfect practitioner of chivalry, Gawain has paid so much attention to outward form that he has become not much more than a shell himself, with little of the warm blood of humanity left in him. The other knights are not like this, or not so much like this, because they do not allow the demands of chivalry to drive them so hard. They temper their chivalry with practicality and common sense. This is where Malory and the *Gawain*-poet part company. Both see the unnaturalness of chivalry as its most threatening aspect, but whereas Malory sees this flaw in social terms, dividing the knights and engulfing them all, willy-nilly, in ruin, the *Gawain*-poet shows it to be ruinous only for Gawain. His story makes the point, implicitly, that a knight must not allow chivalry, with its limitations, to become a rival to, or substitute for, religion. Gawain has allowed it to take over his life, and in doing so he has turned his potentially positive qualities (such as his seriousness and sense of commitment) into damaging negatives.

So at the end of the story Gawain is in an impasse. In Christian terms he is mired in pride, refusing to take responsibility for his own fall, unable to accept that like everyone else he is imperfect, and dangerously close to despair, the unredeemable sin. Had he accepted the Christian view of human fallibility he would not have been so hard on himself. Had he had a deeper faith in the Christian afterlife, he would have been better able to resist the lady's offer of the girdle. Had he been more willing to accept

'Christian' forgiveness from the Green Knight, he would not have felt the need to wear the girdle as a perpetual reminder of his disgrace. The meaning of the girdle in Arthur's court is that, as a symbol of both honour and dishonour, it points to the very different outcomes of two different approaches to chivalry. The king and the court, who see chivalry more as a source of the good life than as anything else, adopt the girdle in a spirit of celebration; if in doing so they are insensitive to Gawain's hurt, that is part and parcel of their pragmatism. The poem sees the knights' way of life as flawed, whichever aspect of it one looks at. The games and the glamour end in Morgan, and the code of honour leaves Gawain, the pearl of knights, a broken man.

Postscript

In the light of the poem's concerns, its choice of Gawain as hero, rather than any other famous Arthurian knight, is far from arbitrary. Not only was Gawain by tradition *the* knight of courtesy, he is also found characterised in some earlier romances as a knight who is unable to see beyond chivalry to the possible transformation of chivalric values into spiritual ones. By far the most attractive 'Christian' story for the romance writers was the often-told story of the search for the magical Holy Grail, sometimes identified with the dish from which Christ ate at the Last Supper. No doubt the particular attraction of the Grail for Arthurian authors was that it pretended to give romance magic an authentic religious foundation, and it inspired stories with a strong spiritual dimension. In these stories chivalry was spiritualised, so that a knight's performance in the Grail quest was taken as an index of his chivalric as well as spiritual attainment.

For his conception of Gawain, the *Gawain*-poet appears to draw particularly on a tradition represented chiefly by the Vulgate *Queste del Saint Graal* 'The Quest of the Holy Grail' (*c.*1225), from the French Vulgate cycle of romances. This cycle became the authoritative Arthurian text, drawn on by many authors from all over Europe, until the end of the middle ages.[56] In this work Gawain is a kind of summation of worldly chivalry which is set alongside the superior spiritual chivalry of Perceval and Galahad. For Perceval and Galahad, but not Gawain, chivalry and magic become fully interpenetrated by spiritual values, and both of

them, but not Gawain, achieve the Grail.[57] This intertextual possibility supports the idea that the English poem, though it has
nothing to do with the Grail, has a hidden dialectic which points
to how potentially dangerous the code of chivalry is when it is
allowed to take precedence over religious faith.

Notes

1   Putter, *Introduction*, p. 74.
2   *Ibid.*, pp. 75–82.
3   Indicating an oral delivery and/or claiming a written source is not unusual in
    Middle English romances.
4   See below, p. 167, and note 8.
5   Spearing, 'Poetic identity', especially, pp. 38–9, 44–5.
6   Though *outtrage* here is usually glossed simply 'exceedingly strange,
    extraordinary', the Middle English word usually has the derogatory conno-
    tations of modern *outrageous*.
7   The link between the English court in the fourteenth century and King
    Arthur is clearest in Edward III's institution of the Order of the Garter,
    inspired by the Arthurian Round Table; see Maurice Keen, *Chivalry* (New
    Haven and London: Yale University Press, 1984), p. 191. At the end of
    Gawain the Arthurian court decides to establish a knightly order in honour
    of Gawain, with an emblem which, like a garter, has feminine associations.
    This episode may be intended in part to encourage the audience to link
    Arthur's order with Edward's, and hence the chivalry of the poem with
    courtly life in their own times.
8   This is the view of J. A. Burrow, *A Reading of Sir Gawain and the Green
    Knight* (London: Routledge and Kegan Paul, 1965), p. 7: 'No mere eulogist,
    it is certain, would have described Arthur as "sumquat childgered"; for this
    phrase does undoubtedly imply a criticism.' But the precise sense of
    childgered, and therefore the degree of criticism implied in its use, are
    unclear, as this is the only occurrence of the word. 'Childish, boyish, high-
    spirited' is the likely range of meaning. In a full discussion of the word in the
    Tolkien-Gordon-Davis edition of *Gawain* (p. 75), it is compared with the
    noun phrase *child gere* 'childish games, childish behaviour', found in *The
    Wars of Alexander* and *The Ormulum*.
9   See especially *The Alliterative Morte Arthure* in *King Arthur's Death*, ed.
    Larry D. Benson, rev. Edward E. Foster (Kalamazoo: Medieval Institute
    Publications, 1994). There is a long description of the giant (lines
    1074–1103), which makes him five fathoms tall and monstrously ugly in
    every detail of his appearance.
10 Putter, *Introduction*, p. 62, quoting this line, suggests that the 'fairyland' from
    which the Green Knight comes is to be differentiated from the 'natural'
    world of the Arthurian court: 'the line that separates reality from romance no
    longer falls between the world inside the text and the world outside it, but
    becomes a division internal to the text itself'. My own view is different.

11 *Of Giants* (Minneapolis: Minnesota University Press, 1999), p. 159.

12 The word *barlay*, found uniquely here in Middle English, is of uncertain origin, but editors usually identify it with the modern dialect word *barley*, used by children in their games to call a truce or caim a turn.

13 A. C. Spearing, *Criticism and Medieval Poetry* (London: Edward Arnold, 1964), has a detailed analysis of the style of this speech as expressive of Gawain's courtesy (pp. 39–43).

14 For *sapiencia* and *intelligencia*, see 2 Chronicles 1.9–12 and 2 Kings 3. 9–13.

15 This work, one of a group of allied texts known collectively as the *Ars Notoria*, has been given a raised profile since the publication of Claire Fanger, ed., *Conjuring Spirits: Texts and Traditions of Ritual Magic* (Stroud: Sutton, 1998).

16 Frank Klaassen, 'English manuscripts of magic, 1300–1500: a preliminary survey', in Fanger, *Conjuring*, pp. 3–31, notes a work with the title *Tractatus de Penthagono Salomonis* found in MS York, Austin Friars A8, 362, a large collection of magical works (p. 9). Richard Kieckhefer, 'The devil's contemplatives', in Fanger, *Conjuring*, pp. 250–65, notes that in the *Liber Iuratus* ('Sworn Book' or 'Sacred Book') of Honorius of Thebes, a work which, like the Solomonic *Ars Notoria*, claims divine authorisation, a magician is told to construct a 'seal of God' with a pentagram at its core, to be used for conjuring spirits, and possibly also to help in attaining the beatific vision (pp. 255–6).

17 Lynn Thorndike, *A History of Magic and Experimental Science*, 8 vols (New York: Columbia University Press, 1923–58), vol. 2, pp. 279–80.

18 Phillipa Hardman, 'Gawain's practice of piety in *Sir Gawain and the Green Knight*', *Medium Ævum* 68 (1999), 247–67.

19 Susan M Powell, 'Untying the knot: reading *Sir Gawain and the Green Knight*', in Susan M. Powell and Jeremy J. Smith, eds, *New Perspectives on Middle English Texts* (Cambridge: D. S. Brewer, 2000), p. 59.

20 Compare the term 'knot' or 'nut' used for the star-shaped sword formation, created by interlocked swords, which is held aloft at the end of the traditional English sword dance.

21 Stephanie J. Hollis, 'The pentangle knight: *Sir Gawain and the Green Knight*', *Chaucer Review* 15:3 (1981), 271–81, also discusses the language of the pentangle passage, and of Gawain's speeches after the Green Knight's revelations, as indicative of externality. She suggests that Gawain's knightly identity is to be understood as an entity attached to him (274).

22 Richard Hamilton Green, 'Gawain's shield and the quest for perfection', *English Literary History* 29 (1962), 121–39, reprinted in Robert J. Blanch, ed., *Sir Gawain and Pearl: Critical Essays* (Bloomington: Indiana University Press, 1966), pp. 176–94, quotes from a religious work by Robert Holcot: 'In the history of Britain it is written that King Arthur had a picture of the glorious Virgin painted on the inside of his shield, and that whenever he was weary in battle he looked at it and recovered his hope and strength' (p. 184). In Chretien de Troyes's romance *Erec and Enide* (ed. and trans. C. W. Carroll, New York and London: Garland, 1987), Erec draws inspiration from his sight of Enide praying: 'Erec looked towards his lady, who was very softly praying for him. As soon as he saw her, his strength was renewed; because of

her love and her beauty he regained his great courage' (Carroll's translation
of lines 911–16).

23   The inclusion of *cortaysye* in this list is an indication that Gawain's courtesy
goes beyond verbal courtesy. In the later middle ages the word 'courtesy'
developed a wide range of meaning through its use in romance literature. At
one end of its spectrum of meaning it meant formal politeness of speech and
behaviour, the usual modern meaning. In the middle of the spectrum it
embraced the idea of the knight as courtier, a devotee of the social arts and a
servant and lover of women. At the other end of the spectrum the word
acquired moral connotations. All in *Gawain* practise courtesy in the first
'polite' sense as a matter of course; this kind of courtesy is the common currency of chivalry. All attend to the second sense also, especially Gawain. But
only Gawain takes on the third sense, making courtesy the centre of the
value-system which underpins his chivalry.

24   In the list of virtues loved by Chaucer's Knight, i.e. 'Trouthe and honour,
fredom and curteisie' (*Canterbury Tales*, I, 46), the first two together may be
regarded as equivalent to the *Gawain*-poet's *trawthe*.

25   Keen, *Chivalry* notes that the same or similar virtues are associated together
in romances, from Chretien onwards, as characteristic of good knighthood (p.
2). He notes that Raymond Lull, in his influential treatise *Libre del Ordre de
Cavalayria* (*c*.1270), refers to the same list of knightly qualities, and comments that 'they do not seem to be in any direct way derivative from theological treatments of virtue (though of course, as Lull saw, they can be
brought into line with them)' (p. 11). Keen's study is invaluable for its examination of the complex interrelations between chivalry and religion. The drift
of his argument is that, in life as in literature, chivalry, though thoroughly
imbued with medieval Christian values, is in its origins and history essentially secular and separate.

26   The pentangle passage tends to focus the distinction between those readers
who see Gawain's faith as of paramount importance to him and those who do
not. For a thoroughgoing example of the former line of interpretation see A.
D. Horgan, 'Gawain's pure pentaungle and the virtue of faith', *Medium
Ævum* 56 (1987), 310–16. Horgan interprets Gawain's *trawthe* as 'faith' (311)
and explains the pentangle as follows: 'I take it, then, that the pentangle passage is intended as a symbolic account of a perfect Christian knight: one who
can give a good account of himself in battle, not led by his senses into sin,
trusting in the power of Christ's redeeming sacrifice for his salvation, full of
fortitude because he looks to Mary's intercession if he should be in peril of
his life, and with his faith in God issuing forth in generosity and fellowship,
purity, courtesy and pity' (313). Ross G. Arthur, 'Gawain's shield as *signum*',
in Blanch, *Text and Matter*, pp. 221–7, argues that *trawthe* is used in the pentangle passage in the sense of absolute truth or God, so that the pentangle figure 'is a statement that Gawain believes in and relies on God as infinite truth'
(p. 223).

27   On standard rhetorical aspects of the seasons passage see Alain Renoir,
'Descriptive techniques in *Sir Gawain and the Green Knight*', *Orbis Litter-
arum* 13 (1958), 126–32, and Derek Pearsall, 'Rhetorical *descriptio* in *Sir
Gawain and the Green Knight*', *Modern Language Review* 50 (1955), 129–34.

28 Cf. Proverbs 14.13: 'the end of that mirth is heaviness'.

29 E.g. Psalm 90; see especially verses 4–6: 'For a thousand years in thy sight are but as yesterday when it is past .. they are like grass which groweth up . . . in the evening it is cut down, and withereth.'

30 'In May, whan every harte floryshyth and burgenyth (for, as the season ys lusty to beholde and comfortable, so man and woman rejoysyth and gladith of somer commynge with his freyshe floures, for wynter wyth hys rowghe wyndis and blastis causyth lusty men and women to cowre and to syt by fyres), so thys season hit befelle in the moneth of May a grete angur and unhappe that stynted nat tylle the floure of chyvalry of all the worlde was destroyed and slayne' (Malory, *Works*, p. 673).

31 W. A. Davenport, *The Art of the Gawain Poet* (London: Athlone Press, 1978), in his discussion of the coupling, refers to 'the moralist's emblems of transience and mutablility in the two faces of woman, Youth and Age'. He considers that the younger woman's being led by the hand presents her as 'one subordinate to and manipulated by another', and suggests that she is 'merely a facet of the old woman' (p. 160).

32 The game is described, in characteristic narrative style, with tactful suggestiveness, in lines 69–70: 'Ladies laghed ful loude, thagh thay lost haden, / And he that wan was not wrothe, that may ye wel trawe.' ['Ladies laughed very loudly, though they had lost, and he who won was not angry, you may well believe that.'] Kissing is not explicitly mentioned, but it is hard to see what kind of game it might be unless one involving a kiss as a forfeit.

33 This point is made more fully in J. J. Anderson, 'Gawain and the hornbook', *Notes & Queries* ns 37 (1990), 160–3.

34 Hardman, *Piety*, pp. 251–4.

35 This view is in general accord with that of, amongst others, Derek Pearsall, 'Courtesy and chivalry in *Sir Gawain and the Green Knight*: the order of shame and the invention of embarrassment', in Brewer and Gibson, *Companion*, p. 352: '[Gawain] is dutiful and pious, and has a care for his "costes" (750), or observances, when he finds himself apparently far from human habitation and praying-places on Christmas Eve, but he has no inward sense of religion, of the reforming or re-forming power of faith.' See below, pp. 202–3.

36 The arch way in which the New Year's game at Arthur's court is described (lines 66–70) suggests that the knights and ladies who played it might well have adopted such a tone in talking to each other.

37 'In relying on this pagan talisman to deliver him from the death he fears, he is falling short in that fortitude which ought to spring from his devotion to the Blessed Virgin' (Horgan, 'Gawain's pentaungle', 314). An example of a hero who rejects supernatural assistance (and pays for it with his life) is the suitor in Marie de France's story *The Two Lovers*, who carries his bride-to-be up a mountain, as he is required to do, without drinking the magic potion which will give him the necessary strength (referred to by Richard Kieckhefer, *Magic in the Middle Ages*, Cambridge: Cambridge University Press, 1990, p. 109).

38 Kieckhefer, *Magic*, pp. 103–5, notes that there was no universal acceptance of the claim of Bishop Marbod of Rennes (in his influential lapidary *The*

Book of Stones, late eleventh century) that the benign powers of precious stones came from God. Some thought such powers might be demonic, others were sceptical of the whole idea of them. *Gawain, Pearl,* and *Cleanness* all allude to the special powers of jewels.

39   In this reading of the confession scene Gawain does not confess to taking the girdle because he does not admit to himself that he has sinned in doing so. There is then no contradiction between a failure to confess the girdle and the narrative's statement that he confessed all his sins, *the more and the mynne*.

40   Geraldine Heng, 'Feminine knots and the other in *Sir Gawain and the Green Knight*', *PMLA* 106 (1991), 500-14, finds a 'women's plot' in which Gawain is merely 'a player drawn into Morgan's game' (501). She sees the 'tenuous and incomplete' love-lace as a slippery sign of multiple reference which eventually overtakes Gawain's fixed and perfect pentangle.

41   In the later middle ages girdles, including decorative ones, were as likely to be owned and worn by men as by women. See examples in *MED* s. girdel.

42   Michael W. Twomey, 'Morgain la Fée in *Sir Gawain and the Green Knight*: from Troy to Camelot', in *Text and Intertext in Medieval Literature*, ed. Norris J. Lacy (New York: Garland, 1996), pp. 91–115, points out that Morgan's role as instigator in *Gawain* is paralleled (with some correspondences of detail) by her role in an episode of the French prose *Lancelot*, which also explains her hatred of Guinevere.

43   In the well-established tradition Arthur was the result of a one-off sexual encounter between King Uther Pendragon and Ygrayne, wife of Gorlois, Duke of Cornwall.

44   Edward Wilson, *The Gawain-Poet* (Leiden: Brill, 1976), argues that in Bercilak's court there is 'an atmosphere of intricacy and ingenuity in no apparent relation to ethical values' (p. 122), and 'a deep devotion to form and subtlety for their own sakes, a devotion which is not "halched" in other more substantial virtues .. intricacy turns to intrigue, and ingenuity becomes deceit'. (p. 124).

45   This is my own reading of these lines. Other editors read them differently, putting a stop at the end of line 2445.

46   Helen Cooper, 'The supernatural', in Brewer, *Companion,* pp. 277–91, refers (p. 290) to the Grail castle, unknown to others, which appears to Perceval in Chretien's *Conte del Graal*, and the fairy castle and palace created by Oberon for the sake of the hero in *Huon of Bordeaux*, as examples of other romance castles created by magic for specific purposes.

47   Anne Rooney, *Hunting in Middle English Literature* (Cambridge: D. S. Brewer, 1993), points out that the poet, in having Bercilak despatch the boar on foot with a sword, uncharacteristically departs from the pragmatism of the hunting manuals and follows romance tradition instead. 'He clearly divorces Bertilak from the realm of the limited real hunter to place him amongst the ranks of heroic literary hunters' (p. 174).

48   On magicians at court see Kieckhefer, *Magic*, pp. 96–100. Kieckhefer's summary statement that 'courtly society was ridden with magic and fear of magic' (p. 96) expresses his substantial agreement with Edward Peters, *The Magician, the Witch, and the Law* (Philadelphia: Pennsylvania University Press, 1978), pp. 110–37. The poet may see the mixture of the courtly, the

religious, and the occult in Gawain's pentangle, as he explains it, in terms of the unsophisticated beliefs of many of his courtly contemporaries. The spirit of such beliefs, including belief in the power of amulets and talismans, is well caught by the Middleham Jewel, dated 1430–70, a gold lozenge-shaped pendant set with a sapphire and engraved with representations of the Trinity (with the crucified Christ prominent), the Nativity, the Lamb of God, and a selection of saints. Engraved in the border round the edge of the pendant on the Trinity side is the text (in Latin) of John 1.29: 'Behold the Lamb of God who takest away the sins of the world', followed by *miserere nobis* 'have mercy on us', and then the words 'tetragrammaton' and 'ananizapta'. Hardman, 'Piety', notes that *Agnus Dei* [Lamb of God] talismans were widely used, and looked on more favourably by the church than Solomonic charms. 'Tetragrammaton', a Greek word meaning 'word of four letters', is a term for the 'unspoken' Hebrew name for God (Jehovah, written without the vowels as YHWH), supposedly revealed to Solomon, and 'ananizapta' is a charm-word for use against epilepsy. There are other late medieval instances of these two words occurring together on jewels. It seems that like Gawain's shield this pendant had several functions, including aid to religious devotion, magic charm, and indicator of its owner's courtly taste and status. Cherry suggests that an aristocratic lady was likely to be the owner. See further John Cherry, *The Middleham Jewel and Ring* (York: Yorkshire Museum, 1994), and Richard Marks and Paul Williamson, *Gothic: Art for England 1400–1547* (London: V&A Publications, 2003), p. 233. Compare the late fifteenth-century Coventry ring, which has the inscription: '5 wounds are my medecine: casper, melchior, baltasar ananzapte tetragramaton' (*Gothic*, p. 333).

49 Kieckhefer, *Magic*, pp. 8–12 and *passim*.

50 Leo Carruthers, 'The Duke of Clarence and the earls of March: Garter knights and *Sir Gawain and the Green Knight*', Medium Ævum, 69 (2000), 66–79, notes: 'Although it is commonplace for romance authors to invoke a blessing on the audience they do not do so in the style of preachers, which is the convention followed here. This couplet is typical of medieval English sermons' (67). If Carruthers is correct, the possibility that the last two lines suggest a religious perspective on the story is strengthened.

51 Keen, *Chivalry*, p. 62.

52 Keen, *Chivalry*, refers to 'the concern with outward show and ceremony which [the] statutes [of the secular orders of knighthood] so markedly evince' (p. 198).

53 Putter, *Gawain*, approaching the matter from the point of view of courtesy literature and the 'etiquette of hospitality', also discusses the link between courtesy and deceit. He points out that the *Gawain*-poet's interest in this link is shared by Chretien de Troyes, who in this as in many respects is, amongst the romance writers, closest in temper to the *Gawain*-poet: 'Alongside the discrepancy between faces and feelings which etiquette encourages, there appears the possibility of deceit, a theme that appears with great frequency in the romances of Chretien, his continuators, and *Gawain*.' (p. 99). On the etiquette of courtesy see Jonathan Nicholls, *The Matter of Courtesy: Medieval Courtesy Books and the Gawain-Poet* (Woodbridge: Boydell and Brewer, 1985).

54   Pearsall, 'Courtesy', p. 353, quotes the words of Sir Clegis and Sir Bors in
         Malory, *Works*, ed. Vinaver, p. 130: 'knyghtes ons shamed recoverys hit
         never'.

55   This view accords with that of Pearsall, 'Courtesy', p. 360, who follows Bur-
         row: 'It is not what he did that so fills him with embarrassment, but that he
         was found out in the way that he was; as Burrow says, "Only when he is actu-
         ally dishonoured by the censure of a fellow knight does he feel . . . shame"'
         (John Burrow, 'Honour and shame in *Sir Gawain and the Green Knight*', in
         his *Essays in Medieval Literature*, Oxford, 1984, p. 126).

56   Malory made extensive use of this work, e.g. his own Grail story is an Eng-
         lish version of the Vulgate's.

57   Gawain's limitations lead him to another deadly fate in the *Queste*: '[Gawain]
         epitomizes the courtly ideal: brave, magnanimous, unmatched in courtesy
         and *savoir-faire*, the staunchest and most discreet of friends. The *Quest* cred-
         its him with all these qualities and then sets out to show their bankruptcy in
         the spiritual order. Gawain is not without idealism . . Indeed his intentions
         are always of the best. His fault lies in the fact that he never follows them up
         . . He is so rooted in the creed of his caste, so embedded in the secular that
         the sacred passes him by unrecognized. Inapt as he is for spiritual adventures,
         his virtues find no other outlet than in futile bloodshed, and he proceeds,
         unwilling and unwitting, to slaughter his companions one by one.' *The Quest
         of the Holy Grail*, trans. P. M. Matarasso (London: Penguin, 1969), p. 19. In
         Perceval (or *Conte du Graal*) by Chretien de Troyes (*c.*1181), Gawain is the
         knight of courtesy in the widest sense, a paragon of earthly chivalry, but spir-
         itually undeveloped. He is set beside the more naïve Perceval, who achieves
         earthly chivalry and then goes beyond it, imbuing it with Christian morality
         and spirituality. Another great continental romance which owes much to
         Chretien and which takes a broadly similar view of Gawain is Wolfram von
         Eschenbach's *Parzifal*.

Afterword: the poet and his times

In 1969 Charles Muscatine gave a series of lectures at the University of Notre Dame, which were published under the title *Poetry and Crisis in the Age of Chaucer* (Notre Dame: Notre Dame University Press, 1972). In them he considers the responses of the *Gawain*-poet, Langland, and Chaucer to their troubled times, dominated by the fearsome ravages of the plague – the Black Death. He notes that whereas the problems of the age are everywhere in *Piers Plowman*, there is almost no overt reference to them in the *Gawain*-poet and Chaucer. He concludes (p. 145) that the Gawain-poet 'refines out, in his art, all of the contemporary except the ultimate moral issues'; that Langland 'immerses himself and his poem in the moving current of history, from which both emerge with the marks of crisis upon them'; and that Chaucer 'is somewhere in between, detached yet sympathetically moved'. Earlier (p. 69), he suggests that for the *Gawain*-poet, crisis is 'completely absorbed in his art', and that 'the perfection of his art has become a kind of defense against crisis'.

But 'the perfection of his art' may be read in another way, as heightening, not taking away from, a sense of crisis. I have indicated in my discussions of the individual poems how often they convey a sense of urgency in the speeches, a sense of drama in the situations. *Pearl* is the test case. Of the four poems it is stylistically the most ornate, metrically the most complex, the one in which 'art' is most in evidence. It combines a language of great expressive potential with a demanding poetic form. It has an energy and passion which are all the more impressive for being controlled. I have argued that passages in *Pearl*, which may seem at first to offer little but formality (e.g. the enumeration of the jewels in the walls of the heavenly city) may, for some readers at least, be very powerful (see above, pp. 11–12, 64–8). This is not, in the phrase Muscatine uses in the title for his *Gawain*-poet chapter, 'art as defense'. A more appropriate phrase would be 'art as engagement', for in *Pearl* and his other poems the poet is searching for meaning, and the issues he writes about clearly matter greatly to him. If the implication of Muscatine's comment on Chaucer is that the *Gawain*-poet was not 'sympathetically moved', then I cannot agree. Of the three poets, it is Chaucer who is the least committed and most well defended.

If the sense of urgency in these poems suggests that their issues are close to their author's heart, is there any sense that the poems may respond to historical as well as personal situations? *Cleanness* is the most interesting in this regard. *Piers Plowman* explicitly avails itself of the tradition of clerical explanations of natural catastrophes like the Black Death as God's punishment of sinning mankind: 'thise pestilences were for pure synne' (B. 5. 13). Preachers of the time, who regularly took this line, were ready to compare the visitations of the plague to Noah's Flood and the destruction of Sodom and Gomorrah, which comprise two of the three major narrative episodes in *Cleanness*. Thus the Latin sermons of Thomas Brinton, Bishop of Rochester 1373–89, repeatedly link the plague (and other natural disasters) to the judgement of God on the sins of Noah's world and Sodom and Gomorrah; see e.g. Sermon 48 in *Sermons of Thomas Brinton*, ed. M. A. Devlin, 2 vols, Camden Society 3rd series 85, 86 (London: Royal Historical Society, 1954), p. 216. The language of *Cleanness* conveys an intense reaction against filth, in which physical and metaphysical notions of filth are inextricably mixed. Behind the gruesome imagery of death and decay may lie the poet's horror at the effects of the plague on the human body, and, equally, of his horror at the sinful state of his world and God's reaction to it. One of the many ways in which *Patience* may be seen both as complementing and moving on from *Cleanness* is that it responds to the crisis of its times not with 'repent ye for the end of the world is at hand', but with 'repent ye and accept God's will'. Julian of Norwich, writing at about the same time as the *Gawain*-poet, is able to express a conviction that God is free from anger, that he will see to it that all shall always be well, and that love was his meaning. The message of God's love is present in *Pearl*, *Cleanness*, and *Patience* too, but the poet shows no confidence that people can grasp it. All they can grasp, so the endings of *Pearl* and *Patience* indicate, is the more sombre message of the need to submit themselves to God.

Whereas Julian demonstrates the security of her personal faith in the face of national events, *Pearl*, *Cleanness*, and *Patience* suggest that for the poet national events may have merged with events in his own life to challenge his faith. With *Gawain* too it is possible that the public and the personal intermingle to shake his faith in chivalry and the feudal model of social order. Chivalry is evidently in his blood, and as one who writes for courtly patrons he may be said to have a vested interest in it. At the same time, especially if he is a cleric, he may be uneasy about the conspicuous consumption of the ruling classes in an age which was familiar with famine, when the contrast between the lot of the richest and poorest was extreme. The extravagance of the rich, as indicative of the social and moral decay of England, is another of Brinton's sermon themes; see e.g. Sermon 49, on pride, in Devlin's edition, pp. 218–22. The poem's striking emphasis on the luxury of the courts of Arthur and Bercilak may imply disapproval. In any event the condition of severe deprivation under which so many of the poet's contemporaries lived gives an edge to the poem's presentation of chivalric life as glamorous but shallow.

Nevertheless, though external events may well be a significant extra stimulus for the poet, his world, like Julian's, is primarily an interior world of reflection. His experience of the world around him, like his reading, is raw material for thought which always favours the timeless over the time-bound. He creates dialogues which take his readers to the issues at the heart of the two long-established ideologies of Christianity and chivalry. He is drawn to both ideologies, and the poems show why. In his imaginative worlds their positive and negative aspects are powerfully realised. To a degree, he presents the two systems as alternative ways of seeing things. But his fundamental perception is that the same great obstacle to belief applies to both systems: their major doctrines run counter to people's deepest instincts. He wants to demonstrate their viability, but is compelled in honesty to demonstrate their lack of it. Taken together, the four poems communicate a muted sadness – the poet's sadness that, despite their desire to do so, human beings cannot make work for them great ideals which their culture makes available to them and which promise to lift them above their imperfect world and imperfect lives.

Abbreviations and select bibliography

Only editions, monographs, and journal articles cited in the study are listed.

Abbreviations

AV   Authorised Version (1611 English edition of the Bible). This is the version always used in references and quotations unless otherwise noted.
Douay   *See* Vulgate.
EETS ES   Early English Text Society Extra Series.
EETS OS   Early English Text Society Original Series.
MED   *Middle English Dictionary*, ed. H. Kurath and others (Ann Arbor: Michigan University Press, 1954–2002).
OED   *Oxford English Dictionary*.
Vulgate   The Latin Vulgate Bible, *Biblia Sacra*, cited in the Douay translation.

Editions of the *Gawain*-poems

Sir Gawain and the Green Knight, Pearl, Cleanness, Patience, ed. J. J. Anderson (London: Dent, Everyman, 1996). All references to and quotations from the *Gawain*-poems are based on this edition.

The Poems of the Pearl Manuscript: Pearl, Cleanness, Patience, Sir Gawain and the Green Knight, ed. M. Andrew and R. A. Waldron, 2nd edn (Exeter: Exeter University Press, 2002).

The Pearl Poems: An Omnibus Edition, ed. William Vantuono, 2 vols (New York, 1984).

Pearl, ed. E. V. Gordon (Oxford: Oxford University Press, 1953).

Purity [*Cleanness*], ed. Robert J. Menner (New Haven: Yale University Press, 1920).

Patience, ed. J. J. Anderson (Manchester: Manchester University Press, 1969).

Sir Gawain and the Green Knight, ed. J. R. R. Tolkien and E. V. Gordon, 2nd edn rev. N. Davis (Oxford: Oxford University Press, 1967).

Editions of other texts

The Alliterative Morte Arthure in *King Arthur's Death*, ed. Larry D. Benson, rev.
      Edward E. Foster (Kalamazoo: Medieval Institute Publications, 1994).
Barlam and Iosaphat, ed. John C. Hirsh, EETS OS 290 (London: Oxford Uni-
      versity Press, 1986).
The Bestiary, in J. A. W. Bennett and G. V. Smithers, eds, *Early Middle English
      Verse and Prose* (London: Oxford University Press, 1966), pp. 171–3.
Sermons of Thomas Brinton, ed. M. A. Devlin, 2 vols, Camden Society 3rd series
      85, 86 (London: Royal Historical Society, 1954)
Chaucer, Geoffrey, *The Canterbury Tales*, *The Book of the Duchess*, in *The River-
      side Chaucer*, ed. L. D. Benson and others, 3rd edn (Boston: Houghton Mif-
      flin, 1987). All references to and quotations from Chaucer's works are based
      on this edition.
Gower, John, *The English Works of John Gower*, ed. G. C. Macaulay, 2 vols, EETS
      ES 81, 82 (London: Oxford University Press, 1900, 1901).
The Harley Lyrics, ed. G. L. Brook, 3rd edn (Manchester University Press, 1964).
Langland, William, *Piers Plowman*, B-text, ed. A. V. C. Schmidt, 2nd edn (Lon-
      don: Dent, Everyman, 1995).
Malory, Sir Thomas, *Works*, ed. Eugene Vinaver, 2nd edn (Oxford: Oxford Uni-
      versity Press, 1977).
Pecock, Reginald, *Reule of Crysten Religion*, ed. W. C. Greet, EETS OS 171 (Lon-
      don: Oxford University Press, 1927).
The Quest of the Holy Grail, trans. P. M. Matarasso (London: Penguin, 1969).
Sawles Warde, in J. A. W. Bennett and G. V. Smithers, eds, *Early Middle English
      Verse and Prose* (London: Oxford University Press, 1966), pp. 246–61.
Speculum Sacerdotale, ed. E. H. Weatherly, EETS OS 200 (London: Oxford Uni-
      versity Press, 1936).
Troyes, Chretien de, *Erec and Enide*, ed. and trans. C. W. Carroll (New York and
      London: Garland, 1987).
Vices and Virtues, ed. F. Holthauser, 2 vols, EETS OS 89, 159 (London: Oxford
      University Press, 1888, 1920).

Studies

Aers, David, 'The self mourning: reflections on *Pearl*', *Speculum* 68 (1993),
      54–73.
Aers, David, 'Christianity for courtly subjects: reflections on the *Gawain*-poet', in
      Brewer and Gibson, *Companion*, pp. 91–101.
Anderson, Gary A., *The Genesis of Perfection: Adam and Eve in Jewish and Chris-
      tian Imagination* (Louisville: Westminster John Knox, 2001).
Anderson, J. J., 'Gawain and the hornbook', *Notes & Queries* ns 37 (1990), 160–3.
Anderson, J. J., 'The three judgments and the ethos of chivalry in *Sir Gawain and
      the Green Knight*', *Chaucer Review* 24 (1990), 337–55.
Anderson, J. J., 'The narrators in the *Book of the Duchess* and the *Parlement of
      Foules*', *Chaucer Review* 26 (1992), 219–36.
Andrew, Malcolm, 'The realizing imagination in late medieval English narrative',

English Studies 76 (1995), 113–28.

Andrew, Malcolm, 'Theories of authorship', in Brewer and Gibson, *Companion*, pp. 23–33.

Arthur, Ross G., 'Gawain's shield as *signum*', in Blanch, Miller, and Wasserman, *Text and Matter*, pp. 221–7.

Barr, Helen, '*Pearl* – or the jeweller's tale', *Medium Ævum* 69 (2000), 59–79.

Bennett, Michael J., 'The historical background', in Brewer and Gibson, *Companion*, pp. 71–90.

Bishop, Ian, *Pearl in its Setting* (Oxford: Blackwell, 1968).

Blanch, Robert J., Miriam Youngerman Miller, and Julian N. Wasserman, eds, *Text and Matter: New Critical Perspectives of the Pearl-Poet* (Troy, New York: Whitston, 1991).

Blanch, Robert J. and Julian N. Wasserman, *From Pearl to Gawain: Forme to Fynisment* (Gainesville: Florida University Press, 1995).

Brewer, Derek and Jonathan Gibson, eds, *A Companion to the Gawain-Poet* (Cambridge: D. S. Brewer, 1997).

Burrow, J. A., *A Reading of Sir Gawain and the Green Knight* (London: Routledge and Kegan Paul, 1965).

Burrow, J. A., *The Gawain-Poet* (Tavistock: Northcote House, 2001).

Burrow, John, 'Honour and shame in *Sir Gawain and the Green Knight*', in his *Essays in Medieval Literature* (Oxford, 1984).

Carruthers, Leo, 'The Duke of Clarence and the earls of March: Garter Knights and *Sir Gawain and the Green Knight*', *Medium Ævum* 70 (2001), 66–79.

Cherry, John, *The Middleham Jewel and Ring* (York: Yorkshire Museum, 1994).

Clark, S. L. and Julian N. Wasserman, '*Purity*: the cities of the raven and the dove', *American Benedictine Review* 29 (1978), 285–6.

Cohen, Jeffrey J., *Of Giants: Sex, Monsters, and the Middle Ages* (Minneapolis: Minnesota University Press, 1999).

Condren, Edward I., *The Numerical Universe of the Gawain-Pearl Poet* (Gainesville: Florida University Press, 2002).

Cooper, Helen, 'The supernatural', in Brewer and Gibson, *Companion*, pp. 277–91.

Davenport, W. A., *The Art of the Gawain Poet* (London: Athlone Press, 1978).

Davis, N., 'A note on *Pearl*', in John Conley, ed., *The Middle English Pearl: Critical Essays* (Indiana: Notre Dame University Press, 1970), pp. 325–34.

Fanger, Claire, ed., *Conjuring Spirits: Texts and Traditions of Ritual Magic* (Stroud: Sutton, 1998).

Farrell, Thomas J., ed., *Bakhtin and Medieval Voices* (Gainesville: Florida University Press, 1996).

Fein, S. G. The 'twelve-line stanza forms in Middle English and the date of *Pearl*', *Speculum* 72 (1997), 367–98.

Glenn, J. A., 'Dislocation of *kynde* in the Middle English *Cleanness*', *Chaucer Review* 18 (1984), 77–91.

Green, Richard Hamilton, 'Gawain's shield and the quest for perfection', *English Literary History* 29 (1962), 121–39, reprinted in Robert J. Blanch, ed. *Sir Gawain and Pearl: Critical Essays* (Bloomington: Indiana University Press, 1966), 176–94.

Hardman, Phillipa, 'Gawain's practice of piety in *Sir Gawain and the Green*

Knight', *Medium Ævum* 68 (1999), 247–67.

Heng, Geraldine, 'Feminine knots and the other in *Sir Gawain and the Green Knight*', *PMLA* 106 (1991), 500–14.

Hollis, Stephanie J., 'The pentangle knight: *Sir Gawain and the Green Knight*', *Chaucer Review* 15 (1981), 271–81.

Holquist, Michael, ed., *The Dialogical Imagination: Four Essays* [by M. M. Bakhtin], trans. Caryl Emerson and Michael Holquist (Austin: Texas University Press, 1981).

Horgan, A. D., 'Gawain's pure pentaungle and the virtue of faith', *Medium Ævum* 56 (1987), 310–16.

Hulbert, J. R., 'A hypothesis concerning the alliterative revival', *Modern Philology* 28 (1931), 405–22.

Ingledew, Francis, 'Liturgy, prophecy, and Belshazzar's Babylon: discourse and meaning in *Cleanness*', *Viator* 23 (1992), 247–79.

Kean, P. M., *The Pearl: An Interpretation* (London: Routledge and Kegan Paul, 1967).

Keen, Maurice, *Chivalry* (New Haven and London: Yale University Press, 1984).

Keiser, Elizabeth B., *Courtly Desire and Medieval Homophobia: The Legitimation of Sexual Pleasure in Cleanness and Its Contexts* (New Haven and London: Yale University Press, 1997).

Kieckhefer, Richard, *Magic in the Middle Ages* (Cambridge: Cambridge University Press, 1990).

Kieckhefer, Richard, 'The devil's contemplatives', in Fanger, *Conjuring*, pp. 250–65.

Klaassen, Frank, 'English manuscripts of magic, 1300–1500: a preliminary survey', in Fanger, *Conjuring*, pp. 3–31.

Marks, Richard and Paul Williamson, *Gothic: Art for England 1400–1547* (London: V&A Publications, 2003).

Milroy, James, '*Pearl*: the verbal texture and the linguistic theme', *Neophilologus* 55 (1971), 195–208.

Morse, Charlotte C., 'The image of the vessel in *Cleanness*', *University of Toronto Quarterly* 40 (1971).

Morse, Charlotte C., *The Pattern of Judgment in the Queste and Cleanness* (Columbia: Missouri University Press, 1978).

Muscatine, Charles, *Poetry and Crisis in the Age of Chaucer* (Notre Dame: Notre Dame University Press, 1972).

Nicholls, Jonathan, *The Matter of Courtesy: Medieval Courtesy Books and the Gawain-Poet* (Woodbridge: Boydell and Brewer, 1985).

Pearsall, Derek, 'Rhetorical *descriptio* in *Sir Gawain and the Green Knight*', *Modern Language Review* 50 (1955), 129–34.

Pearsall, Derek, 'Courtesy and chivalry in *Sir Gawain and the Green Knight*: the order of shame and the invention of embarrassment', in Brewer and Gibson, *Companion*, pp. 351–62.

Peters, Edward, *The Magician, the Witch, and the Law* (Philadelphia: Pennsylvania University Press, 1978).

Powell, Susan M., 'Untying the knot: reading *Sir Gawain and the Green Knight*', in Susan M. Powell and Jeremy J. Smith, eds, *New Perspectives on Middle*

English Texts (Cambridge: D. S. Brewer, 2000), pp. 55–74.

Prior, Sandra Pierson, *The Fayre Formez of the Pearl Poet* (East Lansing: Michigan state University Press, 1996).

Putter, Ad, *Sir Gawain and the Green Knight and French Arthurian Romance* (Oxford: Oxford University Press, 1995).

Putter, Ad, *An Introduction to the 'Gawain'-Poet* (London and New York: Longman, 1996).

Radulescu, Raluca L., *The Gentry Context for Malory's Morte Darthur* (Cambridge: Boydell & Brewer, 2003).

Renoir, Alain, 'Descriptive techniques in *Sir Gawain and the Green Knight*', *Orbis Litterarum* 13 (1958), 126–32.

Rhodes, Jim, *Poetry Does Theology: Chaucer, Grosseteste, and the 'Pearl'-Poet* (Notre Dame: Notre Dame University Press, 2001).

Riddy, Felicity, 'Jewels in *Pearl*', in Brewer and Gibson, *Companion*, pp. 43–55.

Rigby, S. H., *Chaucer in Context* (Manchester: Manchester University Press, 1996).

Rooney, Anne, *Hunting in Middle English Literature* (Cambridge: D. S. Brewer, 1993).

Schleusener, Jay, '*Patience* lines 35–40', *Modern Philology* 67 (1969), 64–6.

Spearing, A. C., *Criticism and Medieval Poetry* (London: Edward Arnold, 1964).

Spearing, A. C., *The Gawain-Poet: A Critical Study* (Cambridge: Cambridge University Press, 1970).

Spearing, A. C., 'Poetic identity', in Brewer and Gibson, *Companion*, pp. 35–51.

Stanbury, Sarah, *Seeing the Gawain-Poet* (Philadelphia: Pennsylvania University Press, 1991).

Stokes, Myra, 'Suffering in *Patience*', *Chaucer Review* 18 (1984), 354–63.

Thorndike, Lynn, *A History of Magic and Experimental Science*, 8 vols (New York: Columbia University Press, 1923–58).

Twomey, Michael W., 'The sin of *untrawthe* in *Cleanness*', in Blanch, Miller, and Wasserman, *Text and Matter*, pp. 117–45.

Twomey, Michael W., 'Morgain la Fée in *Sir Gawain and the Green Knight*: from Troy to Camelot', in Norris J. Lacy, ed., *Text and Intertext in Medieval Literature*, (New York: Garland, 1996), pp. 91–115.

Vitto, Cindy L., 'Feudal relations and reason in *Cleanness*', in Liam O. Purdon and Cindy L. Vitto, eds, *The Rusted Hauberk: Feudal Ideals of Order and their Decline*, (Florida: Florida University Press, 1994).

Wallace, David, '*Cleanness* and the terms of terror', in Blanch, Miller, and Wasserman, *Text and Matter*, pp. 93–104.

Wallace, David, ed., *The Cambridge History of Medieval English Literature* (Cambridge: Cambridge University Press, 1995).

Watson, Nicholas, 'The *Gawain*-poet as a vernacular theologian', in Brewer and Gibson, *Companion*, pp. 293–313.

Watts, Ann Chambers, '*Pearl*, inexpressibility, and poems of human loss', *PMLA* 99 (1984), 26–40.

Williams, David, 'The point of *Patience*', *Modern Philology* 68 (1970) 127–36.

Wilson, Edward, *The Gawain-Poet* (Leiden: Brill, 1976).

Index

The Bible and the *Gawain*-poems themselves are not indexed